MW00988051

IN
THE
GROUND

Insider's Guide
to
Oil and Gas Deals

by John Orban, III

4th Edition (4.5)

Meridian Press • Oklahoma City

< www.MeridianPress.com >

M. B. Kumar
July, 2007

This book is set in ITC Century Book,
a type face designed for easy reading, originally selected by
Ed-Be, Incorporated, premier typographers in
Oklahoma City since 1956, succeeded by Be-Graphic Inc.
Typesetting, layout, and design of this 4th Edition is by
Jerry Hamm, Norman, OK.

Published by
Meridian Press, Oklahoma City, OK.

FIRST EDITION	October	1985
SECOND EDITION	January	1987
THIRD EDITION	January	1989
2nd Printing	1/90	
3rd Printing	1/91	
4th Printing	1/93	
FOURTH EDITION	May	1997
Edition 4.3	3/01	
Edition 4.4	7/04	
Edition 4.5	4/06	

ISBN 0-9615776-6-5

Manuscript text: English version 4.5

A reviewer, however, may quote brief passages for a news-
paper , magazine, or broadcast review, if full credit, URL,
and address are given: www.M eridianPress.com, Meridian
Press, PO Box 21567, Oklahoma City, OK 73156-1567, USA

This publication is designed to provide accurate and au-
thoritative information in regard to the subject matter
covered. It is sold with the understanding that by providing
this information, the publisher does not purport to render
legal, accounting, or other professional service. If expert
advice or assistance is required, the services of a competent
professional should be sought.

< www.MeridianPress.com >

To Yuko,

and my Mother and Father

Contents

Foreword

"Is this a good time to invest in oil and gas?"

No one can know how to answer such a question, but one thing is certain. More than at any time in the 20 years this book has been in print, now is the time to understand the business side of the oil and gas business.

Wrenching changes are in progress. Some will alter the structure of the global oil and natural gas industry. This in turn has the potential to affect the daily lives of each and every one of us.

Oil prices fluctuate on a global scale. In 1986, it was feared the price of a barrel of oil might stay as low as $9. The spot price of WTI at Cushing, OK was over $26. in 1999; in 2003, there was speculation that oil could once again, slide briefly to $10. As of 2006, we have seen sustained highs for WTI at Cushing at more than $65. Of course the price of oil is important but so is the fluctuation of price. Volatility has added a new and critical variable to the oil and gas business.

Natural gas prices are destined to follow suit. In the U.S., the price of natural gas was deregulated in 1978. Previously the price was controlled by the Federal government and gas-purchase contracts were long term commitments. Today gas is traded on the spot market, with repercus-

sions in terms of risk and the economics of exploration and production (E&P). Over the life of a
gas well completed in 2006, will the price for the
product be $13. per MCF (sustained Henry Hub
spot price late 2005 - early 2006)? Will a tight
market for North American gas in the near term
cause prices to go even higher? Or will prices
decline to $4. as we import more gas and LNG?

Here in the U.S. the Energy Policy Act of 2005
(signed August 2005) provides a grab bag of tax-
based incentives for: research and development,
renewable energy, alternative energy development, fuel efficiency, secondary recovery (oil),
new technologies, expansion of the developing
LNG industry, conservation, etc. As always, new
tax rules will logically lead to new types of oil
and gas deals and new investment opportunities.

America is one of the few countries in which
you (as an individual or corporate, domestic or
foreign investor) can lease, or even own, the
rights to oil and gas production (mineral rights).

Before you dive into these kinds of opportunities, you need some understanding of how and
why the oil business has come to work the way it
does, today. You also need to appreciate the ever-
increasing rate of change and how change can
affect the business. Ideas that may seem 'common sense' today, were unimaginable, a short
while ago.

Some areas that have the potential to dra-
matically impact the oil and gas business ....

Who owns the oil?

Among the world's top oil companies, the top
10 owners of oil reserves in 1993 were state-
owned. They own 78% of world oil reserves. [1]

Price prediction?

In 1995, the U.S. Department of Energy (DOE) projection for the price of natural gas in year 2010 was $3.50 per MCF. One year later, the same projection had decreased $2.10 per MCF (a 40% decrease). [2]

In the last half of 2005, we have had natural gas prices of more than $13 per MCF.

Where is the business?

Feb 06: One oil guy predicts that the majors are coming back to the U.S. because the long lead time for developing discoveries tends to kill the economics of all but a few overseas deals. [3]

Mar 06: Another oil guy says, " We focus on overseas deals, because the potential is so much greater, and there is less competition." [4]

Where are the people?

In 1993, employment in 'oil and gas production and field services' (345,000) was down 50% from the 685,000 individuals employed in the industry in 1981.[5]

By 2006, one oil field company acknowledged, " ... we'll hire just about any who can walk and talk ... and pass a physical and a drug test." [6]

Wet barrels or paper barrels?

By 1989, the price paid for most of the oil consumed in the free world was determined by the price bid or asked for about 1% of that volume of 'domestic sweet crude' at Cushing, Oklahoma."[7]

By 1994, trading in energy derivatives (futures, options, etc.) was widespread ... and the resulting losses were startling: $1.3 billion (MG Refining & Marketing), $2.6 billion (Sumitomo), $1.4 billion (Showa Shell), $1.5 billion (Kashima Oil), $102 million (Proctor & Gamble), $20 million (Gibson Greetings), etc. [8]

Is there really a 'free market'?

Lower oil prices became a key administration objective in 1985. ... 'We wanted lower international oil prices, largely for the benefit of the American economy,' said Edwin Meese, then White House Counsel. 'The fact that it meant trouble for Moscow was icing on the cake'. [9]

'One of the reasons we were selling all those arms to the Saudis was for lower oil prices', recalls Caspar Weinberger. [10]

The list could go on, but you get the point

It seems likely that the next several years will be characterized, if not defined, by higher oil and gas prices. This Fourth Edition (4.5) was updated to provide a practical look at the business side of the oil and gas business in 2006. The goal is to give you a background from which to assess how technical, economic and even political developments can affect the business of investing in oil and gas.

Thank you for your interest and attention.

John Orban, III
Oklahoma City, OK
March, 2006

Acknowledgments

If not for an article by Toni Mack in Forbes Magazine (June 17, 1996), instead of this revised 4th Edition you might be standing there, holding a dated re-print of an earlier edition! She mentioned MONEY IN THE GROUND in her article, which triggered a flood of calls from around the country. Readers and callers alike made a convincing argument that it was time for a new, up-to-date 4th Edition.

This edition would not have been possible without good information.

A number of writers and editors consistently provide well thought-out commentary on the energy business. I am indebted to many, including (in alphabetical order): Nigel Bance, Roy Boles, Scott Burns, Robert Corzine, Craig Cranston, Jerry Davis, Rich Eichler, Aliza Fan, Loren Fox, Sam Fletcher, Laurie Lande, Sonali Paul, Charles Snyder, Cody Huseby, J. Ishee, A.D. Koen, Dolores Kelly, John Kennedy, Larry Levy, Toni Mack, Onnic Marashian, Mike McCall, Betty McKinnis, Mary Mietus, Ken Miller, Sarah Miller, Chuck Morrison, John Morrison, Larry Nation,

Alan Petzet, Elizabeth Pike, Anne Reifenberg, Rick Robinson, Mike Rounds, Agis Salpukas, Nick Snow, Edwin Snyder, Jack Z. Smith, Kip Stratton, Bob Scott and writers and editors of World Oil, Sana Siwolop, Tom Schwartz, Vern Stefanic, Bob Tippee and writers and editors of the Oil & Gas Journal, Ray Tuttle, Ray Tyson, Bob Vandewater, Jack Westbrook and many others.

Ideas and information gleaned from informal discussions with (and formal presentations by) many professionals who are active in this business on a day-to-day basis are incorporated in this book. I am especially indebted to (listed in alphabetical order): Sandy Beach, Bob Boyer, Porter Bennett, Denise Bode and the staff of IPAA, Don Caldwell, Fred Callon, Lou Christian, Gary Christopher, Richard Clements, Tara Collins, Tim Collins, Keith Davis, Louis Dorfman Jr., Frank Eby, Bryan Erb, Arlen Edgar, Jim Evans, Ralph Fite, Randy Foutch, Jim Gibbs, Mike Gordon, David Hatcher, Jim Hawkins, Bob Hinson, Dave Horner, Al Jaffe, Harry Johnson, Randy King, David Kreuter, Mark Longman, Wib Ladson, Stuart Lang, Joe Manders, Dick McKnight, Pete McMillan, Robert McTavish, George Meacham, Ted Meade, Laverne Michel, David Murfin, Larry Nichols, Jerry Namy, Greg New, Marshall Nichols, Bob Northcutt, Ted Oppel, Georges Pardo, Paul Pause, Bill Pattillo, Brent Poe, Dave Presley, Dave Rippee, Jack Rose, Mark Rupert, Bill Russell, Roderick Salaysay, Dale Schomp, Earl Sebring, Dean Sims, Jim Stafford, Robert Stanger, John Swords, Wayne Swearingen, Gilbert Tompson, Rick Tozzi, Art Van Tyne, Bruce Vincent, Bill Ward, Lew Ward, Myra Ward, Jim Wilkes, Kang Wu, George Yates, and many others.

Jim Gibbs urged the inclusion of several new topics, and these lead to the addition of more new topics, with the end result that the book has nearly doubled in size.

In addition, there are a number of professionals who quietly contributed to the some of the technical discussions of this book, but requested anonimity. Special thanks goes to these 'silent contributors' for their interest and efforts to help make this a user-friendly (as contrasted to a very technically precise) publication.

This book could not have been produced without the active involvement of publishing and information resource professionals, including (in alphabetical order): Eddie Acquino, Glen Behymer, Jeff Behymer, Kevin Bennitt, Sandy Carson, Jack Clady, Pat Countryman, Chester Cowen, Greg Franks, Jerry Hamm, Harley Duncan, Jacequeline Huntoon, Tim Martgan, Melody Morris, Marilynn Rhonne, Oklahoma Historical Society, Cathy Ronald, Mary Ruhl, Vickie Vann, Julie Waddle, Jim Walker, Mike Wilbins, and Ken Wolgemuth.

The Archives & Manuscripts Division of the Oklahoma Historical Society provided the photo that sets off the beginning of each chapter.

Special appreciation goes to Maria Gonzales and Nachamah N. Jacobovits whose efforts provided timely information quoted throughout the book

Responsibility for finished product, of course, rests solely with the author.

Acknowledgments to the First Edition

Some time ago, John McCaslin was kind enough to publish an article of mine in the Oil & Gas Journal. Were it not for the confidence gained from that experience, and interest in the concept of this book, shown by Frank Burke, Vance Maultsby, Billy Mann, Dan Morrison, Boots and Bob Safford, and others, the idea for MONEY IN THE GROUND might not have matured into the pages you are holding.

I am indebted to the people who gave generously of their time and advice. Stephen A. Zrenda, Jr. offered suggestions on improving the manuscript. Bill Herzog critically reviewed the manuscript while on vacation with his family. Jeff Morton provided input to an early draft of the text. Dave Park made himself available to discuss topics that were particularly elusive. George Robinson and Johnny Gutierrez reviewed the manuscript, providing helpful suggestions. Russell D. Chapman offered suggestions that have improved the text in several important areas.

The discussion of depletion in Chapter 10 was substantially improved through inclusion of material from the Touche Ross pamphlet, Oil & Gas Programs, with permission of Richard M. Pollard, National Director of Touche Ross Energy Services. Appendix B includes actual AFE drilling and completion costs compiled by John Hugo; they are presented through the assistance of John Kerr, with permission of Woods Petroleum Corporation. Discussions of government regulations in Appendix C, and partnership classification in Appendix E were significantly improved through the incorporation of material by Stephen A. Zrenda, Jr., with his permission. Bob Northcutt assisted in obtaining the photograph of Healdton field, reproduced with permission of Mac McGalliard and Mrs. Carolyn Franks. Jon Halsey provided the photograph of the Grand Canyon.

Acknowledgements

This book includes material and concepts from diverse areas. I did not discover the principles. I merely pulled them together. Sources are identifies in Notes. Recognized authorities are listed in Recommended Reading.

Various associations spanning several years, fostered this undertaking. Grateful acknowledgment is due all who have contributed to the shape and texture of the book - perhaps not directly in the creation of the manuscript, but certainly in the preparation of the author.

Among my role models at Princeton, John C. Maxwell introduced me to the oil business making possible summer employment as a roustabout with Sun Oil in Morgan City, and Hollis D. Hedberg instilled a fascination with the origin of petroleum. Bill Bonini, Pierre Cote, Tewdwr Davies, the late Erling Dorf, Russ Dutcher, Al Fischer, Robert Hargraves, the late Harry Hess, Sheldon Judson, David Kinsman, Bob Phinney, John Rodgers, Earl Stanford, Fred Vine, and others, introduced me to the concepts first of pure geology, and later the specialized field of petroleum geology.

I thank Fan Adams for a part-time job that was much-needed when I was a student in Tokyo, and Bob Graves for a position that led to broad exploration exposure. Experience was gained in diverse areas though the interest of Alex Massad, and personal involvement of Bob Graves, Carl Burnett and others.

Understanding of scientific exploration came from colleagues at Mobil, including Courtenay Gans and Charlie Menard, and evolved through associations with Rod Avenius, Jim Berry, Bob Brodine, Bill Brown, Clem Bruce, Lou Castelli, Aaron Chauvin, Lou Christian, Chuck Cline, George Coleman, John Delay, Ed Driver, Bill Duggan, John Earl, Art Elliot, John Goff, Jack Hackler, Tuffy Heath, Jim Humphreys, Gene Jones, Nabil Khalil, John Magee, Clem Novosad, Georges Pardo, Dee Pendley, Phil Raveling, Roy Roadifer, Bob Rohloff, Nihat Tank, Lazlo Valachi, Bob Watson, and many others.

While exploring in the Gulf of Mexico and the Middle East, understanding the practical application of geophysics to oil prospecting developed though associations with Ilyas Anwar, Charlie Beeman, Chris Christopherson, Paul Enochson, Don French, Pete Helsdingen, Bill Hurley, Jim McGibboney, Don McLaughlin, Stuart Moncrieff, Percy Pan, Bill Ruehle, Armando Telles, Kieran Thompson,

Lloyd Weathers, and others.

At an ARAMCO meeting in Dhahran, Bill Rogers aptly summarized exploration (Where are the rocks? Are there holes in them? ... etc.) and presented the opportunity to explore in the world's most prolific oil province. Understanding of the special exploration problems of The Arabian platform came from work with Paul Jackson, and developed though associations with Mahmoud Baqi, Sid Bowers, George Covey, Chuck Edwards, Wafik El Guindi, Lee Entsminger, Bob Goodfellow, Jon Halsey, Greg Hatch, John Hoke, Moush Husseini, Folke Johansson, Ian Johnston, Brad Jones, Walter Koop, Warren Latshaw, Bob Maby, Dia Mahmoud, Jim Molnar, Harry Nagel, Ray Nasen, Frank Pruett, Phil Salstrom, Slatz Slentz, B.J. White, Martin Zieglar, and many others.

The opportunity to explore for deep gas in the U.S. was provided by Alan Warren. Familiarity with domestic exploration developed though associations with Bill Chaney, Dwight Johnson, Debbie Morgan, and Carl Newman. Familiarity with non-geologic aspects of the exploration business came through discussions with Kerry Adams, Al Blanc, Don Caldwell, Fred Callon, Don Clutterbuck, Jim Ervin, Digger Gray, Meade Hufford, Richard Ingham, Tim Larason, Harold R. Logan, Jr., John Lockridge, Billy Mann, Harold Smith, Kirby Smith, Mike Tatum, Les Youngblood, and others. Familiarity with specific oil and gas deals and programs developed from conversations with many, many independent oilmen.

I have benefitted greatly from ideas and perspectives which developed out of countless associations, but the responsibility for the material in this book is solely mine.

In the events leading to publication, Ken and Dianna Brooks were instrumental in computerizing the effort. Susan Coman provided helpful suggestions. Glen Behymer took processed words and turned them into attractively-set type. The professional quality of the book was achieved though his guidance.

Special thanks goes to Jack Clady who created the cover design. He also created the many fine illustrations. Many of the concepts presented in the book might be even more difficult! to understand, were they not graphically depicted by his artwork.

Introduction

A valuable commodity to some, a strategic material to others, petroleum is our society's primary source of energy.

It took millions of years to create petroleum. Nature has buried this limited resource deep in basins around the globe. More than 40,000 commercial oil fields have been discovered worldwide.[12] Vast sums have been spent exploring for this oil. Even greater investment will be required in the future.

Modern exploration is directed at oil and gas accumulations trapped beneath the surface of the earth. Early knowledge of petroleum came from seeps where oil or gas flowed naturally out of the ground. The Oracle at Delphi in ancient Greece was located near a burning spring (a natural gas seep). Ancient Chinese burned natural gas to accelerate the evaporation of water used in the mining of salt.

The United States is third in world oil production after the Soviet Union and Saudi Arabia. The nation's first gas well was drilled in 1821, near Lake Erie in Fredonia, New York. More than a hundred years earlier, French missionaries had seen natural gas seeps in the area ignited by Indians during religious ceremonies. The nation's first oil well was drilled near an oil seep in Pennsylvania, in 1859.

Today there are 600,000 producing oil wells, and

200,000 producing gas wells in the United States. More than 2,500,000 property owners receive a share of the revenue from oil and gas produced on their lands. An additional 5,000,000 investors own working interests in these wells. Many 'owners' are limited partnerships, some having thousands of limited partners. As many as eight million Americans and thousands of corporations receive income directly from ownership of oil and gas.

Finding oil used to be seen as a lucky gamble. The search involved little more than guesswork. Today a vast technology has developed around the exploration and production of petroleum. There are risks, as in any venture, but they have become manageable. Hundreds of thousands of drilled wells, and millions of man-years of experience, provide information on the basis of which these risks can be evaluated.

The number of oil and gas wells drilled in the U.S. averaged about 25,000 per year during the recent 10 years (after reaching an all-time high of more than 82,000 wells in 1984 - at a cost of more than $25 billion in 1984 dollars). Typically 5% - 10% of domestic exploration expenditures has come from outside the oil and gas industry in the form of investment by corporate and individual investors.

Some of them believe owning oil in the ground is better than having money in the bank. Perhaps they are right.

This text covers the how's and why's of oil and gas exploration and production. Because they can influence investment choices, the subjects of accounting, taxes, securities and the structure of oil and gas deals are discussed for both the potential investor and the interested observer. Definitions are provided in the glossary.

Wells drilled in U.S. and Crude Oil Price

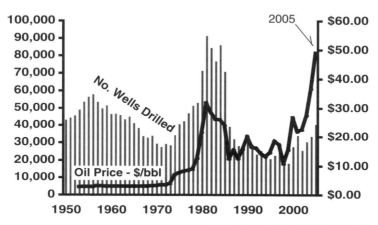

Data from EIA of DOE and IPAA

U.S. Oil and Petroleum Imports
Averaged $107 Billion per year (= **$295,850,000** per day)
for the period 2000-2005

U.S. Trade Balace Deficit and Oil Imports

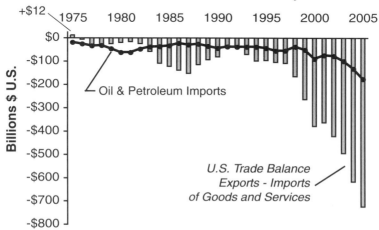

Data from EIA of DOE and DOC

19

Chapter 1

PETROLEUM

"Rock Oil"

Petroleum is 'rock oil'. It includes crude oil, natural gas, and natural gas condensate. Petroleum is generally fluid, and thus mobile. This makes exploring for it more complicated than exploration for a solid mineral like coal. Most oils and all gases are lighter than water and this tends to narrow the range of places petroleum is likely to be found. Among its other physical and chemical properties, this natural buoyancy with respect to water is the property upon which scientific exploration for petroleum is based.

As it comes from the ground, petroleum can range from crude oil that is black or brown or green, to natural gas that is odorless and colorless. Crude oil may flow as readily as alcohol, or it may be as soupy and viscous as honey - depending on its chemical composition and its temperature. The higher the temperature, the easier it flows. Oil

---

" . . . to $24.75 a barrel . . . "
WEDNESDAY'S MARKET: Crude-Oil Prices Reach Highest Level in Five Years
by Suzanne McGee
THE WALL STREET JOURNAL, Thursday, Sept. 12, 1996.

---

gives off a diagnostic glow when exposed to ultraviolet light, allowing positive identification of even small traces of it. Oil and gas are both very poor conductors of electricity. The electrical resistance of a layer of rock can indicate the presence of petroleum, which might not otherwise be detectable.

Oil and gas are hydrocarbons (chemically composed of hydrogen and carbon). They are an excellent source of heat energy. When burned, the hydrogen and carbon combine with oxygen to form water and carbon dioxide, and heat. Take methane gas, for example, the simplest of the hydrocarbons:

methane + oxygen = water + carbon dioxide + heat
CH_4 + $2 O_2$ = $2 H_2O$ + CO_2 + heat

Petroleum is usually found as a mixture of different hydrocarbons, ranging from methane, to complex oils with dozens of carbon atoms and many more hydrogen atoms.

Impurities (nitrogen, helium, carbon dioxide, as well as a number of mineral compounds including table salt) are frequently found associated with oil and gas. Sulfur and its chemical compounds are the most troublesome. Hydrogen sulfide is a noxious, poisonous gas, which dissolves in water to form a dilute solution of sulfuric acid. Over time, it corrodes pipe and steel equipment used in drilling and producing operations. Petroleum containing hydrogen sulfide (H_2S) is called sour crude (or sour gas).

An accumulation of crude oil usually contains natural gas dissolved in the oil (solution gas). If more gas is present than can be dissolved in the oil, the oil is saturated, and the excess gas, being lighter than the oil, accumulates above it as a 'gas cap'. Picture an inverted bottle of salad dressing in which the salad oil floats on the vinegar, and the air (gas cap) floats above the salad oil.

A typical petroleum accumulation is shown in Figure 1.1. A less typical, but nonetheless not uncommon type of accumulation is shown in Figure 1.2. This is heavy oil, found at or near the surface above the Karamay oil field in central China.[13]

Heavy oil is generally believed to result from (mobile) liquid petroleum, that has migrated upwards toward the earth's surface, where at relatively shallow depths, it has then been degraded (or 'biodegraded') by contact with the biosphere, freshwater environments, and/or the atmosphere[14]. Heavy oil reserves are found in many basins around the world. The world's largest known petroleum accumulation is in the Eastern Venezuela Basin (where volumes of oil are estimated at as much as 1,200,000,000,000 barrels = 1.2 trillion barrels of reserves in place). Most of these reserves

> "America's oil and gas industry is in better shape now than it was 15 years ago. Today's domestic industry is better managed and relies more on sophisticated, cost-efficient technology than at any time in its history."
> "Point of View" by Jim Linn , TULSA WORLD, Tuesday, January 23, 1996

are in the form of heavy oil found along the southern flank of the basin in the Orinoco tar belt, which measures about 400 miles long and 40 miles wide.[14] In North America, the world's second largest heavy oil accumulation is found in western Canada's Athabasca tar sands (in an area approximately 750 miles by 400 miles); these sands are estimated to contain nearly 900,000,000,000 barrels = 900 billion barrels of heavy oil reserves in place.[15]

U.S. heavy oil, totals more than 80 billion barrels of reserves in place, found primarily in California, Alaska, and Wyoming. Under current technology, it is projected that oil prices in excess of $45 would be required, before development of many of these reserves would become economical.[16] Deposits of very heavy oil, at depths of less than 200 feet, have been mined in northeast Missouri.

It is worth noting that the presence of oil seeps or heavy oil accumulations at the surface has sometimes been taken as an indication of potential oil accumulations at depth. Hence seeps have been regarded as an important exploration indicator. Of course the debate continues as to whether the presence of oil at the surface indicates that a) oil accumulations exist at depth, or b) any oil that may have originally accumulated at depth, has since escaped and migrated to, and is now to be found at, the surface.

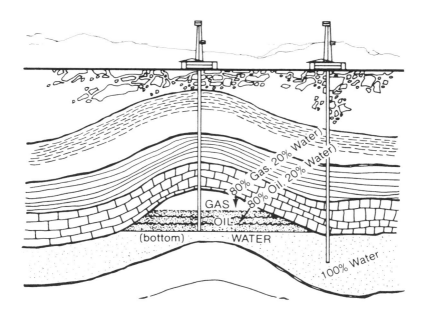

Figure 1.1 Typical Petroleum Accumulation

The Origin of Petroleum?

No one knows! In the U.S., it is generally believed that oil comes from living things. Buried under thousands of feet of overlying sediments, animal and plant remains are subjected to high pressures and temperatures. Fatty proteins are thought to undergo chemical and physical alteration to form oil and gas – in the manner that a peat bog at the earth's surface might become buried and successively transformed, first into bituminous coal, then into anthracite (and potentially ... into diamonds?).

A strong case can be made for such a biogenic origin for oil. Chemical characteristics of certain liquid crude oils are strikingly similar to those of the solid organic matter contained in nearby shales. Although the evidence is less compelling, there are also indications that certain other crude oils could have non-biogenic origin.

There is less consensus about the origin of natural gas. Some types of organic matter may naturally transform into natural gas (as opposed to crude oil). Heat and temperature are believed necessary to produce crude oil, but excessive temperature and pressure may ultimately crack crude oil molecules into successively lighter, simpler hydrocarbons ... and ultimately into the simplest hydrocarbon, methane gas, CH_4.

Laboratory experiments would support this. Drilling experience also indicates that the deeper one drills: (1) the greater the likelihood of encountering natural gas (as opposed to crude oil), and (2) the greater the likelihood that such natural gas may consist largely, if not entirely, of methane.

To date, the deepest well in the U.S. was drilled in southwest Oklahoma, to a final total depth of 31,441 feet. The thickness of sedimentary rock in Oklahoma, however is believed to continue to depths of 50,000 feet or more. There is theoretical support for the belief that under the extreme pressures at these undrilled depths, a variety of thermodynamic reactions may cause methane to be transformed into carbon dioxide, hydrogen sulfide, hydrogen, or other gases, depending on the chemical composition of the reservoir rocks.[17]

Does methane represent liquid crude oil that have been cracked into simpler hydrocarbon molecules? Or is it possible the interior of the earth naturally contains methane, and the deeper one drills, the closer one gets to the source?

Experimental drilling in a meteor impact zone (the Siljan Ring structure) in Sweden has found evidence of methane where it would not be expected according to the biogenic-origin-of-gas theory. For most earth science professionals, the results to date are ambiguous. Although the project is expensive (costing $50,000,000 or more so far, to drill through more than 20,000 feet of Sweden's hard granite) further experimental drilling can be expected in the future.[18] For now, a growing minority of earth scientists may be ready (however reluctantly) to concede that natural gas (and perhaps even crude oil?) could have dual origins – either biogenic or non-biogenic.

Figure 1.2 Heavy Oil
As found in Karamay Field, Xinjiang, China
Photo courtesy of Oil & Gas Journal, May 4, 1987

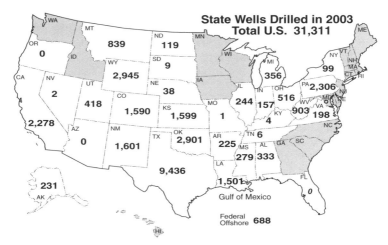

Wells drilled in U.S. by State - 2003
Source: IPAA

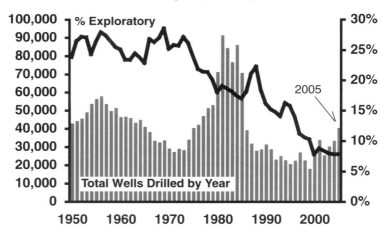

Total Wells Drilled in U.S.
With Percentage Exploratory Wells

Data from EIA of DOE and IPAA

Chapter 2

GEOLOGY

Where are the rocks?

Petroleum Geologist

Legendary petroleum geologist Wallace Pratt observed that "... oil is found ... in the minds of men"[19]. In other words, the petroleum geologist holds the key to scientific exploration for oil and gas. By applying science and reasoning to raw data, he generates prospects. Oil and gas accumulations are three dimensional - characterized by thickness (feet) across a definable area (acres), and measured in terms of 'acre-feet'. The geologist classifies pertinent geologic information and spatial relationships, sorting and rearranging them until they make good geologic sense. From this knowledge and experience, he can recognize clues that may lead to a new prospect. He produces a report consisting of maps and cross-sections, that explains why his prospect is expected to contain petroleum in quantities sufficient to warrant drilling for it.

If employed by a major oil company, a geologist is normally paid an annual salary. About 40% of the 33,000 petroleum geologists in the U.S.[20] work for smaller independent oil companies and consulting firms, and may be paid an annual salary plus some form of participation in revenues from

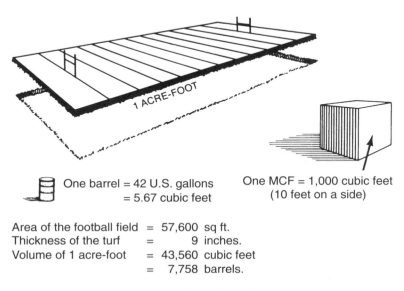

One barrel = 42 U.S. gallons = 5.67 cubic feet	One MCF = 1,000 cubic feet (10 feet on a side)

Area of the football field	=	57,600 sq ft.
Thickness of the turf	=	9 inches.
Volume of 1 acre-foot	=	43,560 cubic feet
	=	7,758 barrels.

Figure 2.1 An Acre-Foot

the oil and gas discovered on their prospects. Independent geologists often generate prospects and provide exploration services in return for cash and/or some form of participation in production revenues.

Finding Oil & Gas

"The present is the key to the past." Natural earth processes we witness today have gone on for millions of years. The basement and foundation of the continents consists largely of granite. Through natural exposure to the elements, granite becomes physically and chemically altered to form soil and grains of sand. These are eroded, and then transported by ice, wind, and water to the oceans (or sometimes, inland lakes). Layer upon layer of these continental sediments settle on the seafloor. By understanding processes that control the transport and deposition of different types of sediments, the geologist also understands spatial relationships of the sediments. Clean quartz sands are found along a wave swept coastline. Black muds are found in lagoons. He applies this knowledge of sedimentation to rocks millions of years old.

Large oil fields have rarely been found among volcanic islands or in the deep ocean basins. Granite also does not occur in the ocean basins. It forms the foundation of the five continents, and appears to be a critical factor in the efficient generation of petroleum. Natural weathering and erosion of granite produces a special family of clays. Buried with organic matter and subjected to high temperatures over millions of years, these clays undergo chemical and physical changes that help expel water and petroleum from them, as the petroleum is formed.[21] Erosion of granite also produces quartz sand. Deposited near the clays, sands contain empty spaces between the sand grains into which petroleum can flow.

More than six hundred basins containing sedimentary rocks (sedimentary basins) have been identified around the world. Some are filled with layers of rock 50,000 feet thick. All these basins have three characteristics in common:

- pressure increases with depth from the surface;
- temperature also increases with depth;
- the holes and voids among the sediment grains were originally water-filled (the sediments having been transported and/or deposited in water).[22]

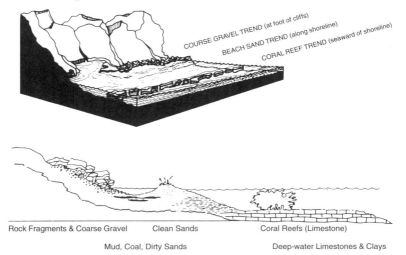

COURSE GRAVEL TREND (at foot of cliffs)
BEACH SAND TREND (along shoreline)
CORAL REEF TREND (seaward of shoreline)

| Rock Fragments & Coarse Gravel | Clean Sands | Coral Reefs (Limestone) |

Mud, Coal, Dirty Sands   Deep-water Limestones & Clays

Figure 2.2 Sediments Follow Predictable Patterns

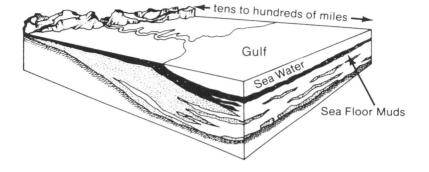

Figure 2.3 Typical Sedimentary Basin

About one quarter of these basins have produced most of the world's petroleum found to date. Some of them produce mostly oil, some produce gas, and some produce both oil and gas. Petroleum-producing basins have the four geologic conditions necessary for an oil or gas accumulation:

1   a layer of rock containing organic plant and animal material that naturally transforms into petroleum (source rock)

2   a layer of rock with interconnected holes and voids, into, and out of which, petroleum can flow (reservoir rock)

3   a layer of rock through which oil and gas cannot flow (seal)

4   trap: a special geometrical configuration of these rock layers such that oil and gas generated from the source rocks can mi-

33

grate upward into the reservoir rock, but will be unable to migrate further because of an overlying seal.[23]

The majority of commercial oil fields have been found at depths between 2,000 feet and about 15,000 feet beneath the earth's surface. At greater depths, temperature and pressure increase to the point that the complex hydrocarbon molecules of oil, tend to be cracked into the simpler hydrocarbons that make up natural gas. Commercial natural gas accumulations are mostly found at depths ranging from 2,000 feet to more than 25,000 feet.

A rock must have two characteristics in order to act as a petroleum reservoir – porosity and permeability.

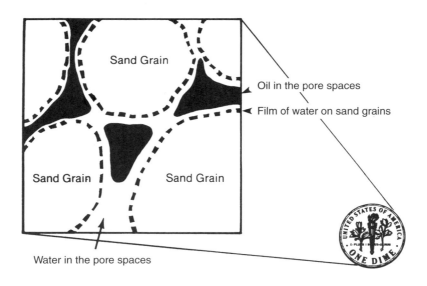

Figure 2.4 Porosity

Picture a bathtub filled with grapefruits. Pour in water, and it fills the empty spaces (porosity) which exist between the grapefruits. Open the drain, and almost all of the water will rush out of the tub.

Imagine a second bathtub filled with golf balls. Pour in water. This second tub will hold nearly as much water as the first one. The individual empty

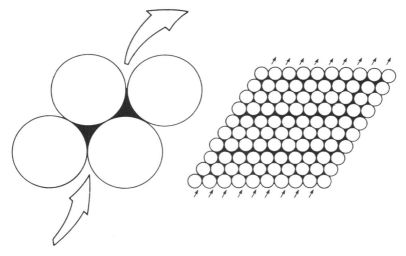

Oil and flow more easily throught sandstone formed of large sand grains.

Figure 2.5 Permeability

spaces between golf balls are smaller, but there are a lot more of them. Now when you open the drain, water will only trickle out slowly compared to the first tub. The two bathtubs have nearly the same porosity (roughly about 25%), but permeability (ability to flow) among the golf balls is much lower than among the grapefruit.[24] (If you find this difficult to accept, you may want to clear out the bathroom before your next trip to the supermarket...)

Petroleum reservoir porosities are measured in percent, with typical commercial reservoirs having porosities that might range from about 7 - 40%. Permeability is measured in units called darcies (and millidarcies which are 0.001 darcy); commercial reservoirs can exhibit permeabilities ranging from a low of, say, 10 millidarcies, to a high of perhaps as much as 50 darcies (in other words, from 0.01 darcies - 50.0 darcies). [25]

A trap may be formed by natural variations in the succession of sediments as they are deposited: source rock, overlain by reservoir rock, which is then overlain by a seal (stratigraphic trap). It may also be formed by the bending, folding, and breaking of layers of rock in response to great movements of the earth's crust (structural trap).

Petroleum exploration involves two tasks. The first is to find a sedimentary basin that contains source rock (without which no petroleum would be generated). The second is to find a trap in the basin which might contain an oil or gas accumulation. In Western China, where major oil and gas production is a relatively new development, much exploration is directed toward identifying sedimentary basins that contain source rock (without which petroleum will not be generated). In the continental U.S., where more than one hundred years of drilling has already established which basins have generated hydrocarbons, exploration is more narrowly focused on finding a trap which might contain an oil or gas accumulation.

Various tools are available to the geologist as he develops a prospect. Aerial photography and infrared satellite pictures can reveal trends on the

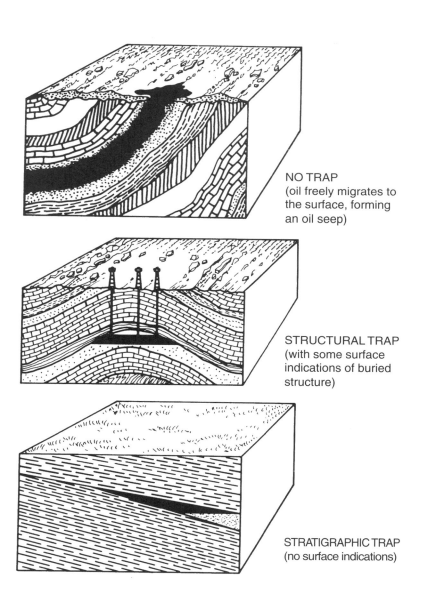

NO TRAP
(oil freely migrates to
the surface, forming
an oil seep)

STRUCTURAL TRAP
(with some surface
indications of buried
structure)

STRATIGRAPHIC TRAP
(no surface indications)

Figure 2.6 Oil & Gas Accumulations

earth's surface too subtle to be recognized from ground level. Skilled interpretation of them can often locate geologic structures buried thousands of feet below.

Several tools combine the sciences of geology and physics (geophysics). Measurements of variations in the earth's gravitational and magnetic fields can provide information about the structure of layers of rock buried deep beneath the surface.

One of the most effective geophysical tools for locating structural traps is the seismograph. Sound waves are transmitted deep into the earth. Microphones (geophones) are placed along the ground to record the echoes reflected from buried layers of rock. The principle is similar to radar and so-

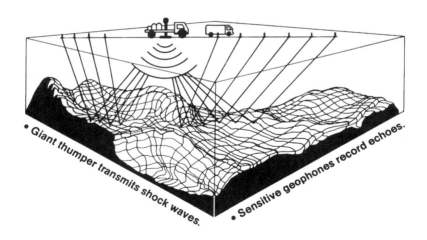

Figure 2.7 Seismic Surveying
Depth to rock layer can be estimated from the time it takes for echoes to be reflected back to the surface

nar. Geophones are arranged in a line and connected to a recording computer by electrical cables. Computer processing produces an image of the geologic structures below the surface. In particular geologic environments (such as offshore in the Mississippi River delta, or the delta of the Niger River) it is sometimes possible to directly detect the presence of oil and gas thousands of feet below the surface from seismic images, with a surprisingly high degree of success.

"Large discoveries are more probable elsewhere (outside the U.S.) but are no longer economically preferable on the basis of sheer size. Part of the reason for that is the comparatively long time required for start of production from large fields in remote areas."

"J.S. Herold: North American E&P back on track"
Oil & Gas Journal, July 15, 1996

The health care industry now applies the same seismic principles in the ultrasonic scanning of bones and organs hidden beneath the skin.

Traditional seismic land crews generally work 12 hours per day, 6 days a week, and can cover up to about three linear miles per day, depending on the terrain and the weather. Even under the best of circumstances, however, seismic surveying ('shooting') can be expensive – ranging from about $3,000 per linear mile to more than $12,000 per linear mile, depending on the relief and difficulty of traversing the surface terrain.

Newer three-dimensional seismic (3-D) data field work involves involves a very similar procedure,

Flat-Lying Rock Layers

White Rim Trail.   *Photo by Jacqueline E. Huntoon*
Canyonlands Nat'l Park, UT.   *Penn. State University*
View of top of cliff-froming White Rim Sandstone from top of Junction Butte.
Re-printed by permission of AAPG

Folded Rock Layers

Lulworth Cove, U.K.   *Photo by Author*

Figure 2.8

except in 3-D work, the geophones are laid out in several parallel east-west lines, so that they form a rectangular grid over an area that extends both east-west and north-south. The reflected echoes are recorded along the grid, and processed by computer to generate a three-dimensional image of the sub surface. As with traditional seismic data collection, terrain and relief significantly influence cost. Onshore in the U.S., the current cost of shooting and processing 3-D data currently ranges from perhaps $30,000 - $50,000 per square mile, depending on terrain and the design criteria of the shoot.

The geologist's most reliable information comes from wells previously drilled in the vicinity of his prospect. Suppose a well is drilled into a new sand, never before seen in nearby wells. From which direction did the ancient sediments come? Where were the river channels? the river delta? the ancient shoreline? By mapping and reconstructing the ancient geography, a geologist can anticipate where to go to find more of that sand.

More detailed investigation may reveal the geometrical configuration of a trap in which the sand could be filled with oil or gas. Oil or gas reservoirs are thin layers of rock that can extend across tens of square miles or more. From movements of the earth's crust, they are often folded and rumpled, like blankets on an unmade bed. The dip (tilt or angle of inclination) of a rock-layer measured in a well would indicate the direction buoyant oil or gas would naturally tend to flow.

After analyzing available data, the geologist creates two final maps of the reservoir rock-layer. One is a structure map. Like a topographic map of the

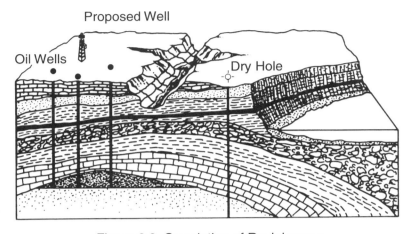

Proposed Well

Oil Wells

Dry Hole

Figure 2.9 Correlation of Rock Layers
Recognizable rock layers can extend across hundreds of square miles.
In the sub-surface they can be correlated from well to well. Often some
of these can be inspected where they crop out at the surface.

earth's surface, it shows the high areas and low areas ('hills' and 'valleys') of the rock-layer, across the prospect. Since oil and gas are mobile and lighter than water, they will naturally move into high areas, to become trapped in places from which there is no avenue of escape (a fold shaped like an inverted soup plate, for example). A second map shows where the best porosity exists in the reservoir rock.

A good prospect should be structurally high compared to the surrounding and nearby area (to have captured any buoyant hydrocarbons migrating through the area). It should have abundant porosity (to be able to hold a large accumulation).

A developmental prospect involves a reservoir that has already been found to produce oil or gas in the area around the proposed well. An explor-

3-Dimensional View of a Real Situation
(Prospect is described by maps.)

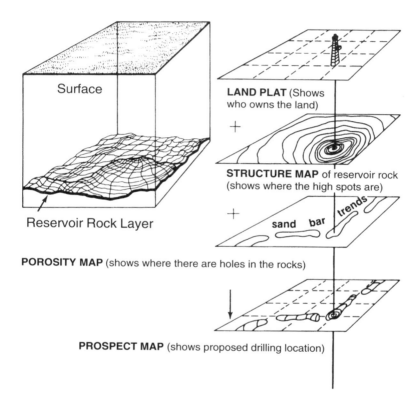

Surface

Reservoir Rock Layer

LAND PLAT (Shows who owns the land)

STRUCTURE MAP of reservoir rock (shows where the high spots are)

sand bar trends

POROSITY MAP (shows where there are holes in the rocks)

PROSPECT MAP (shows proposed drilling location)

Figure 2.10 Typical Prospect

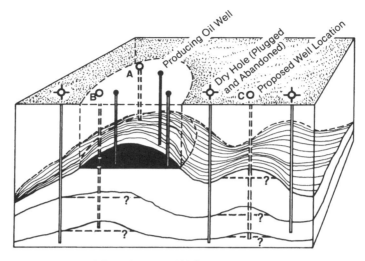

A *Development Well*
B *Exploratory Well (deeper pool test)*
C *Exploratory Well (new field wildcat)*

Figure 2.11 Exploratory vs Development Drilling

atory prospect seeks to find new production from a reservoir that has not yet been proven productive in the area of the proposed well.

The Costs and Their Tax Significance

Expenditures involved in prospect generation are referred to as G&G (geological and geophysical) costs. They may include data acquisition and analysis, and geologic and geophysical surveys. Most G&G costs associated with exploratory drilling were long considered capital expenditures, and commonly lumped together with lease acquisition costs (please see discussion under Land). Some G&G costs involved in development drilling were treated as currently deductible expenses.

The Energy Policy Act of 2005 revised the tax treatment of G&G expenses. For the previoius 80 or so years, they have been treated as capital expenditures to be capitalized and depreciated. Under the new legislation they can be written off over a period of 2 years. While this isn't quite as favorable as treating them as currently deductible expenses, it does serve to help improve the economics of petroleum exploration and development.

It seems both reasonable and appropriate now as more (and more advanced) Geological and Geophysical effort is commonly applied to the pre-drilling evaluation of a prospect. Important (and in terms of dollar costs, signficiant) pre-drilling G&G expenditures might include: 3-D seismic, reservoir analysis, ERTS satellite image data, surface geochemical data, and the analysis and integration of these and other data into detailed subsurface mapping of a new drilling location.

Real Geologists ...

- don't eat quiche; they don't even know what it is. Real geologists like raw meat, bear, and tonsil-killer chili.
- don't need rock hammers. They break samples off with their bare hands.
- don't sit in offices. Being indoors makes them crazy. If they wanted to sit indoors all day, they'd have become geophysicists.
- don't need geophysicists. Geophysicists measure things nobody can see or feel, make up a whole lot of numbers about them, then drill in all the wrong places.
- don't make exploration budgets. Nervous managers make exploration budgets. Only insecure mama's boys try to stay within exploration budgets. Real geologists ignore exploration budgets.
- don't use compasses out in the field. That smacks of geophysics. Real geologists always know exactly where they are and the direction of the nearest place where cold beer is available.
- don't have joint-venture partners. Partners for for wimpy bed-wetters who don't know how to "think big".
- don't write reports. Bureaucrats write reports, and you know what they're like!

After J. Gardner, Editor, Geolog, the news magazine of the Geological Association of Canada.

Chapter 3

LAND

Who owns the land?

Landman

The petroleum landman's job is to acquire the right to drill for oil and gas on the tract of land which overlies the geologist's prospect. He negotiates the purchase of drilling rights from the landowner, and corrects (cures) defects in the legal title to property that is leased. (A cursory review of title is conducted at the time non-producing leases are acquired. Thorough title examination is generally made only after drilling operations are scheduled.) The landman also assists in complying with government reporting procedures.

If employed by a major oil company, the landman is normally paid an annual salary. There are over 7,750 petroleum landmen in the U.S.[26] Many work for smaller independent companies. They may be paid an annual salary plus some form of participation in future revenues from oil and gas discovered on property they have leased. Independent landmen may work on a day rate for cash and/or some form of participation in production revenues.

Historical Perspective

U.S. law pertaining to ownership of land is largely based on English common law under which land has been granted to individuals, for more than 800 years. (Early grants were often for service to the king such as military service in battle). American oil and gas law has also been influenced by Spanish custom. In the 18th century, the King of Spain granted land to settlers of North and South America, but retained rights to 1/5 of all production from mines developed on these lands (a share of production for the royals (or 'royalty').[27]

Land measurement in the original thirteen colonies was founded on the English system of irregular measurements and natural (non-systematic) boundaries ('metes and bounds').[28] Charles Mason and Jeremiah Dixon were the English surveyors who established the first professional boundary survey in the colonies. The Mason-Dixon line (which runs east-west between Pennsylvania and Maryland, and then north-south between Maryland and Delaware) has become a symbolic division between the North and South. One of the earliest American surveyors was young George Washington, who later became the first President of the United States.[29]

During the American Revolutionary War, the cash-starved revolutionary government often granted land (claimed by the original thirteen colonies) as compensation (in lieu of wages) to American soldiers who had fought for the nation's independence. After the war, Federal lands were viewed as a potential source of revenue. Tracts could be sold for settlement, with the proceeds going to pay off the large national debt that had accrued during the course of the war. Congress

Figure 3.1 Historical Influence on U.S. Lands

COUNTY AND STATE: Caddo County, Oklahoma

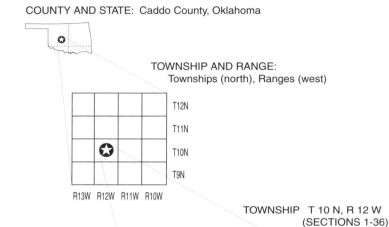

TOWNSHIP AND RANGE:
Townships (north), Ranges (west)

TOWNSHIP   T 10 N, R 12 W
(SECTIONS 1-36)

SECTION: Section 9 (9-10N-12W)

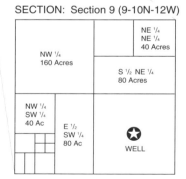

WELL: John Smith #1 c SE ¼ 9-10N-12W (Center of SE
Quarter, Section 9, Township 10N Range 12W,
Caddo County, Oklahoma)

Figure 3.2 Township and Range

passed the National Land Act of 1785, establishing a uniform land measurement system. It was modified after an earlier proposal of the nation's third President, Thomas Jefferson (whose father was a surveyor.) In most states, land is now measured according to this township and range system. (See Figure 3.2.) It establishes uniform squares, six miles on a side ('townships'); they, in turn, are subdivided into 36 uniform squares one mile on a side ('sections').[30]

Some areas of the U.S. retain peculiarities of land ownership which existed at the time these territories became states. Counties are known as 'parishes' in Louisiana, reflecting the influence of early

"Rise of oil, gas hedge funds cited in volatility of U.S. energy prices"

by Paul Monies in THE OKLAHOMAN, Wednesday, March 1, 2006

French land administration along the lower Mississippi River valley, before Louisiana became a state (in 1812). Present day land administration and ownership in Texas bears the influence of land grants in the south and southwest made by the Spanish land commissioner, before Texas became a state in (1845).

Under the constitution of the United States, some government functions are administered by the Federal (national) government, others by the state government. Education, intrastate commerce, and intrastate transportation, for example, are administered at the state level. Exploration and production of natural resources within state borders are also administered by the state.

Oil and gas law can differ significantly from state to state. Petroleum is fluid. In some states, the law is based on the concept that petroleum is mobile and is not owned until it is produced (law of capture). In other states, law is based on the concept that petroleum is a mineral, and as such, it is treated the same as solid minerals (ownership in place).[31]

Acquiring The Rights To Drill

Under U.S. law, land ownership is three dimensional. The landowner (fee simple owner) of a tract of land holds the right to use, occupy, and enjoy the surface of the land and the air space above it (surface rights), plus all rights to minerals beneath it (mineral rights).[32]

The fee simple owner may divide (in legal parlance: "sever") the rights to his land either vertically or horizontally. In the case of horizontal severance, the surface rights and the mineral rights become two separate and distinct estates, and each may change hands independently of the other. If mineral rights have been severed, then the owner of a farm or ranch (surface ownership) does not own title to the minerals beneath the surface of his land (minerals ownership). Minerals ownership generally includes the right of access to as much of the surface as may be necessary to explore for and to produce the minerals. Please refer to Figure 3.4.

The minerals owner holds the exclusive right to explore for, and to produce (remove), oil, or gas, or other minerals from his property.[33]

Instead of undertaking exploration and production of these minerals himself, he may lease or sell these minerals rights to another party. These rights may be sold or leased in whole or in part, with or without restrictions (as to certain minerals or to certain depth intervals below the surface, etc.).

An oil company evaluates the geologist's prospect. If they believe they can make money by drilling for oil and gas on a particular tract of land, the company's landman will negotiate with the min-

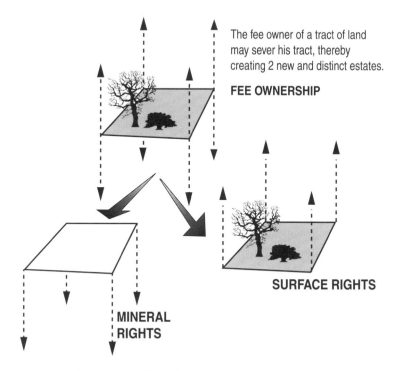

The fee owner of a tract of land may sever his tract, thereby creating 2 new and distinct estates.

FEE OWNERSHIP

SURFACE RIGHTS

MINERAL RIGHTS

Figure 3.3 Fee Ownership and Severance

POTENTIAL DISPOSITION OF MINERAL RIGHTS

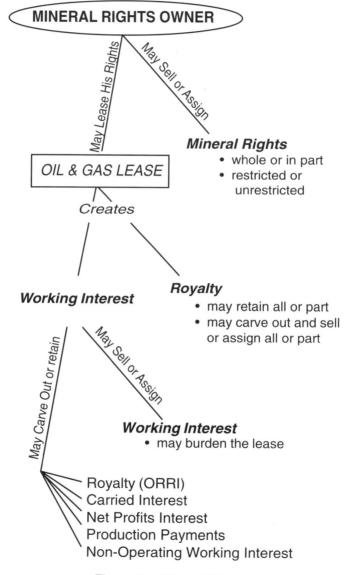

Figure 3.4 Mineral Rights

erals owner for the permission (the legal right) to drill a well. If an agreement can be reached, the minerals owner may grant exploration and production rights through the execution of a written lease agreement (a 'lease'). The typical lease agreement covers at least five fundamental areas:

BONUS - Cash paid by the oil company to the minerals owner to obtain the lease (to obtain the exclusive right to produce and sell minerals from the leased property). During the last 20 years, the bonus amount has probably ranged from $1.00 (or less?) per acre to $10,000.00 (or more) per acre, depending of the prospectivity of the land being leased.

ROYALTY - A cost-free share of the proceeds of any oil or gas produced on his land, retained by the minerals owner, payable as the minerals are produced and sold.

PRIMARY TERM - The period of time a lease is in effect (provided that delay rentals or shut-in royalties are paid and current). Nowadays it might typically range anywhere from 6 months to several years. Historically, it has ranged as long as 75 years or more.[34]

DELAY RENTALS - Cash payments made by the oil company to the mineral rights owner to postpone the drilling of a well. An oil company often seeks the exclusive right to drill a well, but may want to wait on the outcome of nearby exploration drilling activities before deciding whether or not to spend the money to drill their own well. The landowner typically prefers to see a well drilled immediately.

SECONDARY TERM - The period of time (after the expiration of the primary term) that a lease may be extended by the drilling of a well, or by the establishment of production (commonly "for so long as oil and gas be produced in paying quantities").[35]

Interests Created by a *Lease*

A lease agreement creates two specific interests: a 'royalty interest' and a 'working interest'.

The royalty interest is a right to a cost-free share of the proceeds resulting from production of oil and gas (on the tract of land covered by the lease agreement). The landowner generally retains the royalty interest (although he may sell or assign it to a third party). In most states, royalty interests are expressed as a fractional part of the whole (1/8 or 3/16, for example). Some of the fractions commonly seen in lease agreements and their percentage equivalents, in increasing amount:

1/16	=	6.25 %
1/8	=	12.50 %
5/32	=	15.63 %
1/6	=	16.67 %
3/16	=	18.75 %
1/5	=	20.00 %
1/4	=	25.00 %
5/16	=	31.25 %

The working interest is the exclusive right to explore for, and produce, oil and gas on the tract of land covered by the lease. It includes the obligation to pay 100% of the costs of exploration and production of any oil or gas found. The working-interest owner is entitled to all revenues from production attributable to a lease, after deducting revenues accruing to the royalty interests. The working interest owner may reduce his share of revenues (burden the lease) by carving out revenue interests and transferring them to others.

One of the revenue interests commonly burdening a lease is the overriding royalty interest (ORRI). It is a cost-free share of the proceeds from gross production. Although it appears similar to the landowners royalty, an 'override' is created by the working-interest owner when he carves out part

"Crude Oil Drops below $65 a barrel"

The Oklahoman, Friday, September 2005

of his share of the revenues. It is an assignment of rights to specified revenue under the lease agreement and is in effect only as long as the lease is in effect, and can be sold or assigned to a third party. After such assignment, the working-interest owner's share of the costs is still the same (100%), but his share in the revenues (his 'net revenue interest') is now reduced by the landowners royalty and any overriding royalties (or other burdens). For example:

Gross revenues from production	100.0 %	
- landowner's royalty	12.5 %	(= 1/8)
- overriding royalties	5.0 %	
- any other burdens	0.0 %	
Net revenue interest	82.5%	

States are subdivided into local geographical areas (counties). Ownership and the transfer of title to a tract of land (also lease agreements and assignment of overriding royalties) are recorded at the courthouse of the county in which the land is located. If not properly recorded, title has not vested in the owner, which creates substantial risk of loss. County records are available for public inspection.

"Entrants, returnees to Libya face tight equipment market"

Oil & Gas Journal, January 23, 2006

Government Land Administration

A landman deals not only with the landowner and the county courthouse, but also with various state agencies.

When application is made for the drilling of a well, the state regulating agency establishes the "drilling and spacing unit" (surface-area density) for oil wells, and for gas wells, for each of the anticipated reservoirs. In theory, one well should be able to produce most of the petroleum that can be recovered from the area of the reservoir that lies within the spacing unit.

To efficiently exploit oil and gas reserves contained in the reservoir, a single well should be able to produce most of the recoverable petroleum from within that reservoir's drilling and spacing unit.

The fractional ownership of a well, is proportional to the working-interest ownership of acre-

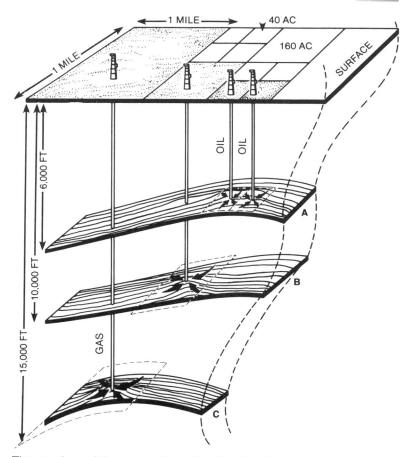

The spacing unit is assigned by estimating the (size of the) area, from which recoverable hydrocarbons are likely to be effectively drained by a single well.

In the diagram

Reservoir A   Wells producing OIL from Reservoir A (6,000 feet) are spaced at 40 acres (1 well per 40 acres).

Reservoir C   Wells producing GAS from Reservoir C (15,000 feet) are spaced at 640 acres (1 well per 640 acres).

Reservoir B   Wells producing GAS from Reservoir B (10,000 feet) are spaced at 160 acres (as shown). OIL wells might be spaced at 80 acres.

Figure 3.5 Spacing Units

age within the well's spacing unit ("drilling and spacing unit" or DSU).

Assume a well is proposed in the northeast quarter of a section, and you have leased the mineral rights to 80 acres of land located in this quarter-section (which consists of 160 acres = 1/4 of the 640 acres in a square mile).

- If the spacing unit of the well is set by the state at 160 acres, you would have a 50% working interest in the proposed well (and would be obliged to pay 50% of the well costs to receive 50% of the revenue, net of royalties); your 80 acres /160 acres in the quarter section = 1/2 = 50%.

- If, on the other hand, the spacing unit is set by the state at 640 acres, you would have a 12.5% working interest in the proposed well (and would be obliged to pay only 12.5% of the well costs to receive 12.5% of net revenues); your 80 acres /640 acres = 1/8 = 12.5%.

The spacing unit for wells producing from a particular reservoir is determined on the basis of physical principles and efficiency of exploitation. Both temperature and pressure increase with depth below the earth's surface. Oil flows more readily at higher temperature. Gas becomes more compressed under greater pressure. The spacing unit for high pressure gas at 15,000 feet, would likely be 640 acres or more, while the spacing unit for oil at a depth of 2,000 feet might only be 10 acres. Please see Figure 3.5. In the case of a reservoir at a depth of 10,000 feet, a single well might be able to drain *gas* from an area of 320 acres

EXAMPLE 3.1

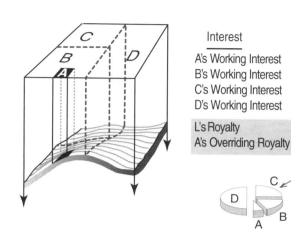

Share of :

Interest	Costs	Revenues
A's Working Interest	6.25%	5.4687%
B's Working Interest	18.75%	15.6563%
C's Working Interest	25.00%	20.8750%
D's Working Interest	50.00%	41.7500%
L's Royalty	0	12.50%
A's Overriding Royalty	0	3.75%

A leases from *L*, 160 acres owned by *L*. *L* retains a 1/8 (= 12.5%) royalty interest.

State authorities set the spacing unit for the well *A* proposes to drill at 160 acres.

A keeps 10 acres (10/160 = 1/16 = 6.25%) and burdens the remaining 150 acres with a 4% overriding royalty.

A sub-leases the 150 acres to *B*, *C*, and *D*, delivering to them an 83.5% net-revenue-interest lease (= 100% less *L*'s 1/8 royalty, less *A*'s 4% override.)

CALCULATION:

Working Interest (W/I)		less Burdens		W/I Net Revenue Interest
Acreage	W/I	(W/I x Royalty)	(W/I x ORRI)	NRI
A 10	1/16 = .0625	1/16 x 1/8 = 0.0078	1/16 x0 = 0	0.05468
B 30	3/16 = .1875	3/16 x 1/8 = 0.0234	3/16 x4% = 0.0075	0.15656
C 40	1/4 = .25	1/4 x 1/8 = 0.0313	1/4 x4% = 0.01	0.20875
D 80	1/2 = .5	1/2 x 1/8 = 0.0625	1/2 x4% = 0.02	0.4175
160	1.0	0.125	0.0375 = 0.8375	
Acres	Working Interest	Landowner's Royalty	Overriding Royalty	Net Revenue Interest

around the well, but it might be able to drain *oil* from an area of only 160 or even 80 acres.

The Costs and Their Tax Significance

The expenditures involved in acquiring leases are called lease acquisition costs (also 'leasehold' costs). They are capital expenditures and include lease bonus payments, delay rental payments, and various costs related to acquiring a lease such as legal fees. Geological and geophysical (G&G) costs are also commonly included under leasehold costs.

Photo Courtesy of Mac McGalliard and McGalliard Historical Collection, Ardmore Public Library, Ardmore, OK

THE HEALDTON FIELD IN SOUTHERN OKLAHOMA (IN 1914)

Figure 3.6 Before State Regulation of Spacing Units

Chapter 4

DRILLING

Getting to the rocks

Operator and Drilling Contractor

Because of the high costs and the risks involved in drilling a well, the co-owners (fractional working-interest owners) of a property may join together, in a single, common effort (a joint venture). They normally enter into a joint operating agreement (JOA), under which one of the working-in-

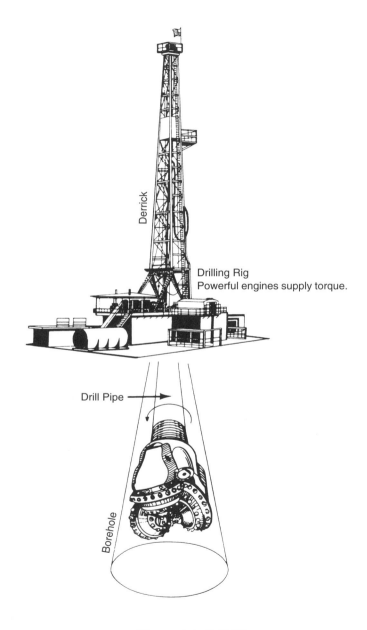

Figure 4.1 Drill Bit

terest owners is designated the operator, and the other working-interest owners are non-operators.

On behalf of all working-interest owners, the operator manages the drilling, testing, completion, and production of the well. Although the operator may be an individual, most operating companies are staffed with experienced personnel who supervise operations. The operator solicits bids from drilling contractors for the drilling of a proposed well, or he may have drilling rigs and his own drilling personnel. He provides reliable estimates of the

"As Gas Guzzling Becomes a Way of Life, Oil Imports Soar"
Suburbia Can't Kick the Nozzle by Agis Salpukas
THE NEW YORK TIMES, Tuesday, July 23, 1996

various anticipated costs of drilling and completing the proposed well in a document called an authorization for expenditure (AFE). Please see Appendix B. Once it is approved by the working-interest owners and all the required permits are obtained, drilling operations can proceed according to the operator's written plan (sometimes referred to as the drilling prognosis).

The operator provides daily drilling reports to the non-operators. He keeps records, pays invoices, and in turn, bills non-operators for their proportionate share of expenses (joint interest billing - JIB). The operator is compensated for his overhead and direct costs, billing each working-interest owner his fractional share of these costs, according to provisions of the joint operating agreement. The drilling contractor is paid according to a contract for

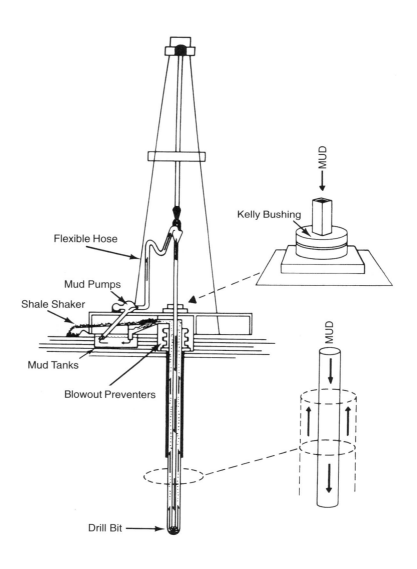

Figure 4.2 Circulation of the Drilling Mud

the drilling of the well. It may be based on a cost-per-day (day rate), on a cost-per-foot of hole drilled (footage rate), or on a set cost for drilling the proposed well to a specific depth (turnkey basis).

Drilling a well is expensive. The cost depends mainly the depth of the well, and on the degree of difficulty encountered in the drilling (and hence the time it takes to drill the well). Success often depends on the quality and experience of the operator. Although working-interest owners have legal recourse to remove the operator (a provision of the joint operating agreement), this is rarely done. Knowledgeable participants try to avoid this sort of problem up front, by not participating in a well unless they know the operator and have confidence in his ability.

Drilling The Well

Field operations begin by placing a stake in the ground at the well location. The staked location is surveyed to make sure it is properly located over the geologist's prospect (and that it is on the tract of land that was leased by the landman). Earth-moving equipment is used to build a road leading to the well site, and to clear and level the ground ('site preparation', 'building a location'). A water well may be needed to supply water for the drilling operations. The various components of the drilling rig are trucked to the location and assembled. Pipe and equipment that will be used in the drilling of the well are laid out, and drilling fluid (mud) is prepared.

A mobile drilling unit may be used to start the hole from the surface, or the well may be started (spudded) by the much bigger, assembled drilling rig. Once the surface portion is drilled, large diameter steel pipe (surface casing whose diameter might range up to 20") is lowered into the borehole by a crew using special large-diameter-casing handling equipment. A subcontractor cements the casing in place by pumping a slurry of cement into the ('annular') space around the outside of the casing, securing it to the walls of the borehole. Blow-

"World's Oil Supply to Hit Peak in 2010, Then Fall, Experts Say"
ROAR Newsletter, June 1, 2002

out preventers and other safety equipment can then be installed at the top of the casing. Drilling into an unexpected pocket of high pressure gas would be like sticking a pin in a balloon. The blowout preventers can be closed to prevent any uncontrolled flow of oil, gas, or drilling fluid from the well.

Drilling proceeds with a drill bit that has a relatively large diameter (but is still small enough to pass down through the surface casing). It is screwed into a length of drill pipe and lowered into the borehole. The drill pipe is turned clockwise by powerful drilling rig engines (traditionally fueled by diesel fuel, but now increasingly powered by electricity). As the bit cuts the borehole about 30 feet deeper, another joint is added to the string of drill pipe already in the hole.

When a drill bit becomes dull, it must be replaced. To do this, the drill string must be pulled out of the borehole, hoisted into the derrick, and disassembled. Each third joint is unscrewed. The 3-joint stands of drill pipe (about 90 feet tall), are leaned against the derrick of the oil rig.

After replacing the bit, the string of drill pipe is reconnected and run back into the borehole, three joints at a time. Drilling can resume once the drill bit is back on the bottom. Operations continue around the clock with three crews (of five or more men) each working eight-hour shifts (a shift may be referred to as a tower, but in the field is generally pronounced so that it sounds like a 'tour').

Drilling may be interrupted for any number of reasons. Drilling breaks, circulating bottoms up, logging, coring, and setting casing are situations that are anticipated, and provided for in the written drilling plan. (These operations are all described in the Glossary.) Drilling is normally intended to follow a straight line vertically down from the surface (as required by government regulations and the joint operating agreement), but peculiarities of the rock-layers may cause the borehole to veer off slanting in one direction or another. Drilling is frequently interrupted to measure the inclination of the borehole (directional survey) and to whatever may be necessary to get the hole back on a vertical course. Lost circulation, fishing, and drill stem testing may result in unanticipated interruptions in the drilling. (Please see the Glossary.)

Drilling through layers of rock having different pressure characteristics may require one or more strings of (intermediate) casing. Casing serves to keep different pressure regimes isolated from each other. (A second string of intermediate casing might also be called for in drilling through loose sandy sediments which might otherwise tend to cave off the walls and into the borehole, or in any of a number of particular borehole conditions.) Before running casing, the drill string is pulled out of the hole. Sensitive electronic devices (logging tools) are then lowered down into the borehole on a wireline. Logging tools measure characteristics of the layers of rock that have been penetrated: electrical resistivity, density, porosity, natural gamma-ray radiation, and inclination, as well as the diameter and other characteristics of the borehole. Measurements are electronically recorded on computers in a truck-mounted laboratory at the surface, and graphically displayed on paper or film as a curve (wiggle trace) plotted against depth. Traditionally, most of these characteristics could not be measured after steel casing has been set in the hole, but recent new technologies (not yet widely applied) suggest that it may now be possible to record valid measurements of these parameters, even through the casing. Drilling is resumed with a smaller bit that can pass down through the intermediate casing.

When a carpenter drills through wood, his drill bit is designed so that wood shavings are automatically conducted out of the drilled hole (usually only a few inches deep). Drilling a well through thousands of feet of rock requires a different technique.

The borehole is always filled with a heavy drilling fluid (drilling mud). During drilling operations,

mud is (continuously) pumped down into the borehole through the drill pipe. It flows from the drill
pipe into the borehole, through nozzles in the drill
bit; it then circulates back up to the surface
through the space (annulus) between the drill pipe
and the walls of the borehole (or intermediate casing). If the borehole should drill into a pocket of
high pressure gas, it is the weight of the drilling
mud in the hole that will balance and contain pressures exerted by the gas. Mud also helps stabilize
the walls of the borehole; it cools the bit; and it

Rising U.S. dependence on LNG carries risks

"The United States is increasingly going overseas to meet
its natural gas needs ..."

by Brad Foss, AP Business Writer,
The Oklahoman, Wednesday, February 15, 2006

carries chips of rock cut by the drill bit up to the
surface where they are screened out of the mud
system by the shale shaker. The job of the mud logger is to collect the rock chips (cuttings) and examine them under a microscope for visual indications of porosity, and shows of oil and gas.

Once the borehole penetrates the primary objective reservoir of the prospect, logging tools are
again lowered into the borehole to measure and
record various rock parameters. A geologist is usually on hand to witness this operation. He makes a
preliminary evaluation of the log data at the
wellsite, to detect the presence and quality of any
petroleum in the penetrated layers of rock.

This sets the stage for the critical phase in exploration for oil and gas, the casing point election.

The Costs and Their Tax Significance

Drilling costs fall into two categories: equipment (tangible) costs and intangible drilling and development costs (IDC).

Equipment costs are amortizable capital expenditures for assets which have a future useful life and can be salvaged (casing for example). In Federal income tax calculations, equipment costs provide scheduled annual deductions (depreciation allowance) from gross income. (The formerly available investment tax credit was repealed by the Tax Reform Act of 1986.)

Intangible drilling and development costs (IDC) include such items as wages, repairs, and hauling; plus consumables such as fuel, water, drill bits, and mud used in the drilling of wells. Some of these expenditures may appear to be capital expenditures by nature. Nevertheless, the taxpayer is permitted to elect to treat them as expenses, completely deductible from income (as allowed according to passive/non-passive income classification) in the year paid or incurred.[36]

Photo Courtesy of Oklahoma Historical Society

Figure 4.3 Unidentified Blowout

Pressures in a Well

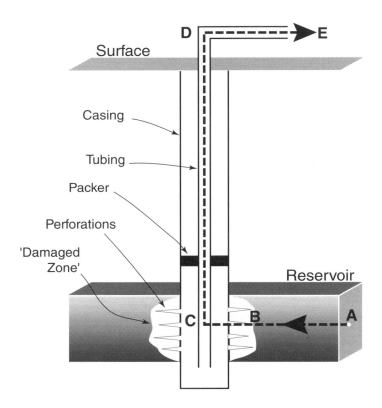

A Natural reservoir pressure

B "Sand Face Pressure" (interface between zone around well bore damaged by invasion of drilling fluid and reservoir).

C Bottom hole pressure.

D Wellhead pressure (shut-in)

   Flowing tubing pressure (flowing).

E Separator pressure

Chapter 5

CASING POINT ELECTION

Are there holes in the rocks?

Here is what separates the men from the boys. Or as a business associate likes to say, "This is where the rubber meets the road!".

The well has been drilled to the planned total depth (TD) and logs have been run. Additional investment will be required to complete the well (to make it ready for commercial production).

The setting of surface and intermediate casing are normally included in a drilling plan. Production casing is run only if the well appears to be capable of commercial production.

'Casing point election' refers to the working-interest owner's decision. Let's assume this is you. Should you participate in the completion of the well

"There is at least a 50-50 chance that OPEC will become irrelevant as a price-controlling organization within the next two years."

The End of OPEC as We Know It? by Charles T. Maxwell
THE WALL STREET JOURNAL, Wednesday, December 27, 1995

by paying your share of production casing and other costs? Or should you plug and abandon (P&A) the well as a dry hole (noncommercial)?

Immediately after the well reaches the planned final total depth, and logs are run, the geologist integrates all available information about zones of interest (intervals of penetrated rock with either porosity or hydrocarbon shows). Such information includes:

- visual examination of the rock cuttings,
- ultraviolet inspection of oil shows,
- chemical analysis of gas dissolved in the mud system,
- porosity inferred from rate of drilling (drilling breaks), and
- analysis of wireline log data.

He then compares the characteristics of these zones with the corresponding rock-layers penetrated in nearby wells (both producers and dry-holes). On the basis of his evaluation, he recommends that well either be completed in one or more zones, or plugged and abandoned.

Time is critical. The drilling contractor's equipment and personnel are standing by, waiting on orders (and costing thousands of dollars a day). As working-interest owner in the well, you have the right to perform your own evaluation (or have your own geologist perform an evaluation for you) of the zones penetrated in the well. You must notify the operator of your decision, usually within 48 hours of receiving copies of the wireline logs.

The operator will complete or abandon the well, according to the election of the majority of the working interest owners.

If the majority of the working interest elect to complete the well, all working interest owners are obliged to pay their proportional share of the assessed completion costs. If you do not consent to bear your proportional share of the expenses involved, you are said to have 'gone non-consent'.

The effect of 'going non-consent' is that the other

"One of the reasons we were selling all those arms to the Saudis was for lower oil prices," recalls Caspar Weinberger.

Excerpts from VICTORY by Peter Schweizer
published by Atlantic Monthly Press

working interest owners will have little choice, other than to pay your share of the completion costs. You will be penalized by a reduction in your share production revenues, as spelled out in the joint operating agreement (JOA). The specific terms vary, but as a non-consenting party, you may have forfeited rights to your share of production revenues (if any), until after the other working interest owners (those who paid your share of

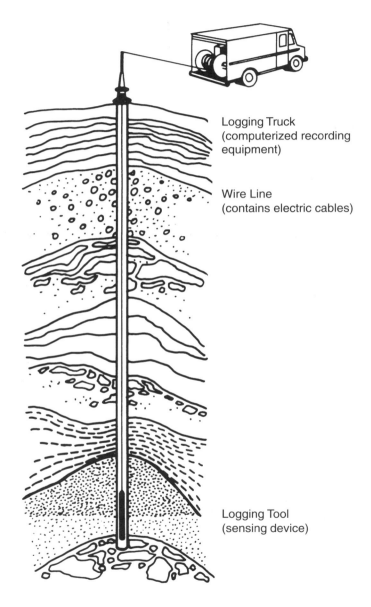

Logging Truck
(computerized recording
equipment)

Wire Line
(contains electric cables)

Logging Tool
(sensing device)

Figure 5.1 Logging a Well

completion costs) have recovered as much as 300% of the costs, which they paid in your stead). In many, cases, this means that for all practical purposes, you

> Lower oil prices became a key administration objective in 1985. For many in the Reagan administration, the main advantage was to the United States. "We wanted lower international oil prices, largely for the benefit of the American economy," says Edwin Meese, then White House Counsel. "The fact that it meant trouble for Moscow was icing on the cake."
>
> *Excerpts from VICTORY by Peter Schweizer*
> *The Journal of Commerce, Monday, July 15, 1996*

are effectively out of the money in this well.

If in the case of a successful well, you as working-interest owner fail to notify the operator of your election within the time period specified in the joint operating agreement, the result is the same as 'going non-consent'. You would be deemed to have 'gone non-consent', and will be penalized by a severe reduction in your share of the production revenues as described above.

The Costs and Their Tax Significance

The authorization for expenditure (AFE) itemizes costs of drilling the well before casing point (BCP), separately from completion costs that will be incurred after casing point (ACP). Completion costs can range from about 35% to as much as 100% of the drilling costs. Please see Appendix B.

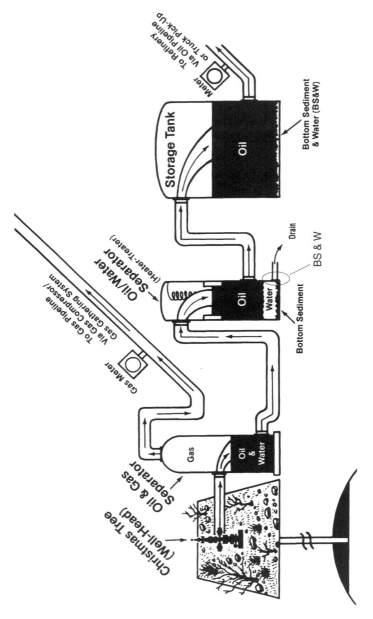

Figure 6.5 From Christmas Tree to Refinery

Chapter 6

COMPLETION

Is there oil in the holes?

Petroleum Engineer

The petroleum engineer plays a critical role in the completion of a well. On the basis of his analysis of mechanical procedures and equipment used on nearby wells, and wells with similar reservoirs in similar geologic settings, he develops a completion plan. After the well is completed, he evaluates

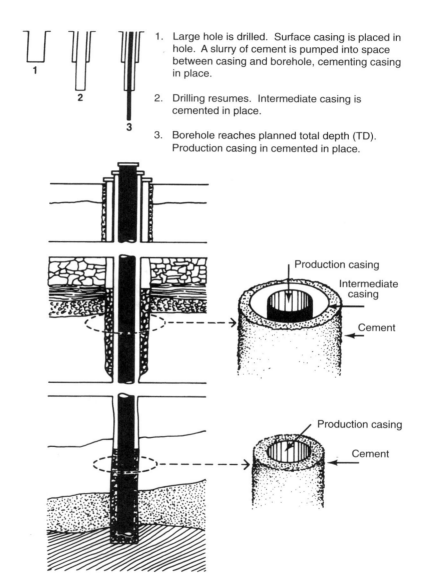

1. Large hole is drilled. Surface casing is placed in hole. A slurry of cement is pumped into space between casing and borehole, cementing casing in place.

2. Drilling resumes. Intermediate casing is cemented in place.

3. Borehole reaches planned total depth (TD). Production casing in cemented in place.

Figure 6.1 Casing

production test data and calculates the volume of reserves attributable to the well, and estimates the well's production capabilities.

There are about 31,000 petroleum engineers in the U.S.[37] If employed by an oil company, a petroleum engineer is usually paid an annual salary. Independent petroleum engineers may consult on an individual basis, for compensation in cash and/or a share of production revenues.

Getting The Well to Flow

Once the decision has been made to complete the well, production casing is run in the borehole and cemented in place. Production tubing is run down

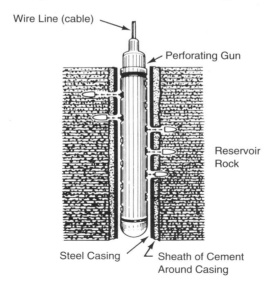

Wire Line (cable)

Perforating Gun

Reservoir Rock

Steel Casing

Sheath of Cement Around Casing

Bullets are shot through the casing into the reservoir rock

Figure 6.2 Perforation

inside the casing, to the level of the reservoir to be tested. The portion of the casing that may extend below the reservoir is plugged off. An expandable barrier (a packer) is installed above the reservoir level to block off the donut-shaped space (annulus) around the tubing. These plugs and barriers straddle the reservoir so that it will be in communication with the surface (by way of the production tubing.)

A perforating gun is lowered down through the drilling mud on a wire line, and positioned at the

---

Cushing (OK) pipeline to Canada reopened;
Re-dedication starts flow of oil to state refiners.
" …Canada is the largest supplier of crude oil to the U.S. … there is potential for the exports to the U.S. to double in the next 10 years… the pipeline flows give Cushing - and the region's other refiners - access to crude supplies from the vast Oil Sands of Alberta, Canada."

Adam Wilmoth in The Oklahoman, Friday, March 3, 2006

---

level of the zone of interest. It is electronically detonated from the surface, shooting a few dozen holes that penetrate through both the steel casing, and the sheath of cement around the casing and into the walls of the borehole. The gun is pulled back out of the hole.

Valves at the surface can be opened, allowing natural pressures in the rock thousands of feet below the surface, to force fluids from the reservoir through the perforations in the casing, into the blocked-off interval of the borehole, and up to the surface through the production tubing.

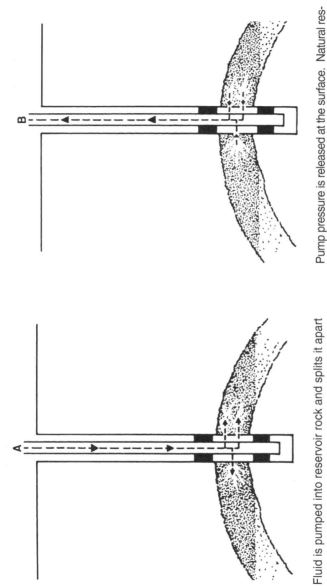

Pump pressure is released at the surface. Natural reservoir pressure forces frac fluid back into the borehole and up to the surface (followed by reservoir fluids).

FRACTURING ENHANCES FLOW FROM THE RESERVOIR

Fluid is pumped into reservoir rock and splits it apart

Beads prop the fractures open.

Figure 6.3   Frac'ing

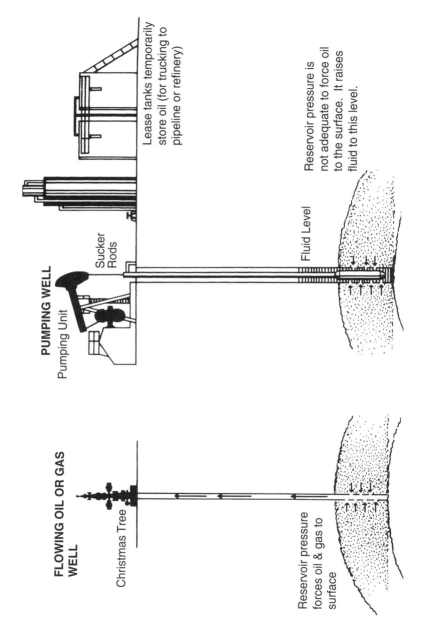

Figure 6.4 Completed Wells

To minimize costs, a big drilling rig might be replaced at this point with a smaller, less expensive, mobile completion rig. Attempts are made to get the zone to flow naturally. This commonly involves bailing out (swabbing) fluid from inside the production tubing. If pressure in the tubing can be lowered below the natural pressures in the pay zone, the well should flow naturally. The natural flow rate is compared to historical production of nearby wells completed in the same zone. If it does not live up to expectations, special treatment may be called for.

Reservoir rock can be physically or chemically treated to stimulate the flow. Fracturing is a physical procedure. A ('frac') fluid is pumped under great pressure down the borehole and into the reservoir. The force is sufficient to split open the reservoir rock. Sand grains or other small beads ('proppant') that have been mixed in the 'frac' fluid at the surface, are carried down the borehole into the open fractures. As the pumping pressure is reduced at the surface, the beads remain behind, to prop open the fractures, making it easier for oil or gas to flow from the rock to the borehole.

Acid treatment (acidizing) is a chemical procedure: acid (often HCl) is pumped into a reservoir containing limestone. It has little or no effect on pure quartz sand reservoirs, unless they happen to contain some limestone (which naturally occurs in some areas.) The purpose is to open and enlarge pore spaces in the rock, by dissolving some of the limestone in the acid.

Before oil and gas production can be tested, the frac fluid or acid fluid (the 'load') must be recovered. (The load fluid might be water, diesel, oil pre viously produced from the same reservoir, a gel, or some other fluid.) In the case of a deep gas reservoir, when pumping pressure is released at the surface, natural pressure in the reservoir may force the 'load' out of the reservoir, back into the tubing, and up to the surface, followed by a flow of the oil-gas-water mixture that naturally occurs in the formation. In the case of a shallow oil reservoirs, however, the natural reservoir pressures are generally lower, and the load must be recovered by bailing ('swabbing') out the tubing, using a special apparatus designed for this purpose.

Once the load has been recovered, it is possible to test the well under various controlled conditions to establish the producing capability of the reservoir. A potential test, for example, measures the maximum amount of oil or gas that a zone will produce during a twenty-four hour period ('open flow potential'). Results are reported to the state regulatory agency.

If a well encounters more than one zone of interest, the operator might make a series of trial completions. Starting with the deepest zone, he would move up the hole, testing one zone after the other for flow and fluid composition. On the basis of these production tests, the well would likely be completed in the deepest zone capable of commercial production.

The Christmas tree is an assemblage of valves, pressure gauges, and flow control devices. Installed at the top of the casing, it replaces the blowout preventers used during drilling operations, and allows connection to the oil and gas flow lines at the surface.

Equipment is installed at the surface to process the natural fluid flowing from the reservoir. Gas is separated from the liquids, and then run through a dehydrator to remove water vapor. Additional equipment may be needed to remove hydrogen sulfide, carbon dioxide, and other contaminating gases, to make the gas acceptable for transmission through a gas pipeline.

If the liquid portion contains both crude oil and water, it is run through a heater-treater. Chemicals, heat, and the force of gravity are used to separate water from the oil. The oil is then ready to flow into an oil pipeline, or into a temporary storage tank from which it can be periodically picked up by truck.

The Costs and Their Tax Significance

Like drilling costs, completion costs fall into two categories: equipment (tangible) costs and intangible drilling and development costs (IDC).

Equipment costs are amortizable capital expenditures for assets such as production casing, production tubing, the Christmas tree and other equipment that have a future useful life and can be salvaged. In Federal income tax calculations, equipment costs provide scheduled annual deductions (depreciation allowance) from gross income. (The formerly available investment tax credit was repealed by the Tax Reform Act of 1986.)

Intangible drilling and development costs (IDC) include such items as rental equipment, wages, consumable supplies, and subcontracted cementing, fracturing, and acidizing services. Some of these expenditures may appear to be capital expenditures by nature. Nevertheless, the taxpayer is permitted to elect to treat them as expenses, deductible from gross income (as allowed according to passive/non-passive income classification) in the year incurred or paid.[38] (Please see discussion of intangible drilling costs, Chapter 10.)

Chapter 7

PRODUCTION

Getting it out of the ground

Keep It Flowing

The production history of a well follows a predictable cycle. It starts with robust initial production and declines over time as the accumulation of petroleum is depleted, and the original pressure in the reservoir is used up. Eventually the produc-

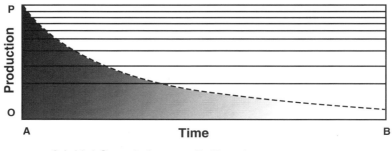

Generalized Decline In Production From A Well

A Initial Completion   **B** Abandonment

For a commercial well:

A-B   might typically range from 3 to 50 years
O-P   might typically range from 30 to >1500 barrels of oil per day

Note: Shaded area under the curve equals the volume
produced over time.

Figure 7.1 Decline Curve

ible hydrocarbons are exhausted, or it becomes no longer profitable to produce them, and the well is plugged and abandoned.

In the typical situation, only about 1/3 of the hydrocarbons originally contained in the reservoir are economically producible under current technology. In other words, we know where to find more oil than all the oil that has been produced to date. It is not yet economically attractive to try to produce it, under current technology ... but this is changing rapidly, as a result of quantum advances in new production technologies.

The physics of oil and gas production involve flow from high to low pressure. Hydrocarbons contained in a layer of rock at a depth of 10,000 feet, are under the pressure exerted by the weight of

PRIMARY RECOVERY

Naturally occurring reservoir pressure moves oil form reservoir rock to the wellbore.

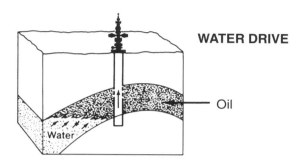

WATER DRIVE

Oil

Water

GAS CAP EXPANSION DRIVE

Gas

SOLUTION GAS DRIVE

Oil

Gas Bubbles

Oil with gas dissolved in it.

Gas dissolved in oil forms bubbles which expand and help force the oil up to the surface.

Figure 7.2 Primary Recovery

the overlying and surrounding rock and water. This pressure may, by itself, supply enough force to cause oil and gas to flow from the reservoir, into the wellbore, and up to the surface (water drive). In the case of a gas-and-oil accumulation, the driving force may be supplied by the gas. Gas that is dissolved in the oil, comes out of solution as the fluid is produced, like the bubbles in a freshly opened bottle of soda (solution gas drive). If additional gas is accumulated in a gas cap above the oil, it also expands, to provide flowing energy (gas cap expansion drive).

Water drive, gas cap expansion drive, and solution gas drive are examples of primary recovery. Please see Figure 7.2. The method and efficiency with which a well produces petroleum is largely determined by the natural conditions in the reservoir. Commercial recovery of oil by primary production might vary from as little as 5% to as much as 55% of the oil originally contained in the reservoir (the "oil-in-place"). Primary recovery of 25-35% of the oil-in-place might be typical.[39]

The water drive mechanism is most efficient, followed by gas cap expansion drive. Solution gas drive is the least efficient. (Secondary recovery methods may be used to try to produce some of the oil remaining in the reservoir after primary production has run its course. Please see discussion in the glossary.)

The completion of a well can be designed to produce reservoir fluids from a single pay zone, or from multiple pay zones. Two or more closely-spaced zones (with similar reservoir pressures) can be completed and produced simultaneously,

SECONDARY RECOVERY
Naturally occurring reservoir pressure is no longer sufficient to move oil to the wellbore. Various fluids are injected into the reservoir to improve recovery.

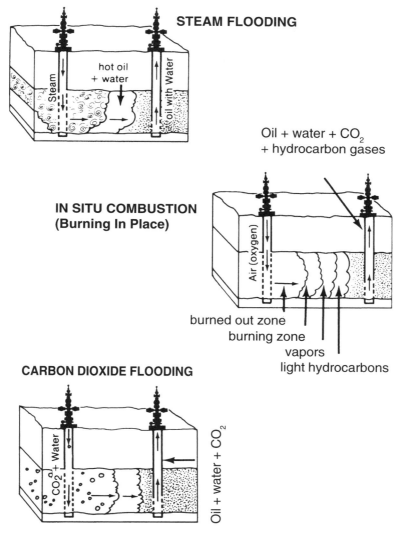

STEAM FLOODING

hot oil + water

Steam

Oil with Water

Oil + water + CO_2 + hydrocarbon gases

IN SITU COMBUSTION (Burning In Place)

Air (oxygen)

burned out zone
burning zone
vapors
light hydrocarbons

CARBON DIOXIDE FLOODING

CO_2 + Water

Oil + water + CO_2

Figure 7.3 Secondary Recovery

95

through a single string of tubing ('co-mingled'). An alternative is to make separate completions in each of two or three zones so that they can be produced simultaneously, but separately, through different strings of production tubing (multiple completion) in the same (single) wellbore.

Producing a gas well can be a fairly straightforward operation - just like letting air out of a balloon. Gas that occurs (naturally) compressed in the reservoir expands as it flows to the surface. Flow is regulated by valves and equipment installed on the surface.

Producing an oil well is usually more complicated. Oil is heavier than gas. Greater pressure is needed to force it out of the reservoir and up to the surface. Like water, oil is relatively incompressible. It will not expand significantly even when released from the natural (confining) pressures in the reservoir. Impurities such as water, gas, tiny bits of rock, and sediment must be removed before

"With new geological data and better measurement tools in hand, USGS sees more resource potential today than it did 6 years earlier − 44% more oil and 67% more natural gas ..."

Bob Tippee, Journally Speaking "Frontiers remain for U.S. exploration"
Oil & Gas Journal, April 3, 1995

the oil will be acceptable for transmission through an oil pipeline (or to a tank for temporary storage).

As reservoir pressure declines through production, there will come a time when oil will no longer flow to the surface. It can be pumped out of the well. A submersible electric pump may be placed down inside the casing. Perhaps more commonly, a piston-like bailing unit is driven by motorized equipment at the surface. It operates on the same principles as in a hand-pumped water well of days gone by (but still not uncommon in rural areas lacking electricity).

Each barrel of produced fluid usually consists of crude oil and water. During the life of a well, the proportion of water increases. This 'formation' water contains dissolved salts, often in concentrations many times that of seawater. To dispose of it in streams or rivers would contaminate freshwater resources. Most states have passed increasingly stringent laws governing the disposal of oil field waters. In the typical case the unwanted formation water is stored in a tank at the surface. It is periodically collected by a tank truck and transported to a now-depleted producing well that has been converted to a disposal well. The formation water is then injected back into the reservoir. An important oil-field service business in most oil-producing regions consists of providing access to disposal wells, and the trucking of formation waters to them, and charging a fee for this service.

If an oil well produces a large volume of water along with the oil, trucking away the formation water may become uneconomic. In this case, it may be better to drill an additional well (to be used as disposal well) near to the producing well, so that the unwanted salt water can be pumped back into the same reservoir.

Production may continue uninterrupted, for many years. More commonly, the well equipment requires maintenance. The fluids produced may contain acids and salts that corrode steel pumps, pipes, and tubing. Installed equipment may need replacement and repair. After a well has been on production for a long time, extensive remedial work may be required.

A mobile 'workover' rig is used to perform a variety of these types of remedial services. Workover operations include pulling the production tubing out of the well for maintenance, cleaning out the inside of the production casing, unblocking the perforations in the casing, re-perforating, re-stimulation by fracturing or acidizing, and squeezing cement to plug leaks in the casing.

The Costs and Their Tax Significance

The costs associated with production from a well are called production costs or lease operating expenses (LOE). (Lifting costs refer to a portion of production expenditures that may be involved in lifting the oil from the level of the reservoir up to the surface.) Expenditures for maintenance and workover operations are classified as expenses, currently deductible from income, as permitted according to passive/non-passive income classification. The drilling of a salt water disposal well, however, is held to have a future useful life, and as such, is classified as a capital expenditure.[40]

Chapter 8

SELLING OIL AND GAS

Who gets what?

Producing a gas well is a relatively simple proposition. It amounts to basically turning on a valve. Selling the gas, however can be rather complicated.

Producing an oil well can be complicated, involving much surface and downhole equipment including expensive pumping, units, etc., but selling the oil is pretty straightforward.

Oil

Oil is liquid. It can easily be collected and stored in tanks at the well location and periodically trucked to a refinery or to an oil-pipeline connection. In recent years the price paid in the U.S. for a barrel of oil has fluctuated right along with world oil prices. Prices for crude oils (identified by geographical source, which assumes certain quality standards and transportation requirements) are quoted on a daily basis in financial newspapers around the world. Prices received vary geographically and according to oil quality, and may be adjusted weekly, monthly, or from time to time in response to market conditions. (Before 1980, the price of oil produced and sold within the U.S. had been regulated by the Federal government.)

Crude oil sales in the U.S. generally fall into one of three situations:

- final sale is made at the lease, or
- crude is transported to a purchaser and then sold, or
- crude oil produced at the lease is exchanged (swapped) for other oil (geographically located somewhere else), and the other oil is then sold.

The sale of produced crude oil involves two main considerations.

Who purchase the crude at the wellhead? The two main purchasers includes major oil companies who need the crude as feedstock for their refineries, and crude oil gathering companies. There are an estimated 85,000 miles of crude oil gathering pipelines in the U.S.[41] Gathering companies aggregate large volumes through their crude oil gathering systems, and then sell it in bulk to refineries. In other words there are many sellers, and in most regions, only a handful of regular buyers (often as few as two or three).

What influences the price paid at the wellhead? Crude oil is not a unique commodity. Every producer in the world is competing for market. The price a producer receives for his crude oil mainly depends on 1) the specific grade (quality) of the oil , 2) location of the well or field (access to pipeline and refineries), and 3) the number of purchasers competing to purchase his crude oil. The price crude purchasers are willing to pay, is largely determined by their (the purchaser's) perceptions of the supply and demand in the near term.

In any producing region, there are likely to be as many as a dozen or so *potential* buyers; the actual sales typically go to those purchasers who, because they own capital assets in the area, are able to consistently offer the best price in the region.

The actual price received for oil produced at the wellhead, is the price that local oil purchasers are willing to pay for it. This 'posted price' has become increasingly volatile during the past 10 years, along with the proliferation of crude oil futures market trading. 'Postings' are influenced by (indeed based on) futures market prices for future delivery contracts traded on the New York Mercantile Exchange (NYMEX). The reality of this situation is that even a rumor about what OPEC might or might not do regarding increasing or curtailing its future crude production, influences NYMEX crude oil futures markets. This in turn can influence the spot market, and hence the posted price which oil purchasers are willing to pay for oil produced in the U.S.

Natural Gas

Natural gas is a gas. It is physically possible to compress and liquefy it for ease of transport. This is being done in foreign countries such as Indonesia and Algeria that have major natural gas production, but have no local market for it. The product is called liquefied natural gas (LNG). There are four port terminals in the U.S. capable of receiving and gasifying LNG transported by tankers - in Everett, Massachusetts; Lake Charles, Louisiana; Cove Point, Maryland; and Elba Island, Georgia. In recent years, only the facilities in Massachusetts and Louisiana have been in operation.

LNG is formed by compressing and cooling natural gas to extremely low temperatures (minus 260° Fahrenheit, which is -162° Celsius). This cooling process reduces the volume of the gas by a factor of about 600 to 1. The investment required for equipment needed to liquefy natural gas, to transport it (at -260° F), and then to re-gasify it, is staggering. Imported LNG is projected not to exceed 1-2% of total U.S. consumption for the foreseeable future, although this could change depending on the market price of natural gas. Current guessing suggests that in the absence of new LNG technologies, the cost of landed LNG will not effectively compete with conventional (pipeline) natural gas, unless U.S. natural gas prices remain consistently above $3.00 per MCF for some extended period of time. [42]

In the United States, it is currently economically feasible to move gas from the well, to the end user, only by transmission through a natural gas pipeline. Even the capital investment required to lay a gas pipeline is substantial. There are an estimated 90,000 miles of natural gas gathering pipelines plus 280,000 miles of interstate gas transmission pipelines plus 850,000 miles of distribution gas pipelines in the U.S. (an estimated total of more than 1.2 million miles of natural gas pipelines).

The actual price received for gas at the wellhead is determined by the gas sales contract. Typically, these contracts are for a period of 30 days or more, and the price received for the gas is based on either 1) the spot market price (spot market prices for contracts traded on the New York Mercantile Exchange), or 2) a local or regional 'index price' (the index is determined by a daily survey of natural gas prices in the area or region), or 3) a percentage of the proceeds (POP) of the price received for

"Executives defend oil profits. While we paid more at the pump, companies made record profits"

by Chris Casteel inThe Oklahoman, November 10, 2005

the gas (after it is transported to and processed through a gas processing plant, to make it acceptable for transmission in an interstate pipeline).

The spot market price of gas is cyclical and depends on the season. Most of the variation in natural gas prices can be attributed to weather patterns and season. Higher prices are generally obtained in the winter when gas is used for heating purposes; lower prices are obtained in the summer when electricity is more commonly the source of energy for air conditioning. Extreme or sudden unexpected weather events can also influence NYMEX natural gas spot market prices. For example, a hurricane in the Gulf of Mexico might cause offshore gas production facilities to be shut-

> "U.S. rise in trade deficits worrying to economists"
> *Headline, The Oklahoman, March 16, 2001*

in and evacuated, and even damaged or destroyed, which in turn affects the availability of natural gas to meet demand. This would likely influence the spot market for natural gas, and hence the price received by many gas producers for natural gas under their gas sales contracts. The volatility of natural gas prices exceeds that of any other commodity traded on the NYMEX.

U.S. Natural Gas Industry - Some Background

Natural gas produced and consumed in the same state is called intrastate gas; gas produced in one state and consumed in another state is interstate gas. Under the U.S. Constitution, the Federal government has the authority to regulate interstate commerce. Before 1985, natural gas prices were regulated by the Federal government. As of 1985, the prices of several categories of newly discovered interstate gas (accounting for perhaps as much as 50% of the gas produced in the nation) were no longer regulated by the Federal government, but are established according to supply and demand. As of 1989, all natural gas prices in the U.S. were 'deregulated'.

Prior to deregulation of natural gas prices, natural gas transmission companies ('pipelines') purchased gas under long term contracts. The contract commonly included a schedule of delivery intended to span the expected life of a well or field (perhaps 10 or even 20 years). The difference between the price paid for gas at the well, and the price at which it was sold to the end-user (hundreds of miles away) would pay back the investment to lay the pipeline plus the costs of transmitting the gas, and in addition, generate a profit for the gas transmission (pipeline) companies.

During the 1980's and early nineties, there was considerable public and political debate over gas-purchase contracts. The supply of gas exceeded demand, and end-users were unhappy about the price they had to pay for natural gas, which seemed out of proportion to the then-current 'glut' of natural gas. In many cases, the transmission (pipeline) companies, however, were bound by provisions in long-term contracts to purchase ('to take') gas from the producers or pay a penalty (so-called take-or- pay contracts). Such provisions had been widely considered necessary, in order to induce investment in the exploration and drilling of wells from which income might not be realized for a number of years.

Beginning in the middle to late 1980's, gas-sales contracts became shorter in duration, and the wellhead price at which gas was purchased by transmission (pipeline) companies or third parties, began to reflect end-user market conditions.

After much public debate, expensive litigation, and many bankruptcies resulting from (or at least related to) take-or-pay contracts, the Federal government stepped in to establish some rules to regulate (or actually 'deregulate') the domestic natural gas industry. In 1992, the Federal Energy Regulatory Commission (FERC) promulgated its 'Rule 636'. Prior to this ruling, interstate natural gas transmission companies ('pipelines') generally purchased natural gas at the wellhead, and then resold this same gas (along with a variety of services, including transportation and storage of the gas) to customers at the other end of the pipeline. After Rule 636, services which had traditionally been handled by the pipeline companies before Rule 636 (specifically the purchasing of gas to be transported, and then the reselling of the transported gas,) were 'unbundled' from the transmission (transportation) and storage of the gas.

Under Rule 636, interstate pipeline companies and their affiliates, can provide transportation, storage and related services, but cannot own the gas for resale.

Before Rule 636:

More than one producer sold gas to a pipeline which in turn resold the gas to a single purchaser at the other end of the pipeline.

After Rule 636:

Open access to transportation on the interstate pipelines makes it possible for many producers/sellers to sell their gas to a wide range of purchasers, including: natural gas aggregators at the upstream end of the pipelines, natural gas marketers, specific downstream industrial customers, natural gas utilities (local distribution companies - LDC's), electrical generation utilities . . . And in the future? Maybe natural gas producers or their aggregators or marketers will sell gas directly to individual residential customers. (This would be analogous to the way that first, long distance telephone service, and now, even local telephone services, are being marketed to businesses and individuals across the country.)

In some cases, purchases of natural gas are made directly between a large end-user and a natural gas producer; in other cases a public utility will purchase gas directly from a producer, or from a third party natural gas marketing firm, and then resell the gas to businesses or residences served by the utility; temporary storage of the natural gas purchased is now handled by the purchaser, or the seller, or some third party, depending on the arrangement under which natural gas is sold and purchased.

The 'post-Rule 636' environment represents a big change for the structure of the natural gas industry. It seems to have made the business even more complex than it was before. The justification for this deregulation, however, is

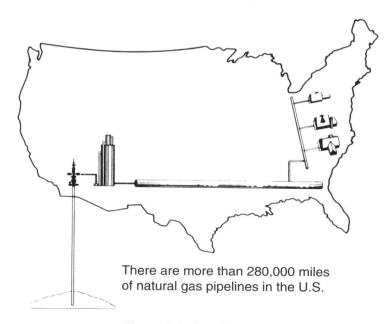

There are more than 280,000 miles of natural gas pipelines in the U.S.

Figure 8.1 Gas Pipelines

that ultimately a market-driven natural gas industry will provide cheaper energy for the nation in the long run. During the period 1985 - 1995, natural gas prices received at the well head have come down by about 35%, while gas prices at the residential burner tip remain virtually unchanged.

The argument is made that U.S. industry will be better able to compete effectively in the global marketplace if U.S. businesses have direct access to the lowest cost, most efficient energy sources. In other words, U.S. business can compete more effectively if its energy costs are not saddled with the high cost of inefficient government regulation and administration. Interestingly, an analogous 'deregulation' of the U.S. electric power industry is just now being undertaken with the expectation that it also will increase competition between energy producers and energy sources. The presumption is that such healthy competition will result in lower energy costs. Whether these cost savings will be realized directly at the individual consumer's residential level is a point that is now being argued (and will likely continue to be argued) by a variety of consumer groups and coalitions.

Quality Testing

The sale of oil is subject to tests required by the purchaser, to affirm that the oil meets certain minimum quality standards. In the U.S. oil (or gas) is measured by volume (at standard temperature and pressure, 60°F; and one atmosphere = 14.7 pounds per square inch). Bulk volume of oil sold must be corrected for any contained bottom sediment and water (BS&W). Details of test measurements including temperature, density (gravity), and BS&W of the oil, the date, name of lease, the number of the oil tank measured, and witnesses for both the producer and purchaser are recorded on a document called a 'run ticket'. [43]

Gas is also sold subject to purchaser's tests. Natural gas is a complex mixture of different hydrocarbon gases. The price generally increases with the amount of liquid hydrocarbons (condensate) it contains, and the amount of energy generated when the gas is burned (typically measured in Btu per MCF - British thermal units per thousand cubic feet of gas). Gas is also tested for the presence of water (moisture) and non-hydrocarbon gases (such as helium, nitrogen, carbon dioxide, etc.) that may not have been completely removed by the separation equipment at the well.[44]

The daily volumes of oil, gas, and water produced from a well are monitored by the operator. Production must be kept within allowable limits set by state regulating agencies. Allowables are established for a particular well or field taking into account its maximum efficient rate (MER) of production, and market conditions for the oil or gas produced.

In the typical case the operator's pumper checks on the production facility daily. In future, it is expected that much of this function will be performed remotely, via electronic metering, recording and monitoring devices and possibly even remote video camera viewing (all solar-powered!). These types of improvements should serve to settle the all-too-frequent disputes between royalty owners, operators, and state tax collectors, about the volumes of oil and gas produced from a particular well.[45]

Sales Price At The Well-Head

The price at which the oil is sold, is adjusted for impurities such as sulfur, salt, etc. that may not have been completely removed by the separation equipment at the well. If the oil contains significant amounts of wax (paraffin), there may also be a substantial negative adjustment to the price, as paraffin tends to clog up equipment, leading to the necessity of frequent maintenance and cleaning procedures.

The Costs

The purchaser of oil or gas from a property generally prepares the division order. Based on information (abstract of title) supplied by the operator, it lists all the royalty and working-interest owners of a producible oil or gas well, and their respective shares of production. Before commercial production is established, the division order is circulated to each revenue interest owner for his signature.[46]

This process typically takes 60 days or more, and accounts for some of the total time lag (often as much as six months or more) between the date of first oil or gas sale and the date an interest owner receives his first revenue check. Royalty and working-interest owners receive their share of monthly revenue from production according to the division order:

ROYALTY INTEREST	*WORKING INTEREST*
GROSS revenue	**GROSS revenue** – royalties, ORRI, other burdens
_____	_____
NET revenues	**NET revenues** (revenue to the net revenue interest, "NRI")
– state production tax – Federal withholding tax – handling fees & taxes	– state production tax – Federal withholding tax – handling fees & taxes – lease operating expenses
_____	_____
NET income	**NET operating income**

PRODUCTION TAX (also called 'severance tax') is levied by each state on oil and gas produced within its borders. It ranges by state, from no tax, to about 15% of gross production (with the average state being about 7%).[47]

Please see Appendix A for production tax rates by state. State severance tax is a deductible expense in computing Federal income tax.

FEDERAL WITHHOLDING TAX is Federal income tax deducted from payments to interest holders who do not provide a Federal tax identification number or Social Security number on the division order. This might apply primarily to 'nonresident aliens' (foreign entities not physically residing or based in the U.S.)

HANDLING FEES & TAXES include a seemingly endless variety of costs or 'adjustments' (always negative!) that may be deducted from a production revenue check. These include such items as:

Transportation fees: the purchaser's charge for transporting oil (typically per barrel per mile) from lease storage tanks at the well location, to the purchaser's refinery or pipeline-gathering facilities.

Gas gathering fees: fees paid to the owner of a gas-gathering system (local pipeline) to transport produced natural gas from the wellhead to the nearest gas pipeline connection.

Compression fees: in the case of low-pressure gas wells, fees paid to boost the gas pressure (by running the gas through a compressor) so that it can be injected into a higher-pressure gas pipeline.

Dehydration fees: charges for special procedures necessary to remove from gas, moisture which was not removed by the gas separation equipment installed at the wellhead, before the gas will be accepted by the pipeline company. (This might also represent a price penalty levied by the accepting gas pipeline company, on natural gas that fails to meet previously agreed-upon gas quality standards).

Tribal Gross Production Taxes: taxes paid to some native American Indian tribes, in the case of oil or gas produced on their lands.

Marginal Well fee: in Oklahoma, a fee levied (under Senate Bill 684) on each taxable barrel of oil and MCF gas produced. The proceeds fund a commission on wells that are only marginally economic (commonly knows as stripper wells, and of which there are many in the state).

Energy Education & Marketing Act fee: in Oklahoma, a voluntary fee collected at the wellhead. The fee was proposed by the oil industry and approved by the legislature, to fund public education and awareness about the oil industry. In the case of revenue interest owners who do not wish to participate in the program, a refund can be obtained from the state taxing authority, upon submission of the appropriate application for refund. (A similar 'checkoff' program is in effect in Kansas; other producing states are expected to follow this trend.)

Other fees: On a state-by-state basis, there are a wide variety of additional or similar fees that may be deducted from production revenue. The operator or entity issuing the check or the state agency that regulates oil and gas production would be the place to go for further information.

In most cases, these various fees are deductible expenses in computing Federal income tax, but check with your tax advisor for the specifics of fees levied in your state.

LEASE OPERATING EXPENSES (LOE) are paid only by the working-interest owners of the property. (A royalty is a cost-free share of production.) In the case of a well-behaved gas well, these costs might average as little as 1% of gross production. In the case of a problem oil well needing extensive pumping and remedial work, and producing enough water to require a salt water disposal well, they could easily average 50% of gross production, or more. These costs may be amortizable capital expenditures or currently deductible expenses, depending on their nature.

Note: When the net operating income begins to converge on lease operating expenses, it becomes uneconomic to continue to operate the well.

Something must change, typically either:

a) rework the well to increase production (and net operating income),

b) sell to a lower cost operator,

C) shut-in and wait for higher oil prices, or

c) plug and abandon.

Economic Limit

Different Operating Expense Scenarios

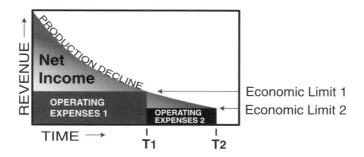

As production (normally) declines over time, revenue* also declines until net income approaches the cost of operating the well. When operating expenses equal net income, operation of the well becomes uneconomic, and the well has reached its economic limit.

A large high-overhead major oil **Company 1** might be forced to dispose of a property at time T_1, whereas a very cost-efficient independent oil **Company 2**, could continue profitable operation of the same well until time T_2.

As shown in the diagram, operating expenses for some independent oil companies (**Company 2**) may be as little as half that of some major oil companies (**Company 1**). If T_1 represents 15 years from first production, the interval T_1 - T_2 might be as much as 10 additional years of production or more.

It is also possible that the well is continually operated by the same company. In this case Economic Limit 2 might represent some combination of application of new technologies and better operating efficiencies which result in lower operating costs and longer productive life of the well.

* Assuming constant oil prices

Economic Limit

Different Oil Price Scenarios

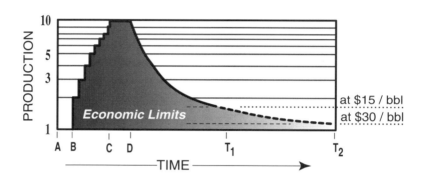

A-B   Generating prospect and selling the deal.

B   Discovery well is drilled.

B-C   Development of the field.

C-D   Peak production.

D-T_1 Production declines to the point that the economic limit of the field is reached at time T_1 (under oil prices at $15 per barrel).

    or . . . . .

D-T_2 Production declines to the point that the economic limit of the field is reached at time T_2 (under oil prices at $30 per barrel).

Chapter 9

TAXES - General

Since the Boston Tea Party

Historical Background

American resistance to British revenue taxes on tea led to the Boston Tea Party in 1774. This set the stage for the Revolutionary War, American independence from British rule, and the adoption of a constitutional form of government. Taxation has played a critical role in U.S. history ever since.

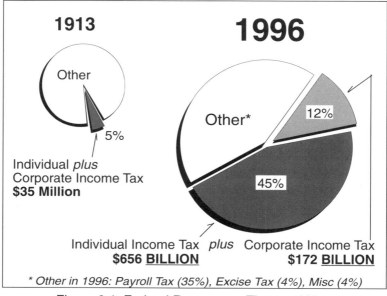

Figure 9.1 Federal Revenues - *Then and Now*

The Sixteenth Amendment to the Constitution was adopted in 1913. It gives the U.S. Congress the power to "lay and collect taxes on incomes, from whatever source derived". Congress passed the Revenue Act of 1913, and that year Federal income tax collections were $35 million (5% of Federal revenues) from individuals and corporations.[49]

In 1983, Federal income tax collections were $326 billion (54% of total Federal receipts); $289 billion came from individual income taxes and $37 billion came from corporations.[50] The impact of Federal income tax has increased to the point that it influences, if not dominates, most large financial and business transactions. The feasibility of any proposed business deal cannot be clearly understood, without analysis of its tax implications.

Much of the Federal revenue law is contained in the Internal Revenue Code of 1986 (which is essentially the Code of 1954, as now modified by the Tax Reform Act of 1986). Federal tax rates have been altered as the Federal government has responded to conditions of the national economy ranging from inflation to unemployment. Details of specific tax provisions have been changed from year to year, but the gross character and effect of the Federal income tax has not. The U.S. Department of the Treasury is responsible for administering and enforcing the revenue laws. It issues regulations covering broad aspects of tax laws enacted by the Congress. A subdivision within the Treasury Department, the Internal Revenue Service (IRS), collects taxes and processes and audits income tax returns.[51]

> "U.S. energy policy for many years has served, on balance, to maintain the dominance of Persian Gulf producers, wittingly or unwittingly. Maintaining this policy has cost U.S. consumers and taxpayers a minimum of $300 billion since 1973, at a very conservative estimate."
>
> *THE JOURNAL OF COMMERCE Monday, July 29, 1996*
> *Energy Security For America by Norman A. Bailey & Criton M. Zoakos*

The Internal Revenue Service (IRS) is not part of the legislature (which makes the law) nor is it part of the judiciary branch (which interprets the law). In its administrative capacity it answers taxpayers questions and issues rulings as to Federal income tax implications of proposed transactions of rather specific nature.[52] A taxpayer has the le-

ORGANIZATION CHART OF U.S. GOVERNMENT

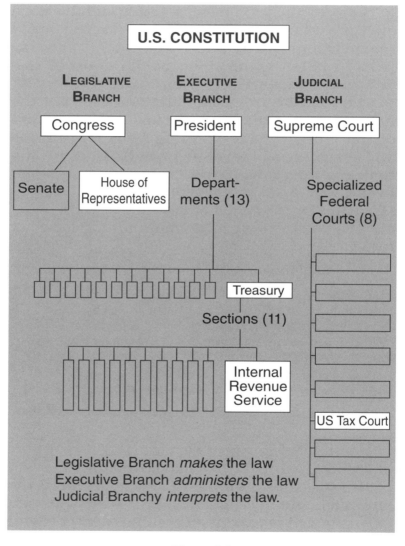

Figure 9.2

gal right to contest rulings of the IRS and the Treasury Department, through hearings before: the United States Tax Court[53] (without paying the tax) or U.S. Claims Court (after having paid the tax).

'Federal tax law' encompasses the Internal Revenue Code, regulations issued by the Treasury Department, rulings by the Internal Revenue Service, and court decisions (especially those of the U.S. Tax Court). In other words, it is continually being revised, modified, reinterpreted, and is studied by legions of the nation's approximately 300,000 accountants and the country's more than 800,000 lawyers. (One has to wonder how different the U.S. economy might be, if the awesome amount of human and financial resources that are now annually devoted to the study of 'Federal tax law' were reallocated into other income-producing fields - such as new business generation, or the like.)

Philosophy of Tax Incentives

The main purpose of U.S. tax law is to raise money needed to operate the Federal government. Through its powers of taxation the Congress exerts huge influence on economic activities held to be significant to society. This influence may take the form of income tax incentives that encourage or discourage activities which are deemed desirable or undesirable, but which are not considered to be appropriate for direct government spending or control. As Presidents and congressmen of different political philosophies have come and gone, tax provisions reflecting their political persuasions have been added to, and deleted from, the Internal Revenue Code.

The Internal Revenue Code ('the Code') is constantly being interpreted, and changed, and reinterpreted through legal appeals and tax-court decisions. Without an understanding of the social, economic, and political considerations that may have influenced the enactment of a specific provision of the Code, many (some observers might say 'most') aspects of the Code appear illogical, if not even counterproductive.

Hopes for shale oil are revived
"Sometimes called the resource of the future …. "
by Perry A. Fischer, Editor, World OIL, August 2005

Under the Sixteenth Amendment, all income is subject to Federal income taxation. Over the years, however, the Federal government has awarded special tax benefits to encourage investment in areas that would help achieve certain national objectives. Some examples:

- benefits for home-owners encourage home ownership and subsidize the home-building industry,

- benefits for rehabilitation of old real estate have resulted in the preservation of historical buildings and monuments,

- allowances for charitable donations have influenced the growth and role of educational and cultural institutions,

- benefits for investment in research and development projects encourage the creation of new technologies, and

- benefits granted to the oil and gas drilling and producing ventures in the past, contributed to the strength and diversity of the domestic oil industry.

These and other tax benefits have influenced American society in fundamental ways.

Figure 9.3 Tax Incentives

Tax Shelters

The narrow definition of 'tax shelter' should probably be restricted to investments which keep current income untaxed until it is used, as in the case of an Individual Retirement Account (IRA).[54]

A tax shelter is an investment vehicle designed to protect (shelter) an investor's income from Federal income taxation. The relevant tax benefits become available (legally) to an investor, as a result of his investment in carefully structured tax-advantaged deals in certain industries. Depending on the structure and nature of the investment, tax benefits may be realized 1) at the time the investment is made, or 2) they may protect a potential income stream to be realized in the future as a result of having made the investment. Regardless of timing, however, the benefit to the taxpaying investor, is a reduction in his taxes due and payable (coupled ... in theory! ... with the potential for an attractive return on the investment made).

The concept of tax shelters is well established in U.S. jurisprudence, as observed by Judge Learned Hand:

> Over and over again courts have said that there is nothing sinister in so arranging one's affairs as to keep taxes as low as possible. Everybody does so, rich or poor, and all do right, for nobody owes any public duty to pay more than the law demands: taxes are forced exactions, not voluntary contributions. To demand more in the name of morals is mere cant. [55]

The concept of 'taxable income' is the end product of countless legislative compromises and court decisions determining what may be included, exempted, or deducted in computing the taxpayers 'taxes due and payable'. In general, a taxpayer's Federal income tax obligation is calculated according to the following formula:[56]

Gross Income
– Deductions
———————————
Taxable Income   x **Tax Rate**   = Tax Liability
                                     – Tax Credits
                                     —————————————
                                     Taxes Due and Payable

Tax sheltered investments are designed to reduce taxes due and payable by:

- increasing **deductions** (to reduce Taxable Income)
- qualifying for a lower **tax rate** (to reduce Tax Liability)
- increasing **tax credits** (to reduce Taxes Due).

In 1983, the total amount of tax shelter investments offered to the public and registered with the Securities Exchange Commission was more than $23.5 billion.[57] After the Tax Reform Act of 1986, this number declined abruptly, with terrific consequences for all kinds of enterprises that had previously been involved in the 'tax shelter business', including the domestic oil and gas industry.

Following chapters address tax advantages that may be available to investors in oil and gas ventures. They involve some discussion of 'tax accounting' methods and principles as differentiated from those of 'financial accounting'. These two areas of accounting may handle the same accounting item differently (commonly in regard to the timing of the item). They have significantly different objectives, as summarized in a U.S. Supreme Court decision:

> The primary goal of financial accounting is to provide useful information to management, shareholders, creditors and others properly interested; the major responsibility of the accountant is to protect these parties from being misled. The primary goal of the income tax system, in contrast, is the equitable collection of revenue; the major responsibility of the Internal Revenue Serviced is to protect the public fisc.[58]

Because its task is to accurately reflect the financial results of an organization's operation, financial accounting allows for the possibility of errors (likely to be made in the course of taking measurements). It uses probabilities and estimates that are intended to understate net income and net worth. Tax accounting, on the other hand, is expected to be precise. Effective collection of Federal revenues cannot be predicated on the understatement of income.[59]

Generally accepted accounting principles (GAAP) of financial accounting tolerate a range of reasonable accounting treatments, but they do not ensure that identical transactions are treated identically. The tax system, however, should be equitable to the extent that taxpayers in similar situations *should* each pay the same amount of Federal income tax. (Nevertheless, there have been any number of surveys in which ten different IRS agents or accountants have prepared the same tax return, and arrived at ten different amounts as the taxes due!)

What is gross income? What kinds of deductions are available to me? How can I qualify for a lower tax rate? How do I get investment tax credits? These and other questions might be addressed to qualified accountants and financial advisors. Subsequent chapters, however, discuss the concepts of tax advantages that may be available specifically to investors in certain types of oil and gas ventures.

Chapter 10

TAX BENEFITS

For the oil and gas investor

At some point in the life of a business enterprise, U.S. Federal tax law allows a business taxpayer to deduct nearly all business expenditures from gross income in computing his Federal income tax due.[60] In other words, the taxpayer does not pay tax on that amount of income from which he recovers his cost of doing business. Some expenditures are deductible when incurred, others may be deducted in installments over a number of years, or when the enterprise is terminated. Oil and gas ventures involve three main types of expenditures.

EXPENSES are expenditures that are deductible from gross income in the year incurred (as in any other business venture).

AMORTIZABLE CAPITAL EXPENDITURES may be deducted from gross income according to a scheduled annual deduction over several years:

EQUIPMENT COSTS give rise to a deduction called depreciation allowance. (as in any other business venture).

LEASE COSTS are not typical of all business ventures, and hence may give rise to a deduction unique to the mining extraction, petroleum, and other natural resource industries, called depletion allowance (discussed later in this section).

NON-AMORTIZABLE CAPITAL EXPENDITURES are something else again. They typically give rise to a (taxable) capital gain or (tax-deductible) loss on sale or other disposition of the items acquired.

EXPENSES

INTANGIBLE DRILLING COSTS (IDC)

These are expenditures for items that have no salvage value, and are "incidental to and necessary for the drilling and the preparation of wells for the production of oil and gas".[61] They include such costs as:

• surveying, building roads, and preparation of well location

- transporting the drilling equipment to the well site,
- drilling,
- consumable supplies such as water, fuel, mud, drill bits
- cementing, logging, coring, drill-stem testing
- installation of casing (but not the cost the casing itself),
- perforation of casing, fracturing, acidizing, and swabbing,
- installation of production equipment (through the Christmas tree). (Please see Authorization For Expenditure, Appendix B).

At the election of the taxpayer, these expenditures may be classified as (1) expenses deductible from current (as opposed to future) gross income, or (2) amortizable capital expenditures. This election was originally established by administrative ruling in 1916. There has been substantial litigation, but the election has been available in various forms for nearly 80 years.[62]

The significance of the election is timing. If the intangible drilling costs are treated as expenses for the purpose of computing Federal income tax obligations, the total amount of these costs are deducted from gross income (including income not only from oil and gas activities, but also any income aggregated from other sources) in the year incurred (but since 1986, they are now subject to the active/passive limitations of the Tax Reform Act of 1986).

If on the other hand, they are capitalized, then the total amount of these same costs are deducted in installments over a number of years. According to the time value of money concept, a dollar received today is worth more than the same dollar received years in the future. The same holds true for an income tax deduction.

New oil and gas reserves are discovered only by drilling wells, which involves substantial cost and a high degree of risk (as compared with some other types of investments). The drilling of a well often results in a dry hole having zero market value; this is a substantially a different situation from, say, investment in a building, whose market value might increase or decrease with market conditions, but would rarely have zero market value. The opportunity to treat intangible drilling costs as currently deductible expenses may allow the investor to protect some of his income (from other sources) from Federal taxation. This provides incentive for a taxpayer to invest in the exploration for oil and gas.

AMORTIZABLE CAPITAL EXPENDITURES

EQUIPMENT COSTS - DEPRECIATION ALLOWANCE

Drilling equipment costs are expenditures for tangible assets that have a future useful life and have a salvage value. Well equipment costs include such items as casing, tubing, various equipment placed in the borehole in connection with running and cementing casing, and the Christmas tree.[63]

Completion and production equipment costs include surface pumping equipment, flow lines, separators, treating equipment, tank batteries, and salt water disposal equipment.[64]

As with the purchase of equipment in any other business or industry, oil and gas well equipment costs can be depreciated and deducted from gross income through annual depreciation allowance. (From time-to-time in the past, purchase of particular equipment specified in the tax code, has also provided investment tax credits, reducing tax liability.)

Oil field is gushing with job opportunities
"Companies planning to hire thousands. . . ."

The Oklahoman, Friday February 24, 2006

NON-AMORTIZABLE CAPITAL EXPENDITURES

LEASEHOLD COSTS - DEPLETION ALLOWANCE

These are costs related to the acquisition of leases, including such expenditures as: bonuses paid to the landowner for acquisition of a lease, fees paid to brokers to acquire a lease, legal fees to examine and secure proper title to a lease, and legal fees involved in law suits which may relate to ownership of an acquired lease. Geological and geophysical costs (G&G) are also commonly included with leasehold costs.

Under IRS tax rules, leasehold costs are not deductible from gross income in the year incurred (as are expenses). They are amortizable capital expenditures but annual deductions for depreciation are not allowed (as they are in the case of salvageable equipment). If a lease is abandoned prior to establishing production, leasehold costs can be recovered through an abandonment loss deduction from gross income. But what if the well is a successful producer?

Leasehold costs for a producing property may be recovered through the depletion allowance which is unique to the natural resources industries. It functions for the owner of a natural resource, the way the depreciation allowance functions for the owner of a depreciable asset.

THE DEPLETION ALLOWANCE

Mineral deposits under a leased property are natural resources that constitute a special type of capital asset sometimes referred to as "wasting assets". The exhaustion of a mineral deposit through production results in physical depletion. The reduction in the value of a mineral deposit as it becomes exhausted through production results in economic depletion.

Under the Federal income tax system, a taxpayer's cost in acquiring an oil and gas lease is an expenditure for a wasting asset. (Although it is indeed, a capital asset, it is not eligible for deduction from gross income through the depreciation allowance).

Think of each dollar of revenue from the production of oil and gas on a property as consisting of two components: 1) part of the revenue represents true 'income' and 2) part of the revenue represents a 'return of capital'. [65]

According to the principles on which the Federal income tax system is based, the 'income' portion of revenues should be subject to Federal income taxation, but the 'return of capital' portion should not. The depletion allowance is the deduction from the gross income (attributable to a producing property) which allows for this ('return of capital') concept.[66]

Depletion allowance must be computed separately on a property by property basis. As defined in the Internal Revenue Code, 'property' means "each separate interest owned by the taxpayer in each mineral deposit in each separate tract or parcel of land". The ramification of the property unit definition are extensive. For a thorough discussion, please see sources listed under Federal Income Taxation - Oil & Gas in Recommended Resources.

By Federal tax law, the depletion allowance must be calculated by two different methods: cost depletion and percentage depletion. The amount of the deduction is the greater of the two in any given tax year.

COST DEPLETION recovers leasehold costs on a property-by-property basis. To the extent that it is based on the cost of an asset and reflects the gradual loss of value of the asset, cost depletion is conceptually similar to depreciation. It is calculated as the percentage of proved reserves (at the beginning of the year) that are produced (during the year) multiplied by the amount of leasehold costs incurred during the year. (Proved reserves are a scientific estimate of the volume of reserves that are considered to be recoverable under existing technology and economic conditions based on geologic and engineering data).

Proved reserves (estimate)		
in the ground January 1	300,000	barrels
Production thru December 31	30,000	barrels
Percent of reserves produced		
during the year	10%	(= 30,000 / 300,000)
Leasehold costs Jan 1 - Dec 31	$150,000	
COST DEPLETION	$ 15,000	(= 10% x 150,000)

PERCENTAGE DEPLETION is simply calculated as a specific percentage of gross income from oil and gas production during the year (without reference to any costs involved). Although the amount of the percentage was originally 27%, it has been watered down over the years, and as of this writing, for the year 1995 and onward, the percentage is 15%. (The amount of the percentage is specified in the legal statues, and is sometimes referred to as the statutory rate.)

Production during the year	30,000	barrels
Price per barrel (ave)	$20	
Gross income from production	$600,000	(= $20 x 30,000)
PERCENTAGE DEPLETION	$90,000	(= 15% X $600,000)

From the preceding example, the amount of the deduction that is allowed on your tax return is the greater of:

A) cost depletion (= $15,000) or

B) percentage depletion (= $90,000).

In this example, it is $90,000. (Obviously in this example percentage depletion can provide a more significant tax benefit than cost depletion.)

If production expenses for the year were $100,000:

Gross income	$600,000	
− Production expenses	100,000	
− Depletion allowance	90,000	(percentage depletion)
Taxable income	$410,000	

Regarding the characteristics of cost depletion and percentage depletion, note that:

- The percentage depletion amount is based on the price at which produced reserves are sold (oil prices have ranged between about $9 - $32 per barrel since 1986), and is available throughout the life of production

- Cost depletion is a per-unit recovery of the leasehold costs discussed above, but terminates once leasehold costs have been recovered.

- In a period of declining oil prices (1986, for example), unrecovered leasehold costs may be high, relative to the price at which reserves are sold, with the result that cost depletion amount might likely be greater than the percentage depletion amount.

A number of limitations on the deductibility of the depletion allowance have been added to the tax code over the years, including the following. (For the latest developments, check with your oil and gas accountant.)

BARREL LIMITATION

Percentage depletion is limited to 1,000 barrels (or 6,000 MCF of gas) of average daily (domestic U.S.) production.

100 % OF NET INCOME

Percentage depletion for each property is limited to 100% of the property's taxable income before the depletion deduction. (In the first or second year of production, intangible drilling costs can add up to a significant amount. Recall that they can be deducted as expenses from gross income. This may significantly reduce the property's taxable income, with the result that percentage depletion might easily be greater than 100% of the property's taxable income.)

65% OF TAXABLE INCOME

A taxpayer's allowable depletion deduction cannot be greater than 65% of his taxable income for the tax year. (Any amount in excess of 65% may be carried forward to subsequent years — but deductions in those years will still be subject to their respective 65% limitations.)

PERCENTAGE DEPLETION GREATER THAN LEASEHOLD COSTS

If percentage depletion is greater than leasehold costs, the amount in excess of leasehold costs is a 'tax preference' item. (Tax preferences may be subject to an 'alternative minimum tax'.)[67]

EXAMPLE - Oil & Gas Tax Benefits

AL and Ben are U.S. taxpayers. Each has a gross income (and a cash position) of $2,000. Their incomes are both taxed at a (hypothetical) rate of 40%.

AL invests $1,200 in a working interest in an oil deal for which the cost breakdown is:

lease acquisition costs	10% (= $120)
intangible drilling costs	70% (= $840)
equipment costs	20% (= $240)

AL elects to treat intangible drilling costs ($840) as expenses, deductible from any income (passive or non-passive). His equipment costs give rise to a deduction for depreciation of the (five year) equipment equal to 20% of their purchase price, the first year ($240 x 20% = $48.) He gets no tax benefit for lease acquisition costs at this time. His deductions total $888.

BEN invests $1,200 in common stock of Big Oil Incorporated, in anticipation of receiving future dividend payments, and increase in the value of the stock. He gets no deductions for his investment.

AL		BEN
$2,000	Gross Income	$2,000
888	- Deductions	0
1,112	Taxable Income	2,000
40%	x Tax Rate	40%
445	Tax Liability	800
0	- Tax Credits	0
$445	Taxes Due	$800

NET EFFECT OF INVESTMENT ON CASH FLOW:

AL		BEN
$2,000	Gross Income (pre-tax)	$2,000
1,200	Investment	1,200
445	Taxes Due	800
$335	**After Tax Cash Position**	0

NOTE: AL is exposed to certain liabilities which could arise out of operations, and could result in financial obligations substantially in excess of the amount of his investment. BEN's risk is limited to the amount of his investment.

NATIONAL ENERGY POLICY ACT OF 1992

A word about the alternative minimum tax. The Energy Policy Act of 1992 provided for a permanent repeal of the alternative minimum tax (AMT), but with some remaining limitations in the case of intangible drilling costs (IDC). To appreciate the significance of this, it is necessary to understand a bit about the concept of a 'minimum tax', which has been a part of the tax Code since 1969[68] The AMT is a second layer of taxation that is in addition to the regular taxation. The goal of this AMT system is to make sure that all profitable businesses and individual taxpayers who have substantial income (and large deductions or other tax benefits), cannot escape paying some 'minimum tax' (regardless of how clever their accountants and lawyers may have been in trying to reduce or even eliminate their tax obligations altogether).

Under the AMT system, the taxpayer must first calculate his tax liability under the regular tax system to arrive at his 'regular tax liability'. Then certain tax benefits such as deductions for intangible drilling and development costs (IDC - discussed above) and deductions for 'excess' depletion allowance (collectively these are termed 'tax preference items'), were added back in to the taxpayer's income, to arrive at a computed 'alternative minimum tax income' or AMTI. 'Excess' depletion allowance refers to the amount by which percentage depletion calculated under the 'regular' tax system, is greater than the adjusted basis of a producing property at the end of the tax year.[69]

The AMT tax obligation was refigured on this computed 'alternative minimum tax income'. The taxpayers actual tax liability was then whichever of the two calculations was the higher - the 'regular' tax or the 'alternative minimum' tax.

After passage of the Energy Act of 1992, the 'alternative minimum tax' was repealed: A) intangible drilling and development costs - IDC, and B) percentage depletion are no longer considered 'tax preference items'. There continue to be some limitations on the amount of the IDC deduction that is allowed (calculated AMT is not reduced by more than 30%). To arrive at this, the AMT calculations still have to be done.[70] Talk to your oil and gas accountant for the latest on this.

As of this writing there is more and more talk of a significant rethinking of the system of U.S. Federal taxation. The U.S. tax code is an exceedingly complex area and it may not be of general interest to most readers. Recognize that you do have a voice in this matter, however. If you don't like the way this system works, one recourse would be to communicate your feelings about the tax code in general or about these tax provisions in particular to your elected representatives in Congress and in the Senate.

Summary

This following summary addresses the tax significance or tax treatment of the several chronological steps in the course of exploration and production of oil and gas.[71]

THE PROSPECT   **Deductions or Capitalize**

- When acquired from others (an 'external' prospect), the costs involved in generating the prospect are generally categorized as expenses deductible against U.S. income.

- When the prospect is generated in-house (an 'internal' prospect), the costs represent a form of overhead, and are generally lumped together as Geological and Geophysical costs ("G&G"), and must be capitalized as an asset. Tax deductions are available: during production, as depletion, or in the case of no production, when the 'asset' is written off.

LEASED ACREAGE   **Capitalize**

(Either Leasehold or Mineral Rights)

- These costs are capitalized as an asset. Tax deductions are available during production: as depletion or in the case of no production: when the 'asset' is written off. Rentals are deductible as expenses when incurred.

DRILLING THE WELL   **Deductions**

- Drilling expenses ("intangible drilling costs" or IDC) are deductible as current expenses, against U.S. income taxable by the Federal government.

COMPLETING THE WELL   Deductions

- Completion expenses ("intangible drilling and development costs" or IDC) are deductible as current expenses, against U.S. income taxable by the Federal government.

EQUIPPING THE WELL   Capitalize

- Equipment expenses are capitalized as an asset. Tax deductions are available when they are depreciated over 7 years, or when the are depreciated over the economic life of the lease.

PRODUCING THE WELL   Deductions + Capitalize

- Income is taxable when it is earned.

- Lease operating expenses (LOE) are deductible expenses as incurred.

- Production income allows for a depletion allowance - a deduction calculated on either the cost or percentage basis. The maximum amount of the depletion deduction is limited to the 'net income' of the lease. (It is a non cash deduction.)

- Capitalized equipment provides depreciation deductions over seven years, or over the economic life of the lease.

EXAMPLE - Tax Effect of Drilling Investment

	Year 1	Year 2	Year n
1 Actual Expense/Revenue			
Revenues			
Gross Income	**$0**	**$250**	**$200**
Expenses			
Leasehold Expense	($100)		
Geological & Geophysical	($25)		
IDC (Drilling and Completion)	($500)		
Lease Operating Expense		($75)	($75)
Equipment Expense	($100)		
Total Expenses	($725)	($75)	($75)
2 Income (for tax purposes)			
Gross Income	**$0**	**$250**	**$200**
Income Tax Deductions:			
IDC (Drilling and Completion)	($500)		
Lease Operating Expense		($75)	($75)
Depreciation of Equipment		($20)	($20)
Depletion (% @ 15%)		($38)	($30)
Taxable Income	$0	$117	$75
Income Tax *		$41	$26
Additional Tax (AMT)		$41	$26
Tax Loss	($500)		
Tax Savings *	$175*		
(based on 35% tax rate)			
3 Net After Tax Position	**$175**	**$168**	**$148**

EXAMPLE - Tax Effect on Drilling vs Acquisition

ASSUMPTIONS
- Investment is $20,000,000.
  In Case 1, Investment is in Drilling Program;
  In Case 2, Investment is in Production Acquisition.
- 20 BCF gas are produced over 16 years.
- Depletion is the greater of cost or percentage depletion.
- Federal Tax rate is 39.6%; State tax rate is 4.3%.
- Drilling Scenario is by Farm-Out (no Lease or G&G Costs)
- All intangible drilling costs (IDC) are incurred in 1st year.
- $3,000,000 of equipment depreciated over MACRS 7 years.
- Alternative Minimum Tax not considered.

	Deduction	Tax Benefit	NPV of Tax Benefit Disc at 10%
Amounts are in $1,000's			
1 DRILLING Case			
IDC (Drilling and Completion)	17,000	7,174	7,174
Depreciation (Equipment Expense)	3,000	1,266	913
Percentage Depletion	9,004	3,800	1,682
Total NPV of Tax Benefits Discounted at 10%			**$9,769**
2 ACQUISITION Case			
IDC (Drilling and Completion)	none	none	none
Depreciation (Equipment Expense)	3,000	1,266	913
Cost or Percentage Depletion	17,000	7,174	3,681
Total NPV of Tax Benefits Discounted at 10%			**$4,594**

This example is presented courtesy of Christopher Daubert, Senior Tax Manager, Mark Edmunds, Partner, and Duane Snyder, Manager at Deloitte & Touche, LLP.

Average Operating Costs per Barrel of Oil Equivalent
Oil & Gas Leases
1995

Operating Cost Category	Average ($/BOE)	% of Total
Overhead and paperwork	$1.40	24%
Pumper	$1.03	18%
Subsurface maintenance / repair	$0.93	16%
Electricity	$0.65	11%
Surface equip. maintenance / repair	$0.50	9%
Water disposal	$0.42	7%
Direct supervision and other labor	$0.42	7%
Chemicals	$0.25	4%
Trucking	$0.11	2%
Gas for pumps	$0.08	1%
Other	$0.01	0%
Total Operating Cost / BOE	**$5.80**	
Gross price $/BOE	$14.47	
Est'd Net Price per BOE*	$11.77	
Total Opt'g Cost / Est'd Net Price	49%	

*   Estimated, net of royalties and gross production tax.

Data from Survey of Oklahoma Oil & Gas Leases for the Oklahoma Commission on Marginally Producing Oil and Gas Wells,
by David A. Penn, Center for Economic and Management
Research College of Business Administration, University of
Oklahoma, 1996.

Chapter 11

DEAL STRUCTURES

Among oil industry partners

Scientific exploration for oil and gas demands the integration of four essential ingredients:

PROSPECT

The scientifically reasoned hypothesis that a commercially exploitable accumulation of oil or gas exists at a specific defined location. The hypothesis can be tested only by the drilling of a well.

LAND

The exclusive right to drill for, and produce, oil and gas on the specific tract of land where the prospect is located.

DOLLARS

Funds invested to test the prospect through the drilling of a well. They are placed at risk in anticipation of earning an attractive return on this investment.

TECHNOLOGY

The technical know-how to successfully drill and complete the proposed well.

Any exploration company may have (or may have ready access to) one or two of these ingredients. In most cases, however, it becomes necessary

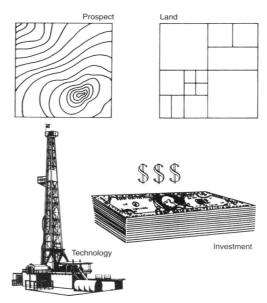

Figure 11.1 Ingredients Needed for Exploration

to make a deal for the other ingredients. Among them, PROSPECT and LAND are uniquely and inextricably linked. There may be any number of potential partners with DOLLARS and numerous operating companies with TECHNOLOGY, but there is only one tract of LAND that goes with the PROSPECT.

What happens if:

- the BLUEJAY COMPANY has a PROSPECT, and
- the GROUNDHOG COMPANY owns a 100% working interest in the tract of LAND where it is located?

They might enter into a farmout agreement to jointly explore and develop the property. In the basic case, they form a tax partnership, with GROUNDHOG contributing his LAND and BLUEJAY contributing the costs of drilling a well. By drilling the well, BLUEJAY will earn a working interest in GROUNDHOG's LAND; GROUNDHOG will retain an interest in net revenues (if any) from the well drilled by BLUEJAY.

One way or another, all four quantities must be pooled together to explore for oil and gas.

During more than a hundred years of negotiations and transactions within the American oil industry, some more or less "standard" deal structures have evolved. They are based on the (commonly held) premise that the relationship between the level of risk and the return on investment changes at different stages in the exploration process. (Purchasing an interest in a producing oil well is generally believed to involve lower risk than buying an interest in an un-drilled prospect). Stan-

Costs	Typical Sequence Of Events in the Drilling of a Well	Revenues
"BEFORE Casing Point"	*Generate Prospect* *Lease Acreage* *Well is Spudded* *Drill to Casing Point and Log*	
"AFTER Casing Point"	*Set Production Casing* *Complete Well* *Flowline Hook-up* *Well on Production* *Remedial Work ?* *PayOut*	"BEFORE PayOut"
"AFTER PayOut"	*Continued Production* *Remedial Work?* *Re-Completion in 2nd Zone?* *Salt Water Disposal Well?* *Well is Abandoned*	"AFTER PayOut"

COSTS are paid
by owners of:

Working Interests

Revenues are shared
by owners of:

Working Interests
Royalties
ORRI
etc.

Table 11.1 Cost and Revenues in Drilling a Well

dard deal structures recognize and take into account, changes in the 'risk - return' relationship during the (predictable) evolution of a property from exploration through development.

In many deals, the sharing of COSTS may be specified to change during each separate stage of drilling/development:

>Before the Casing Point BCP
>
>After the Casing Point ACP
>
>After PayOut APO.

The sharing of REVENUES may also be specified to change during each separate stage of production:

>Before PayOut BPO
>
>After PayOut APO.

Please see Table 11.1. (Except, possibly under the most extraordinary circumstances, no revenue will be generated before the casing point).

The casing point is understood in the oil industry to mean a unique stage in the mechanical operations of drilling and completing a well, specifically: after the well has been drilled to the planned total depth and logged, but before production casing has been run. (Please see discussion under Casing Point Election, Chapter 5.)

Payout, however, may mean different things to different parties, and should be clearly defined (to the point of specifying the accounting method and factors used to establish when it occurs). Payout in the case of single well is different from payout of a prospect (which may involve drilling several wells) or payout of a program (which might include several prospects).

'Pooling of Capital'

One of the foundations of oil and gas taxation which has helped shape the industry as it has evolved to the present day is the concept of 'pooling of capital' as incorporated into the Internal Revenue Code (and described in the IRS General Counsel Memorandum 22730).

For Federal income tax purposes, this concept allows that when a taxpayer (who provides services) receives a royalty interest in a property in exchange for providing ('contributing') his services in the exploitation of that property, the taxpayer will not be deemed to have received taxable income at the time the royalty interest is received. Instead, income will be recognized only as the property generates a stream of revenue.

Assume that a taxpayer contributes materials or services toward development of an oil and gas property. For these services and materials, he receives an interest in the property (an override, working-interest, etc. described below). Under appropriate circumstances, this constitutes a sharing arrangement (rather than compensation for services performed).[72] The taxpayer is not required to pay tax at the time he receives the interest in the property. Instead, he pays tax on his share of revenues from production (if any), as they are received.[73]

This not-taxable-when-received treatment

makes sense. How would it be possible to establish the value of an interest in a property, before a well is drilled? The well might be a dry hole that would generate no income.

On the other hand, suppose the well is a very good one, capable of averaging 250 barrels of oil per day for 10 years. If there is a 1/5 royalty on the lease, a 1/4 working interest might generate net revenues of $3,650,000 (= 250 bopd x 4/5 = 200 bopd x 1/4 = 50 bopd x 365 days x 10 years x $20/bbl = $3,650,000). Imagine having to pay tax on such an amount, at the time of receiving an interest in a not-yet-producing property! Under the 'pool of capital' concept, taxes would become due as the income is received.

A number of criteria must be met to qualify for the non-taxable-when-received treatment.

- The interest in the property must be received in return for services provided in the development of that specific property.
- The interest received must be in the same property for which the services were performed.
- The services-for-interest arrangement must be established before the service work is performed. (An override taken after work has been performed, for example, in place of a salary due, would not qualify.)

When the 'pool of capital' concept does not apply, the taxpayer is subject to immediate taxation in the year the interest is received.

Types of Conditional Interests

Risks are part of the drilling of wells. Typical oil industry deals comprehend these risks by involving interests (in a property) that are conditional with respect to specified outcomes. The carried interest and the back-in interest are two common types of interests, which may be triggered or activated at a specified stage in the development of a well or prospect.

A **CARRIED INTEREST** is an arrangement between co-owners of a working interest (a cost-bearing interest).[74] Please see the glossary for discussion. Suppose:

BLUEJAY has	ZEBRA has
PROSPECT	DOLLARS
	LAND, and
	TECHNOLOGY

BLUEJAY and ZEBRA agree that BLUEJAY shall retain a carried interest in the prospect if ZEBRA will advance the costs of developing the property to a specified point (most typically the casing point). ZEBRA will recover these costs from the proceeds from future production (if any).

If the well is plugged and abandoned without a completion attempt, ZEBRA pays all costs; (ZEBRA carries BLUEJAY to the casing point). BLUEJAY incurs no cost.

If the well is completed, BLUEJAY's carried interest converts to (and begins to function as) a full working interest at the casing point (correspondingly reducing ZEBRA's working interest). BLUEJAY must pay his (full working-interest share) of completion and other costs from that point forward.

If the well is abandoned after an unsuccessful completion attempt, BLUEJAY and ZEBRA each pay their respective shares of completion and abandonment costs.

When production is established, BLUEJAY and ZEBRA each receive their respective shares of revenues (after deducting the landowner's royalty and any other burdens).

Please refer to Example 11.1.

A 'carried interest to the casing point' means the costs of drilling and logging the well are advanced; a 'carried interest through the tanks' (the oil tanks installed at the well for commercial production) means the costs of drilling, logging, and completing the well and installing surface equipment are advanced; (in the case of a flowing gas well, the analogous point might be a 'carried through the meter').

A **BACK-IN** or **REVERSIONARY INTEREST** may be directed to either a working interest (cost-bearing interest), or to a royalty or overriding royalty interest (both of which are cost-free interests). It becomes effective on the occurrence of a specified future event. That event is commonly payout (when exploration and development costs have been recouped out of net revenues). Please refer to Example 11.2.

Production payments and net profits interests are types of conditional interests which may be less common within the oil industry (but are frequently used in deals involving outside investment).

A **PRODUCTION PAYMENT** or **OIL PAYMENT** is a right to minerals in place. It represents a share of production that is limited, either by a specified period of time, or until a specified amount of money has been received. Created from a working interest, it is a cost-free interest in net revenues, similar to an overriding royalty except for time and amount limitations.[75]

A **NET PROFITS INTEREST** is also a right to minerals in place. It is a share of production measured according to the net profits from operations of the property. Created out of a working interest, it is similar to an overriding royalty in that it is effective throughout the life of the working interest, and does not pay development and operating costs. Income to the net profits interest is equal to its share of net revenues reduced by its share of specified development and operating costs (income = net revenues - development and operating costs). The owner of a net profits interest receives no income unless the property generates a net profit.[76]

"The world's big oil firms are engaged in an increasingly desperate scramble for giant low-cost reserves."

THE ECONOMIST May 18th 1996

154

"A Third For A Quarter"

"A third for a quarter to the casing point" is a deal that involves a carried working interest, and is sometimes referred to as a 'standard industry deal'. Geologist generates a PROSPECT and controls the LAND. He contracts for the TECHNOLOGY to drill the well, but he lacks DOLLARS. He finds 3 Oilmen with DOLLARS who each agree to pay 1/3 of the cost of drilling and logging the well to the casing point, in order to receive 1/4 of net revenues (total revenues less any royalties burdening the lease).

The geologist retains a 1/4 carried working interest which will convert to (will become) a 1/4 working interest at the casing point.

If, at the casing point, the well is plugged as a dry hole without a completion attempt:

The Oilmen have gained no income. They paid 100% of the drilling costs and are entitled to 100% of the income tax deductions allowed for intangible drilling costs (IDC) incurred in the drilling of the well. (Typically about 65% of the drilling costs may qualify as IDC.)

The geologist has gained no income, but he has gained the satisfaction of seeing his prospect drilled (without incurring any drilling costs, himself).

If, at the casing point election, the logs look promising and they decide to complete the well, the 3 Oilmen and the Geologist each pay 1/4 of all costs from that point forward, and are entitled to 1/4 of the revenues (net of landowner's royalty and other burdens). (Please see glossary for variations on revenue entitlement).

If the well is completed, but there is no production:

The Oilmen paid 3/4 of the completion costs and are entitled to 3/4 of the deductions allowed for IDC incurred in the completion attempt.

The Geologist paid 1/4 of the completion costs and is entitled to 1/4 of the income tax deductions allowed for IDC incurred in the completion attempt. (Typically about 35% if the completion costs may qualify as IDC.)

If there is production:

Each of the 3 Oilmen receives his share (1/4 = 25%) of revenues and each enjoys tax-free income to the extent of his computed depletion allowance.

The geologist receives his share (1/4 = 25%) of revenues. He enjoys tax-free income to the extent of his computed depletion allowance.

"An Eighth Back"

Geologist generates a PROSPECT and controls the LAND (100% working interest) and contracts for the TECHNOLOGY to drill a well, but needs DOLLARS. Oilman has DOLLARS. Geologist and Oilman strike a deal in which Geologist retains only a 3.5% overriding royalty, but he reserves the right to

EXAMPLE 11.1

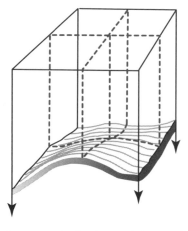

CARRIED INTEREST TO CASING POINT

A leases 160 acres owned in fee by *L*. *L* retains a 1/8 (= 12.5%) royalty interest.

State authorities set the spacing unit for the well *A* proposes to drill at 160 acres.

A burdens the lease with a 4% overriding royalty on the full 160 acres.

He promotes his 100% working interest out to *B*, *C* and *D* on a third for a quarter basis, retaining a 1/4 carried interest to the casing point. He delivers them an 83.5% net-revenue-interest lease.

	Sharing of COSTS Working Interest			Sharing REVENUES Net Revenue Interest	
	Before Csg Pt	After Csg Pt	After Payout	Before Payout	After Payout
W/ I Owners:					
A	0.00%	25%	25%	20.88%	20.88%
B	33.30%	25%	25%	20.88%	20.88%
C	33.30%	25%	25%	20.88%	20.88%
D	33.30%	25%	25%	20.88%	20.88%
	100%	100%	100%	83.5%	83.5%
Royalties:					
A	0%	0%	0%	4.00%	4.00%
L	0%	0%	0%	12.50%	12.50%
	0%	0%	0%	16.50%	16.50%
	0%	0%	0%	100%	100%

back-in for a 1/8 (= 12.5%) working interest after payout.

In this deal, Oilman pays all costs of drilling the well. If the logs look promising and he decides to complete the well, Oilman pays all completion costs.

If the well is abandoned as a dry hole at the casing point:

> Oilman has gained no income, but having paid 100% of all drilling and completion costs, he is entitled to 100% of the income tax deductions allowed for intangible drilling costs (IDC). (Typically about 65% of the drilling costs qualify as IDC.)

> Geologist has gained no income, but he has had the satisfaction of seeing his prospect tested.

If the well is completed but there is no production:

> Having paid 100% of the completion costs, Oilman is entitled to 100% of the deductions allowed for IDC incurred in the completion attempt. (Typically about 35% of the completion costs qualify as IDC.)

> No change in Geologist's situation.

If there is production:

> *BEFORE* PAYOUT

> Oilman will receive 100% of revenues (net of royalties, overriding royalties and other burdens).

> Geologist will receive 3.5% of gross revenues (accruing to his overriding royalty) starting from first production.

EXAMPLE 11.2

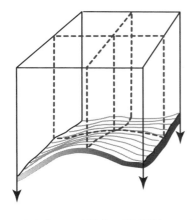

BACK-IN WORKING INTEREST

A lease 160 acres owned in fee by *L*. *L* retains a 3/16 (= 18.75%) royalty interest.

unit for the well *A* proposes to drill at160 acres.

A burdens the lease with a 4% overriding royalty on the full 160 acres.

He promotes his 100% working interest out to *B*, *C*, and *D*, retaining a 1/8 (= 12.5%) carried interest to the casing point and a 1/8 working interest back-in after payout.

A delivers them a 77.25% net-revenue-interest lease, burdened with a 1/8 back-in working interest.

	Sharing of COSTS Working Interest			Sharing REVENUES Net Revenue Interest	
	Before Csg Pt	After Csg Pt	After Payout	Before Payout	After Payout
W/ I Owners:					
A	0.00%	12.50%	25%	9.66%	19.31%
B	33.30%	29.17%	25%	22.53%	19.31%
C	33.30%	29.17%	25%	22.53%	19.31%
D	33.30%	29.17%	25%	22.53%	19.31%
	100%	100%	100%	77.25%	77.25%
Royalties:					
A	0%	0%	0%	4.00%	4.00%
L	0%	0%	0%	18.75%	18.75%
	0%	0%	0%	22.75%	22.75%
	0%	0%	0%	100%	100%

AFTER PAYOUT

Oilman will receive 7/8 (= 87.5%) of net revenues and will pay 7/8 of operating costs. He enjoys tax-free income to the extent of his computed depletion allowance.

In addition to gross revenues which continue to accrue to his override, Geologist will begin to receive one eighth (1/8 = 12.5%) of revenues (net of burdens), and will pay 1/8 of lease operating costs. He receives tax-free income to the extent of his computed depletion allowance.

Other Deals

There is no limit to the creativity that can be applied to any deal, but excessive creativity frequently leads to deals that are too complex to be readily understood.

Chapter 12

LIMITING LIABILITY

and the 'flow-thru' principle

Drilling for oil and gas entails a certain amount of risk. Depending on nature of the rocks being penetrated, and the competence and philosophy of the operator, the drilling procedure can range from an undertaking with rather minimal risk, to an extraordinarily high-risk gamble. The philosophy of the operator is paramount. It has been argued that more than one disreputable operator has occasionally drilled a well 'under-balanced' (with inadequate mud weights) in order to intentionally create a blowout situation; the theory is that the media coverage associated with the blowout serves to advertise the 'success' of the operator in finding oil and gas, and thereby to attract the gullible to invest in future drilling deals with such a 'successful' operator.

"Just as dope prices are set by dope dealers (not by dope addicts), oil importing nations must buy their oil at prices set by competition between oil exporting countries, not by importing nations' consumers, planners, or politicians."

OIL & GAS JOURNAL Oct. 29, 1990
Competition Increases to Obtain Oil Imports by L.F. Ivanhoe

A runaway blowout can result in risk to life and limb, or death, plus very significant physical damages, not to mention legal liabilities from the type of lawsuits which nowadays seem to commonly accompany nearly any misfortune. Anyone considering participation in a drilling venture needs to consider limiting his liability. Reputable operators carry a range of insurance policies, ranging from worker's compensation insurance to blowout insurance. And under the terms of the joint operating agreement (JOA), the protection provided by these policies may or may not extend to other nonoperating working interests; generally they probably do not. In order to protect investors from unlimited liability, a number of legal entities are commonly used in structuring a drilling deal, to protect the investor from unlimited liability. They include corporations (both 'C' corporations and 'S' corporations), partnerships (both general partnerships and limited partnerships) and the relatively new limited liability company (LLC). (Watch your local business news for state legislation that may take up the topics of 'limited liability partnerships' and 'limited liability professional corporations', etc.)

Any definitive discussion of these legal entities falls way outside the scope of this book. Some general review of the legal entities most commonly adopted in structuring oil and gas investments, however, is provided. The limited partnership has become the most widely used vehicle for structuring oil and gas investments, by far. Since 1977 when the first limited liability company (LLC) was established in the U.S., however, this new liability-limiting vehicle has become increasingly familiar in the financing of oil and gas ventures.

Limited Partnerships

A partnership is a business association undertaken by two or more parties, who act as co-owners of the business. The formation and operation of partnerships are governed by state law. Most states have adopted the (Federal) Uniform Partnership and Uniform Limited Partnership Acts. Under these acts, a foreign (non-U.S.) or domestic (U.S.) corporation, individual, or another partnership may be a partner in a general or limited partnership.

A general partnership consists of a single category of partners. Each partner fully shares the general responsibilities, liabilities, and obligations of the partnership, and is called a 'general partner'. Assume for example, that a partnership borrows money from a bank. The bank can force each or any partner (or partners) in a general partnership to repay the partnership's debt (by court action, if necessary). This is in marked contrast, for example, with a corporation, in which the shareholders are owners but do not have any liability for the corporation's debts or obligations.

A limited partnership has two categories of partners: there must be one or more general partners, but there may be thousands of limited partners. The general partner commonly contributes service and expertise, manages the partnership (according to a detailed limited partnership agreement), and has unlimited liability for the debts of the partnership.

Profit from oil a dirty word?
"If politicians pass legislation to punish oil companies for profits, no one should kid themselves about who will pay the price: We all would."

Jonathan Williams of The Tax Foundation, Washington D.C.
in The Oklahoman, Wednesday, February 15, 2006

Limited partners, on the other hand, commonly contribute cash, have negligible rights as to the operation of the partnership, and their liability for the partnership's debts is usually limited to the extent of their contribution to the partnership.

All partnerships are significantly different from corporations. Doing business in the form of a corporation has certain advantages such as limited liability and centralized control. Income earned by the corporation, however, is taxed twice. First, at the corporate level, the corporation pays tax on its income. Then when the corporation's after-tax income is distributed to shareholders in the form of dividends (cash), the shareholder must pay income tax on the dividends he receives.

A limited partnership does not pay Federal income taxes. Who pays tax on income earned by the partnership? The limited partnership calculates and files an 'informational' tax return with the Internal Revenue Service (IRS), but the actual tax-paying obligations "flow through" to the individual partners, according to their share of income or losses from the partnership. This is in marked contrast to a corporation.

The formation of a limited partnership involves the execution of a comprehensive limited partnership agreement. It is signed by all of the general and limited partners. The offering documents commonly run to several hundred pages.[77] The limited partnership agreement, which must be filed with the secretary of state where it is formed, contains, among other things:

- the name, place of business, and proposed type of business of the partnership, the names and addresses of the partners;
- authority, obligations, and responsibilities of the partners;
- initial capital contributions of the general and limited partners (amounts, manner of payment, guidelines for deposit and use of funds);
- procedures for additional financing (borrowing, additional or optional assessments from limited partners);
- the respective participation of the general and limited partners in both costs and revenues of the partnership;
- reports (financial, tax, operating) to be furnished to the limited partners;

- distributions (method for determining amounts of cash available for distributions, frequency of distributions);
- compensation of general partner (commonly in the form of 'guaranteed payments');
- transferability of interests;
- procedures for repurchase of limited partners' interest (by the partnership, the general partner, or other limited partners);
- rights of withdrawal or removal of a partner; and
- the events and rights related to the dissolution and termination of the partnership.[78]

Most Federal income tax elections affecting computation of a partnership's taxable income are made by the partnership ('at the partnership level'). This centralizes a variety of decisions that must be made for all the partners.[79] (The election to expense intangible drilling costs - IDC, however, is made at the partner level.) At the end of the partnership's tax year, the partnership is required to separately report various items of tax significance to the IRS (Form 1065). The partnership provides each partner with a Federal income tax form (Schedule K-1) listing his allocated share of the partnership's income, gains, losses, tax exemptions, tax deductions, and tax credits for the year. He then incorporates these tax items in the preparation of his own corporate or individual tax return.[80]

Because tax items, notably deductions, are "passed through" to the investor, limited partnerships are a popular structure for tax shelters. Ordinarily, the partner enjoys these benefits to the

EXAMPLE 12.1

TYPICAL OIL & GAS LIMITED PARTNERSHIP INVESTMENT

WORKING INTEREST LEVEL

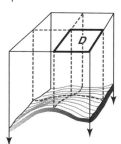

A, *B*, *C*, and *D* each own a 1/4 working interest in a property. They enter into a joint operating agreement (JOA), agreeing to be treated for tax purposes as "co-owners" associated in a 'joint effort'.

A, as operator, manages the operation of the property. *D*, as (non-operating) working-interest co-owner, shares income and expenses in direct proportion to his working interest.

LIMITED PARTNERSHIP LEVEL

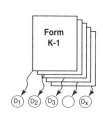

D happens to be a limited partnership with:

D_0 as General Partner,
D_1-D_9 as Limited Partners.

D Limited Partnership pays no Federal income taxes. Each partner's distributive share of partnership income, gains, losses, deductions, and credits is determined according to the partnership agreement, and allocated to him on a Form K-1.

LIMITED PARTNER LEVEL

At the end of the tax year, Partner D_X has

a   items of income, deductions, losses, tax credits (if any) arising from his PASSIVE INTEREST in *D* Limited Partnership, *and*

b   items of income, deductions, losses, tax credits (if any) arising from interests in other PASSIVE ACTIVITIES.

Partner D_X consolidates his net passive income (a + b). If a loss (a negative number), the amount is suspended and carried forward to succeeding years. Otherwise his 3 types of income are aggregated to arrive at Gross Income:

> Passive Income (a positive number, or zero)
> Portfolio Income
> <u>Wages/Income from a Trade or Business</u>
>
> Gross Income
> <u>- Deductions (if any)</u>
>
> Taxable Income   x   Tax Rate   =   Tax Liability
>   <u>- Tax Credits (if any)</u>
>   Taxes Due and Payable

extent of his interest in the limited partnership. The limited partnership agreement may be structured so that tax benefits are allocated disproportionately between the general partner(s) and the limited partners.[81]

"Natural gas prices hit $5"

The Oklahoman, Thursday, September 7, 2000

Financial analysis of a limited partnership considers what a limited partner must put into it (contributions) and what he will get out of it (distributions). A partner may contribute cash, services or property to acquire an interest in the partnership. The value of this becomes his basis in the partnership.

If the partnership generates income in a particular year, a partner may receive cash or property as a distribution from the partnership. He then pays income tax on his distributed share of that income. (Income may or may not be distributed as it is earned.) If the partnership suffers (net operating or capital) losses during a particular year, a partner may receive losses as a distribution from the partnership. He then incorporates his distributed share of those losses as an income tax deduction on his own income tax return. (This deduction is limited, however, to his adjusted basis in the partnership.)[82]

A partner's basis is adjusted according to the results of the partnerships activities. It increases when his share of the partnership's current income is not distributed to him. His basis decreases when distributions to him exceed his share of the partnership's current income, or when the partnership suffers (net operating or capital) losses.[83]

A partner's adjusted basis in a partnership is classified as a capital asset. If a partner sells or exchanges his interest in a partnership interest, any gain or loss may be taxable to him. [84]

Master Limited Partnerships (MLP)

The master limited partnership was a concept pioneered by Apache Petroleum Company in the early 1980's. It served two main functions: 1) to eliminate corporate taxes, and 2) to provide liquidity for the owners of limited partnership interests. A master limited partnership could be formed when the sponsor (general partner) of a series of limited partnerships, combined all of the interest in it's existing limited partnerships, and placed them in one entity, the MLP.

Recall that most sponsors of limited partnerships offered one or more limited partnerships each year, as in the case of the Oil Finder 1984-A Drilling Partnership, the Oil Finder 1985-B Income Partnership, etc. Combining all these many partnerships and their thousands of interest-holders into one master limited partnership probably simplified accounting overhead. If the MLP was then registered to be traded on the stock exchange, it provided limited partnership interest-holders with units that could be traded, in other words liquidity that they otherwise did not have.

A 'roll-up' MLP was formed by combining the interests in separate limited partnerships into one entity, a new master limited partnership. A 'drop-down' MLP was formed when a company created the MLP by spinning off assets such as producing properties owned by the company.[85]

Since an MLP was a partnership and not a corporation, corporate income tax was avoided. Once the Tax Reform Act of 1986 and subsequent rulings were passed, the tax losses generated in the early stages of a drilling limited partnership were deemed to be from a 'passive' activity and could no longer offset an investor's ordinary income from other sources. Hence MLP units created from the combining of such limited partnerships no longer provided the attractive tax benefits enjoyed before 1986.[86]

Royalty Trusts

Long before the concept of the master limited partnership became popular, there had always been interest in finding ways to avoid the 'double taxation' problem of oil and gas assets owned by a corporation. Gulf Oil Corporation created the first royalty trust to achieve this end by placing 60 producing properties in the Gulf of Mexico in the Tidelands Royalty B Trust in 1954.[87] Later in 1979, Mesa Petroleum Company transferred a basket of overriding royalties on producing properties throughout the U.S., into the Mesa Royalty Trust.

These entities allowed investors to 'own' interests in oil and gas producing properties and enjoy income throughout the productive life of the properties - as they gradually liquidated themselves through the normal course of depletion. Since the interests were in royalties and overriding royalties, the interest-holder bore no liabilities for the costs involved in the development and production, or the eventual abandonment of these fields.

Recently this same concept has resurfaced again, this time in Canada. In 1994 about $300 million (USD) was invested in royalty trusts in Canada, by 1996, this number had reached nearly $3 billion (USD).[88]

As in the case of the earlier royalty trusts in the U.S., the Canadian royalty trusts invest in producing oil and gas properties and deliver most of the income from production revenues to the investor, although some may be reinvested by the trust in further development of the reserves. None, however is spent on exploration.

The concept of sharing directly in the revenue from production combined with 'low risk', and 'no exploration and development costs' clearly has appeal to investors. Don't be fooled. Investing in royalty trusts or master limited partnerships amounts to little more than taking a kind of care-taker position, in the waning years of the productive life of an oil field. Lacking any mechanism for aggressive reinvestment in exploration, these types of investment programs will eventually liquidate themselves into oblivion. Always keep in mind that the only proven way to find and develop new oil and gas reserves is to drill for them. Yes, it can involve a high degree of risk and Yes, it can be extraordinarily capital-intensive. Without continuous reinvestment in exploration, however, new reserves will not be found.

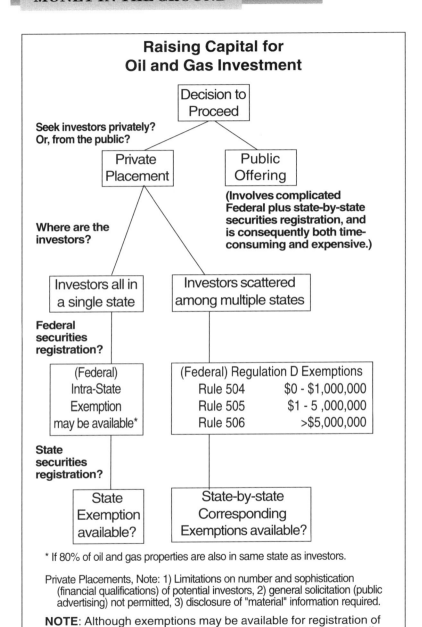

Raising Capital for Oil and Gas Investment

Decision to Proceed

Seek investors privately?
Or, from the public?

Private Placement

Public Offering

(Involves complicated Federal plus state-by-state securities registration, and is consequently both time-consuming and expensive.)

Where are the investors?

Investors all in a single state

Investors scattered among multiple states

Federal securities registration?

(Federal) Intra-State Exemption may be available*

(Federal) Regulation D Exemptions
Rule 504 $0 - $1,000,000
Rule 505 $1 - 5,000,000
Rule 506   >$5,000,000

State securities registration?

State Exemption available?

State-by-state Corresponding Exemptions available?

* If 80% of oil and gas properties are also in same state as investors.

Private Placements, Note: 1) Limitations on number and sophistication (financial qualifications) of potential investors, 2) general solicitation (public advertising) not permitted, 3) disclosure of "material" information required.

NOTE: Although exemptions may be available for registration of offerings, there are no exemptions from securities law fraud!

DISCLAIMER: The foregoing information, while believed to be accurate, does not constitute any representation by the author or the publisher.

Limited Liability Company (LLC)

This new structure appears to be the vehicle of choice for the future of oil and gas investment programs.

Wyoming was the first state to enact legislation (in 1977) providing for the establishment of a limited liability company (the Wyoming Limited Liability Company Act) - specifically for the creation of an oil and gas related business. It was not until the Internal Revenue Service (IRS) issued a public ruling that a Wyoming LLC would be treated as a partnership for tax purposes, however, that this the concept of a limited liability company really caught on as a new viable form of business organization in the U.S.

Nearly all 50 states have now adopted legislation providing for the creation of limited liability companies. Several characteristics of the limited liability company structure appear to be very well suited to the area of oil and gas investment, specifically:

1) Limited Liability,
2) Flow-Through Tax Treatment, and
3) Flexibility in terms of
   a) the number and nature of investors (called 'members'),
   b) form of capital contribution (cash or property), and
   c) allocation of costs, revenues, and tax items. Please see Appendix C for further discussion.

A limited liability company is formed by filing

articles of organization with the secretary of state. Depending on the specific statues of the state, the articles will likely include such information as:

- name and address (and possibly, business purpose) of the limited liability company,
- the latest date on which the LLC is to dissolve,
- street address of it's principal office,
- name and address of the resident agent of the limited liability company,
- (possibly) names and addresses of founding or initial members and managers.

In some states, reports describing the management and capital structure of the LLC may have to be filed with government regulators.[89]

The owners of the LLC are referred to as 'members', and there need to be at least two. The LLC is managed according to an operating agreement, which is a written agreement that dictates the way the LLC is to be run. It is an internal agreement, so there is no requirement that it be filed with government regulators. Depending on the objectives of the LLC and it's members, practically any allocation of profit-sharing or operational, managerial, or administrative structure is possible.[90] In the case of the original Wyoming statutes, for example, members can appoint a manager(s) for the company with authority to act as the agent for the members, or with exclusive authority for ongoing management of the entity.[91] In Oklahoma members may appoint managers, or can perform the function of managers, themselves.[92]

A limited liability company can be recognized by

any of the following qualifiers in it's name: limited liability company, ltd. liability co., limited company, ltd. co., L.L.C., L.C., etc.

The flexibility of the limited liability company structure is impressive and should be of interest to anyone involved in oil and gas ventures. (Note that a limited liability company is governed by an 'operating agreement', just as the activity of an exploration and production joint venture is governed by a 'joint operating agreement'.) Inasmuch as the limited liability company type of entity appears destined to become the business structure of choice in the future, see a copy of your state's statutes for more information. (Also please refer to Appendix C and references listed under Recommended Resources.)

Economic Limit

Secondary Recovery Scenario

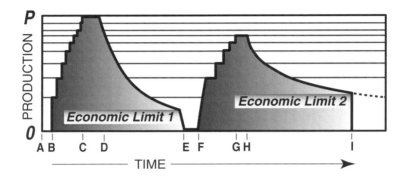

A-B   Generating prospect and selling the deal.

B   Discovery well is drilled.

B-C   Development of the field.

C-D   Peak production.

D-E   Production declines to the point that the economic limit of the field (Economic Limit 1) is reached at time E.

E-F   Field is shut-in pending initiation of secondary recovery (waterflooding, for example).

F-G   As injection wells are drilled and activated, production increases.

G-H   Peak secondary production.

H-I   Production declines to the point that the new economic limit of the field (Economic Limit 2) is reached at time I. (Economic Limit 2 represents greater operating expense than Economic Limit 1 due to the increased cost of operating the secondary recovery system).

Chapter 13

OIL & GAS PROGRAMS

Limited Partnerships for the (non-oil-industry) investor

Historical Perspective

By 1934, four years after the crash of the New York stock market in 1929, total economic production in the U.S. had declined by about 30%. Economic depression focused public and political at-

177

tention on stock market speculation that had contributed to the crash. In rapid succession, Congress passed the Securities Act of 1933 and the Securities and Exchange Act of 1934 to prohibit the types of activities that were believed to have contributed to the collapse of the stock market.[93]

The Securities Act of 1933 requires issuers making public offerings of securities, to file registra-

Dow Jones teaches principles of Islamic investing online. "...Islamic investing is fast emerging as a financial sector..."

THE JOURNAL RECORD, March 28, 2000

tion statements disclosing financial and other pertinent information about both the issuer and the securities being offered for sale. They must be registered with the (Federal) Securities and Exchange Commission (SEC), established under the Securities and Exchange Act of 1934. In addition to the Federal regulations requiring registration with the SEC, each state has also developed its own securities laws regarding the registration of securities to be offered or sold within its borders ('blue sky laws').

What does this have to do with oil and gas? The Securities Act of 1933 defines 'securities' to include any certificate of interest or participation in any profit sharing agreement, investment contract, or *fractional undivided interest in oil, gas, or mineral rights*[94] (Subsequent judicial ruling has defined 'investment contract' as an investment in a common enterprise, with the expectation of profits solely from the efforts of the promoter or a third party.)

As a result of these definitions and rulings, any person intending to offer or sell an interest in an oil and gas deal to the general public (a 'public offering') is dealing with a security, and must file a registration statement with the SEC. Registration involves the preparation of documents disclosing prescribed information about the offering and the sponsoring organization for the benefit of potential investors. Disclosure of this information is intended to enable a potential investor to make an informed decision regarding investment. Disclosure also provides the issuing party some protection against certain legal actions that might otherwise be initiated by a disgruntled investor.

The act of registration does not mean that the security itself meets any specified investment criteria, or is in any way 'approved' by the government. It means only that the issuer has complied with the pertinent regulations which require disclosure of certain information.

The offering of securities that are not intended to be sold to the general public ('private placement offerings') may qualify for exemptions from (Federal) registration with the SEC (under Regulation D of the Securities Act of 1933, as amended). To qualify for such exemption, private placement offerings are generally characterized by a variety of limitations, related to the number of investors (a maximum of 35 under some conditions), the manner in which the offering is made, and the sophistication and financial strength of the intended investors, among other considerations. Exemptions from state registration vary from state to state.[95]

Participation From Within The Oil Industry

Individuals and organizations in the oil industry commonly participate in oil deals through direct acquisition of a working interest or a royalty in an oil and gas property (which is typically co-owned with others). As the operator (or a non-operator) under the joint operating agreement (JOA), an oil industry investor is a participant in a joint venture (as contrasted to a partnership or corporation). This significantly reduces some of the filings and registrations which would otherwise be required under the securities laws. Please see Appendix C.

Investment From Outside The Oil Industry

There is nothing to prevent an investor outside the oil industry from directly purchasing working interests or royalties in oil and gas properties on his own (just as he might purchase stocks, bonds, real estate, or gold coins). If he enlists the assistance of others, however, such a transaction might easily constitute an 'investment contract' in oil and gas properties. As such it becomes a securities transaction, and may be subject to registration requirements and other provisions of securities law. It is generally easier, and much more common, for such an investor to participate in oil and gas deals through an oil and gas fund, specifically designed

REVENUES - COSTS - TAX BENEFITS for Directly Held Interests

INTEREST	WORKING INTEREST (7/8)	ROYALTY INTEREST (1/8)
GROSS REVENUES	Shares of Revenues: 100% (8/8 less Royalty (1/8) = 7/8	Share of Gross Revenues (1/8)
less:	- State Production Tax - (Product) Handling Fee - Federal Withholding Tax*	- State Production Tax - (Product) Handling Fee - Federal Withholding Tax*
NET REVENUES	Net Revenues	Net Revenues

less: EXPLORATION expenses	- Prospect Generation Costs
	- Lease Acquisition Costs
	- Initial Well:
	  Drilling Costs
	  Completion Costs
	  Production Costs	

PRODUCTION & LEASE OPERATING expenses	- Lease Operating Costs
	- Development Wells:
	  Drilling Costs
	  Completion Costs
	  Production Costs	

LIMITED PARTNERSHIP expenses		
INCOME	Net Operating Income	Net Income
Associated TAX BENEFITS	Intangible Drlg Costs Expensed Depletion Allowance	Depletion Allowance

* Federal Income Tax may be withheld from payments to interest holders who do not provide a Federal tax Id. or Social Security number on the division order.

Table 13.1 Working Interests vs Royalty Interests

to accommodate his situation (of wanting to invest in oil and gas, but not being a knowledgeable professional in the industry).

The concept of pooling individual amounts of money so that the accumulated pool of funds can be managed by professionals, has been successfully applied to any number of areas - mutual funds for investment in stock, or real estate investment trusts (REITs) for investment in real estate. Different funds can be designed and managed to achieve different investment goals.

Oil and gas funds represent yet another application of the same basic concept. The average individual investor is not likely to have the expertise in oil and gas activities (or the time necessary to evaluate different prospects to select those in which he might like to invest). In an oil and gas fund (typically a limited partnership), this is done by trained professionals employed by the general partner. (And the general partner is naturally compensated for this service.)

Just as different mutual funds are designed to accommodate different objectives for investment in stocks, there are a variety of oil and gas programs. Drilling programs, income programs, royalty programs, completion programs, and lease acquisition programs are the common categories. In popular usage, the terms 'partnership', 'program', and 'fund' are often used interchangeably; a particular limited partnership formed to invest in exploration and production might be variously referred to as a 'drilling partnership', a 'drilling program', or a 'drilling fund'.

Drilling Funds

A drilling fund encompasses the entire evolution of a prospect: from generation, through exploration and production, and through future development (or through abandonment). The sponsor (general partner) generates prospects in-house (or may acquire them from third parties). He leases exploration rights on the property where the prospects are located, and drills wells to test the prospects. He manages the development, production, and sale of oil and gas from successful wells. For the purpose of marketing these programs to potential investors, a particular drilling program might be described by the sponsor as:

EXPLORATORY

> drilling to find undiscovered reserves in new reservoirs (or significantly extending the limits of known reserves from reservoirs that are already producing).

DEVELOPMENT

> drilling to produce oil and gas from reservoirs proven to be productive in the area (from previous exploratory drilling).

BALANCED

> including both developmental and exploratory prospects.

In a drilling fund, (current) tax deductions (for IDC) and (scheduled) tax credits (if any) typically flow through the limited partnership, to the investor. They can be applied to reduce gross income which he receives from other passive sources. To the extent that the investor has taxable income from passive sources, he can thereby reduce his taxable income. The investor gets the IDC deductions whether or not the program is successful at finding and producing oil and gas. If the results of drilling are successful, revenue from production over the life of the program could theoretically return many times the amount of the original investment. In addition, tax deductions (in the form of percentage depletion) offset some of the income resulting from production. This provides the investor a stream of income, a portion of which, is tax-free over the life of the program.

Income Funds

Income funds invest in the acquisition and operation of oil and gas properties after production has already been established by exploration and development. An income partnership typically purchases working interests in producing (and sometimes in non-producing) properties. As a working-interest owner, the partnership bears operating costs (lease operating expenses - LOE) associated with an oil and gas property; they could involve repair or replacement of equipment, and repair or workover operations on a well. Properties are purchased after geological and engineering evaluation and projection of recoverable reserves; such evaluations and/or projections might be performed by the sponsor's in-house staff, or by outside engineering firms. Income partnerships might drill development wells, but typically, only to the extent that such wells are needed to aug-

REVENUES - COSTS - TAX BENEFITS for Limited Partnership Interests

TYPE of FUND	DRILLING FUND	INCOME FUND	ROYALTY FUND
GROSS REVENUES	Share of Revenues: 100% (8/8 less Royalty (1/8) = 7/8	Share of Revenues: 100% (8/8 less Royalty (1/8) = 7/8	Share of Gross Revenues (1/8)
less:	- State Production Tax - (Product) Handling Fee	- State Production Tax - (Product) Handling Fee	- State Production Tax - (Product) Handling Fee
NET REVENUES	**Net Revenues**	**Net Revenues**	**Net Revenues**

less:
EXPLORATION expenses
	- Prospect Generation Cost
	- Lease Acquisition Costs
	- Initial Well:
	  Drilling Costs
	  Completion Costs
	  Production Costs		

PRODUCTION & LEASE OPERATING expenses	- Lease Operating Costs
	- Development Wells:
	  Drilling Costs
	  Completion Costs
	  Production Costs
		- Lease Operating Costs
		- Development Wells:
		  Drilling Costs
		  Completion Costs
		  Production Costs	

LIMITED PARTNERSHIP expenses	- Organizational Costs - Offering Costs - Management Fees - Interest Costs	- Organizational Costs - Offering Costs - Management Fees - Interest Costs	- Organizational Costs - Offering Costs - Management Fees - Interest Costs
INCOME	**Net Operating Income**	**Net Operating Income**	**Net Income**
Associated TAX BENEFITS	Intangible Drlg Costs * Depletion *	Intangible Drlg Costs * Depletion *	Depletion *

* SUBJECT TO ACTIVE / PASSIVE INCOME RULES (SINCE TAX REFORM ACT OF 1986)

Table 13.2 Drilling, Income, and Royalty Funds

ment production from the properties acquired.

The investor in an income partnership enjoys a stream of cash flow beginning from the date of the closing of the limited partnership. Tax deductions (depletion allowance) offset some of the income from production, providing the investor a stream of income, some of which is tax-free, over the life of the program. Unlike drilling programs, income programs are not expected to provide the investor with tax deductions (for intangible drilling and development costs - IDC).

Royalty Funds

Royalty funds invest in royalties (lessor's royalties and overriding royalties) of producing and non-producing properties. Unlike income programs (which own working interests), royalty partnerships bear no costs or responsibilities associated with the exploration, development, or operation of a property.

The investor in a royalty partnership that purchases royalties in producing properties may enjoy a stream of cash flow starting from the date of the closing of the limited partnership. Tax deductions (depletion allowance) may offset some of the income from production, providing the investor a stream of income, some of which is tax-free, over the life of the program.

Completion Funds

Completion funds are a bit different. They are designed to invest in the costs and equipment required to complete potentially productive oil or gas wells. The decision to participate is made at the casing point election (please see Chapter 5) by the general partner.

In the typical case, a completion partnership might be offered by the general partner of a drilling partnership (in order for the completion partnership to pay for the completion of wells drilled by the drilling partnership). Otherwise, the general partner of the completion partnership would have established agreements with various operators of wells providing the partnership the option to participate in the completion of a well.

In return for paying some or all of the completion costs, the completion partnership acquires a revenue interest in the well or property.

Depending on the nature of agreements with the operator of a well, and its own structure, the partnership may become entitled to (current) tax deductions (for intangible drilling and developments costs) plus depreciation allowance and tax credits (if any) involved in the completion of a well. Such tax benefits would then flow through to the limited partner investor, and can be applied to offset other taxable income which he receives from other passive sources.

Depending on the nature of the revenue interest acquired, the partnership may become entitled to tax deductions for depletion, which would offset some of the income from production, providing the investor a stream of income, some of which is tax-free, over the life of the program.

Depending on the interest acquired and the structure of the partnership, the completion partnership may or may not be entitled to participate in the drilling of subsequent development wells (if any).

Lease Acquisition Funds

Lease acquisition funds are less widely offered, probably because they can be a rather difficult concept to sell, and in any case are perceived to involve a very high degree of risk. Such a partnership might acquire working interests (exploration rights) in oil and gas leases (which one needs to obtain before exploration and development can begin).

At any point in time, the true market value of the leases acquired can fluctuate wildly, depending on the general level of activity and industry interest in the play ... and the results of wells drilled on adjacent leases or in the nearby area. In a very hot play, it is conceivable that the market value of leases (expressed in dollars per acre) could increase tenfold over a period several months. If a succession of dry-holes are drilled in the area, however, and industry abandons the play, it is also conceivable that the market value of the leases could go virtually to zero overnight.

Depending on its structure, the lease acquisition partnership might have a variety of options regarding working interests it acquires: participation in wells to be drilled (if any) during the term of the lease, sale of the lease (if there is a buyer), sub-lease or farmout (if there is a respondent), termination or abandonment.

Limited Partnerships (Front-End) Costs

In oil and gas limited partnerships, certain partnership costs are incurred which are in addition to the exploration costs attributable to the working interest, discussed earlier (such as prospect generation, lease acquisition, drilling, completion, production, and lease operating costs). Limited partnership costs fall into several categories.

Organizational Costs are expenditures incurred in creating the limited partnership: legal fees for preparation of the partnership agreement and creation of the limited partnership, and accounting fees related to the organization of the partnership. Organizational costs may be expressed as a specific dollar amount, and are classified for tax purposes as capital expenditures amortizable over a period of 60 months.

Offering costs (syndication expenses) are the costs involved in marketing limited partnership interests to investors. They include securities registration costs, legal fees for securities and tax advice relating to disclosure of information required by securities law, accounting fees for representations included in the offering documents, sales commissions, and the costs of printing the offering documents and sales material. Offering costs are typically expressed as a percentage of total subscriptions in the limited partnership If they are paid by the partnership, they are classified for tax purposes as non-amortizable capital expenses. Less frequently, however, they might be paid by the general partner. A careful reading of the partnership agreement (offering documents) will determine how they are handled.

Management Fees (and Supervisory Fees) are paid to the general partner for the management of partnership activities. General and administrative expenses may be paid to the general partner for the portion of his overhead costs that are attributable to the partnership; they may be included under the category of management fees or listed separately. Compensation to the general partner may can generally take any of a number of forms:

- a guaranteed payment equal to a percentage of total partnership subscription,
- reimbursement of costs as incurred by the general partner,
- a monthly or annual fee established either by stage of activity (exploration or production, for example),
- a monthly fee per well or prospect, etc.

In most cases, compensation to the general partner is treated as an amortizable capital expenditure.

Interest costs. If the partnership will borrow funds to pay some of these up-front costs the partnership must pay interest on the borrowed capital. (The idea is maximize the amount of limited partners investment going into the program, and then repay the loans out of future production rev-

TABLE 13.1   TYPICAL SHARING ARRANGEMENTS IN OIL AND GAS DRILLING FUNDS

	Carried		Promoted		Reversionary		Functional Alllocation	
REVENUES:	**LP**	**GP**	**LP**	**GP**	**LP**	**GP**	**LP**	**GP**
Before Payout	85%	15%	70%	30%	100%	0%	60%	40%
After Payout	85%	15%	70%	30%	75%	25%	60%	40%

COSTS:

Working Interest Costs (commonly totalling 85-90% of total partnership subscriptions)

	LP	**GP**	**LP**	**GP**	**LP**	**GP**	**LP**	**GP**
Lease Acquisition	99%	1%	85%	15%	100%	0%	0%	100%
Intangible Drlg Costs	99%	1%	85%	15%	100%	0%	100%	0%
Equipment Costs	99%	1%	85%	15%	100%	0%	0%	100%

Limited Partnership Costs (up-front costs commonly total 10-15% of total subscriptions.

Management Fee - often a guaranteed payment of 5-10% of total partnership subscriptions up front, or an annual or monthy fee(as specified in partnership agreement)

Offering Costs - often a dollar amount or 1-3% of total partnership subscriptions (as specified in partnership agreement)

Sales Commissions - often 6-8% of total partnership subscriptions (as specified in partnership agreement)

Gen'l Admin Expense - for the first year, might range from 1-3% of total partnership agreements

Debt Service, etc. - amount and sharing arrangement in accordance with partnership agreement

Different costs may be treated differently by different partnerships.

enues.) Interest is a deductible expense.

Much information is provided in limited partnership offering documents. The treatment of partnership costs is disclosed in the limited partnership agreement. It also addresses the sharing of other costs authorized by the agreement, such as general and administrative expense and interest charges on partnership debt. Although the manner in which information is disclosed conforms to the requirements of securities law, it is usually buried in lots of legalese and accounting tax terminology, not easily read and understood by the casual reader.

Structures of Oil and Gas Limited Partnerships

In a limited partnership, costs and revenues may be disproportionately shared between the general and limited partners reflecting the structures of traditional deals between professionals in the oil industry. Oil and gas limited partnerships can be broadly categorized according to the way costs (for exploration and production), and production revenues are shared between the general and limited partners. Please see Table 13.3.

A.   **'Carried interest' program**

The limited partners pay almost all of the general partner's costs, and the general partner receives perhaps as much as 10-15% of revenues, without incurring exploration and development costs. (The limited partners 'carry' the general partner past those exploration and production steps in which most of the costs are incurred.)

B. 'Promoted interest' program

The general partner's share of revenues (per-haps as much as 30%) is more than his share of costs (15%). This is similar to type A above, but the general partner shares in paying the costs right from the start.

C. 'Reversionary interest' program

The limited partners pay all or nearly all the costs and receive all or nearly all the revenue until they have received cash distributions equal to their costs. Thereafter, the general partner becomes entitled to ('backs-in for') a significant share of revenues (often 25% or more).

D. 'Functional allocation' program (for drilling partnerships)

This structure became popular before the Tax Reform Act of 1986. It is mentioned for the sake of completeness, and because it might be able to play a role in the ongoing evolution of limited liability company deals. Marketing of this type of fund was directed to high-income-tax-bracket investors; the concept was to give all of the IDC tax deductions to the investor, so that he could use them to reduce his (sub-stantial) taxable income other sources. The general partner would pay all of the amortiz-able capital costs. The general partner would then share in production revenues right from the start (40% was common). The purpose of this structure was to maximize the tax ben-efits for the limited partner investor. Under the Tax Reform Act of 1986, limited partner-ships are considered to be 'passive' activities; tax benefits deemed to be from such 'passive' activities can be used only to reduce taxable income from other passive sources (not from other general 'portfolio' income). So this type of deal structure has little appeal under current tax rules.

Each limited partnership is different. The structure is disclosed in the limited partnership agreement. Financial evaluation of a individual partnership involves detailed analysis of the costs and projected revenues, and the manner they are shared between the limited partners and the general partner.

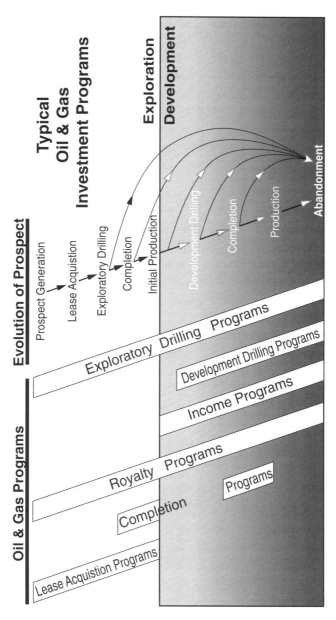

Table 13.4 Oil & Gas Programs

An Oilman's Lament

Running high and looking good!
Just like wildcats do . . . and should.
Fifty feet . . .   sometimes higher,
It fills the owner's soul with fire!

Although there's a stretch in every line,
She's running high and looking fine!
The driller often slips a string,
But that is just a trifling thing.

They cut a sand line, make a splice ...
But they only do this once or twice.
They use a steel line in a pinch,
But the driller is never off an inch!

Geologists now take the dope,
And with shining microscope,
They study shale and sand and lime.
(To think this out takes lots of time ...)
With their colossal brains they ponder,
While wide-eyed farmers stand and wonder.

Lease brokers nearby stand and wait . . .
Geologist: "She's running high and looking great!"
Royalties, overrides, and leases sell;
She's running high and looking swell!

The thrill of it all shakes the very ground.
Then ... they're gone ... before you can turn around.

Three months have passed . . . . another scene:
The rig is gone the grass is green.
A gaping slush pit, cracked and dried.
Shows where an optimist fought and died.

So this it is with wildcat wells.
They're spudded in, with clanging bells.
When plugged, the shouting all has died.
They wonder who the hell has lied.

Later . . . . another optimist is born.
Works late at night, up early morn'.
A wildcat deal . . . no cash in hand, but . . .
"She's running high and looking grand!"

- Author Unknown

This was a particluar favorite of Les Collins (1920-1995)

Chapter 14

ALTERNATIVES

Investor's Choice

There are basically three ways to invest in oil and gas reserves in the ground in the United States:

- buy stock (equity) in corporations that own oil and gas reserves,
- purchase properties which are already producing oil and gas, or
- explore (drill) for new reserves.

All are available to all categories of investors ... individual or corporate, domestic or foreign.

The financial position of an oil and gas producing company cannot really be evaluated solely through the analysis of its financial statements alone. Estimating the value of stock in corporations that own oil and gas reserves, requires some familiarity with the peculiarities of oil and gas accounting methods. Two different accounting methods are used. Although both systematically track revenues and costs, each one is based on different theoretical accounting considerations.[96]

"Full Cost" and "Successful Efforts"

Under full cost accounting a company's aggregate exploration and development efforts are treated as a single activity. All lease acquisition, exploration, and development costs are associated with the total commercial reserves discovered and developed by the company.

Under successful efforts accounting the company's activities are separated into specific defined projects. Costs associated with an unsuccessful exploratory project are expensed, while only the costs associated with a commercial discovery of reserves are capitalized and then depreciated over the producing life of the discovered reserves. In 1988, approximately half of the publicly-owned independent oil and gas companies in the U.S. used the full cost method and half used successful efforts.[97]

Unfortunately, even though the proved reserves are usually the company's primary asset, neither of these accounting methods provide relevant information about proved reserves. When a company makes a major discovery, there is no accounting system for reporting the results of the discovery or its financial significance. Under both systems, a company's success in exploration (revenue) will not be recognized until subsequent years. [98]

Under successful efforts, however, the expense is recognized in the current reporting period (the costs associated with a dry hole are expensed in the current accounting period). This can be significant to the extent that it influences the company's operations. It would not be uncommon for management's decision to drill an exploratory well to be delayed, for fear of the possibility of the well turning out to be unsuccessful, in which case, the expensing of the (often very significant) exploration expense could adversely impacting the financial statements for the current accounting period. [99]

The Securities Exchange Commission (SEC) has made some effort to correct this deficiency through an accounting method that would convey meaningful information about a company's reserves ('reserve recognition accounting'), but the changes have not been implemented. Instead, since December 1982, in addition to its financial statements, a producing company is required to disclose a variety of information called for in Statement 69 of the Financial Accounting Standards Board (FASB), "Disclosures About Oil and Gas Producing Activities". This disclosure is formally known as "standardized measure of discounted future net cash flows relating to proved oil and gas reserve quantities",[100] or more familiarly, 'standard measure'. The information included in the standard measure computations include proved oil and gas reserves owned at year end (with changes during the year), valuation of proved reserves, costs incurred in acquisition, exploration and development during the year, and historical results of oil and gas producing activities. A number of data-vendors market annual compilations of these data sets.

Buying Reserves on Wall Street

Probably the primary attraction of investing in oil and gas through purchasing publicly owned oil company stock is liquidity. Shares are traded daily on several U.S. stock exchanges, and prices are quoted in daily newspapers. across the country.

Purchasing the stock of a corporation that owns oil and gas reserves amounts to an investment not only in the corporation's assets, but also in the skills and philosophy of the corporation's management. Estimating the value of a company's oil and gas reserves can be a complex undertaking.

The process might seem a rather simple computation of calculating the volume of reserves, multiplying by a value per volume, and then providing some sort of discount factor to take into account the fact that some (most?) of the reserves will be produced at some time in the future.

In fact, it is quite a bit more involved. Consider that although the volume of reserves in place can be estimated, the actual volume is never known precisely, or even accurately.

Estimation of 'reserves in place' is more of an art than a science. It depends on information (chiefly porosity, water saturation, and oil column, oil-water contact, etc.) often based only on a single borehole that penetrated the reservoir (and is only about six inches in diameter). This information is then extrapolated across an area as large as hundreds of acres of reservoir.

Estimation of 'recoverable reserves' involves further qualifications about the permeability of the

> "Natural gas imports have doubled from the 1.5 TCF level of 1990 to about 3 TCF in 1996 or 13% of U.S. supply."
> Brent Allen, Vice President of Alpar Resources, Inc. in testimony before the Senate Committee on Energy and Natural Resources, May 7, 1997.

reservoir, the type of mechanism forcing oil or gas out of the reservoir (water drive, etc.), etc.

Even after gathering estimates of 'recoverable reserves' refined from 'reserves in place', there is the question of when will these reserves actually produced. There are two very important considerations here:

a) the 'time value of money' concept, and
b) the market price that can be obtained for oil (or gas) produced in the future.

Since 1978, the U.S. price for oil has fluctuated right along with international prices (adjusted for quality of the oil, geographical location and transportation requirements, etc.).

As documented by published reports, the world market price for oil has been influenced (if not outright manipulated) by conspiracies within the

U.S. government.[101] In other words, it is arguable that there is no 'free market' for oil. (For a thought-provoking read, try Peter Schwiezer's 1994 book, "Victory", published by Atlantic Monthly Press.)

Even assuming a free-market environment, oil and gas prices would naturally be subject to the vagaries of supply and demand, seasonal demand cycles, political instabilities, transportation and production bottlenecks and interruptions, and a host of other factors. Given a non-free-market situation, however, any prediction of future oil prices becomes highly speculative.

The key points to bear in mind, are these:

A) It is impossible for anyone to know the future price of oil, and

B) the volume of the reserves that will ultimately be recovered from a well, depends directly on oil prices that will received in the future (and which cannot be known in advance!).

In general practice, an operator will keep a well in production as long as it is profitable for him to do so. The scenario goes like this. As production from the well declines to the point that production revenues from the well approach the cost of keeping the well in production (lease operating expenses - LOE), the operator faces a tough decision. If product (oil or gas) prices remain low for a protracted period, and lease operating expenses approach net revenues from production, an operator might attempt to 'ride out the storm' by keeping the well in operation in hopes of higher oil prices around the corner. Another operator, with a different financial profile or projected price scenario might be much quicker to provisionally shut the well in; then seeing no improvement in prices, plug and abandon the well.

There is still a lot of oil in the reservoir, but the cost of producing it is more than revenues from production (under the combination of existing technology and oil prices). The well is plugged and abandoned. When this happens, the oil lease terminates, and unless there is a radically favorable change in either recovery/production technology, or oil prices, or both, it becomes unlikely that even in the distant future, anyone will drill a new well or attempt to re-enter the old (original one). The common sentiment is that those reserves have been lost 'forever'.

So ... getting back to the problems of computing a value for oil company stock, the value of the stock can depend very substantially on the value of oil and gas reserves owned by the company, and calculation of the value of these reserves is at best, a 'guess-timation'.

It should also be mentioned, that there may be a variety of tax considerations and market variations which can significantly affect the value of reserves owned by one company in one location, as compared to an equivalent amount of reserves that might be owned by a different company in a different location.

One last note about company stock. Although there is immediate liquidity via the stock markets, there are no significant tax advantages available to the purchaser of oil company shares. In fact there is the disadvantage of 'double taxation' of corporate profits as discussed. The corporation pays Federal income tax on its income. Then the shareholder must pay Federal income tax on any income he receives in the form of dividends, distributed to him out of the corporation's after-tax earnings.

Purchasing Producing Properties

Purchasing production is a means of owning proven oil and gas reserves in the ground. The investor enjoys a stream of income from his investment immediately.

A good buy at the right price is always a good investment. Several aspects of production purchase may be especially attractive under certain circumstances. In addition to reserves contained in the reservoir that are already being produced ('proved developed producing reserves'), a property might also contain reserves in shallower zones (behind pipe reserves), or in deeper, yet un-penetrated reservoirs. Application of newly developing technologies might increase the recoverable reserves from a property. The potential disadvantages of purchasing producing properties include uncertainties about the reserve estimates and future oil and gas markets and prices (discussed above).

Since 1990, the tax effect of purchasing production was enhanced to include not only cost depletion, but now, also percentage depletion, and the limitation on percentage depletion was increased from 50% of net income from a property to 100% of net income from the property. [102]

Drilling For New Reserves

Wallace Pratt, a legendary petroleum geologist, observed in 1939, "Where oil is found, in the last analysis, is in the minds of men. The undiscovered oil exists only as an idea in the mind of some oil finder."[103]

It follows that drilling is the *only* proven way to find new oil and gas reserves. Period.(!)

A few unique technologies have been developed that under special conditions, have demonstrated extraordinarily high predictive value. (The seismic 'bright spot' or 'hydrocarbon indicator' or 'HCI' is one example of what is often referred to as a 'direct detection' technique. It worked so well in the Gulf of Mexico and then in the Niger Delta, that a few major international companies greatly exceeded their normal success ratio for exploratory activity. When management attempted to force the application of this unique technology to basins and geologic environments for which it was not suitable, however, company results inevitably declined to less than normal success ratios for exploratory activity.)

Generally, successful exploration demands coordination of diverse skills working in harmony. Depending on the capability and the philosophy of the parties involved, drilling a well can be a wild and reckless gamble ... or it can be a conservative low-risk no-nonsense operation. Success depends first on the skills of the geologist and the quality of his prospect. Naturally the ability to lease the land at a good price, the technology to success-fully drill and complete the well, and the opportunity to market any oil or gas found are also critical, but as observed by Wallace Pratt and many others since, the prospect is the key to scientific exploration.

Drilling for new reserves may have special attraction for the investor who is a U.S. Federal income taxpayer with taxable income. A significant portion of the costs of drilling and completing a well (IDC) may be deducted (by the owner of a directly-held working interest), from gross income (from other sources) in the year they are incurred, whether or not the well is successful. Depreciation allowance and tax credits (if any) further reduce the taxpayer's taxable income and tax liability. In addition, if the well is successful, the investor will receive (a future) stream of income that is tax-free to the extent of his computed depletion allowance.

The main disadvantage of drilling for new reserves is the combination of high cost and risk. Little can be done about the drilling costs, which respond to market forces (please see Appendix B), but to some extent, risk can be managed.

An estimated 3,000 or so U.S. oil and gas companies are actively discovering new reserves (... down from an estimated 10,000 in 1983.)[104] Each has evolved its own strategy for managing the risk of the undertaking. Some may be better at finding oil and gas, but less effective at managing risk. Others find fewer reserves, but manage risk more effectively. And of course there are some companies that excel in both areas.

Exploration is to a large extent, a growing process. Individuals and organizations learn to profit from past experience and the information gained from previously drilled wells, while new advances in technology become available and are applied.

Several years ago, a survey of several hundred publicly owned oil and gas producing companies characterized about ten percent of them as enjoying a particularly healthy financial condition. One member of the select group was founded almost thirty years ago. In the first year of business, the company drilled 14 dry holes back-to-back, without a single producer. Still in operation under the same management today, it has expanded several fold since it's early days. Both the company and its management and employees developed through years of exploration experience.[105]

This growing process mentioned above, is a critical point that seems to be not well understood by investors or industry watchers. No one wants to drill a dry hole. However, many many times, it is the drilling of a dry hole that leads to a refinement of the understanding of the subsurface geology of the original prospect; this in turn provides sufficient cause to drill another well; and this new well becomes the discovery well of a new oil field.

Indeed, one of the many ploys attempted by some promoters has been to induce outside parties to participate in high-risk exploratory ventures. The concept is to get the other guy to help find out where the oil isn't, and then concentrate one's own resources drilling in areas where the likelihood of finding oil is much higher (based on the information gleaned from the nearby dry holes drilled by others). Other oil companies active in the same area, are well equipped to protect themselves from this sort of ploy. Outside investors too often are not.

The key to protecting yourself from this kind of scenario is to know the people you decide to invest with.

Mechanics of the Investment

Buying publicly traded oil company stock can be as simple as placing an order through a registered stock broker. In the case of purchasing producing properties or drilling for new reserves, a variety of procedures are available. They can be separated into two main scenarios:

- you manage your own investment, or
- you arrange for another party to manage your oil and gas investment under an investment or exploration contract or agreement.

The investor who manages his own oil and gas investments might acquire for his own account: mineral rights, leases, working interests, prospects, royalties, production payments, net profits interests, or other interests in oil and gas properties. In so doing, he accepts all the risks and bears all the liabilities and obligations associated with these interests. He may locate and acquire these interests himself, or as in the typical case of real estate transactions, he might use the services of a consultant. As long as the interests acquired are not "undivided fractional interests in oil, gas or mineral rights", it may be possible that securities laws generally may not apply.

When the investor arranges for another party to manage his oil and gas investments under an investment or exploration contract, however, the transaction will certainly be classified as a security, regulated by applicable securities law. In this case, in addition to the cost of the investment, such a transaction also bears the costs of compliance with securities regulations (at both state and Federal levels), plus whatever compensation is paid to the party managing the investment. During the past 10-15 years, limited partnerships have become the popular avenue by which many individual investors participate in (non-equity) oil and gas investments.

What about risk?

Risk is 'the possibility of loss or injury', and it attends virtually every human endeavor. There is some risk involved in crossing the street, but the typical adult pedestrian has learned to successfully manage the risk involved. He observes the flow of traffic, knows about how long it would take him to get to the other side, and waits for an adequate window of opportunity which will allow him to get to the other side.

In the early days of oil and gas exploration, drilling for oil was seen to be highly speculative ... and in most cases it was! The origins of petroleum were unknown. The science of petroleum geology was in its infancy. The science of geophysics had not been imagined. The systems and processes by which oil production could be controlled and enhanced were unknown. To the curious observer and the wildcat driller alike, the ability to find oil was mysterious. There was no paradigm by which anyone could understand why one well was successful, while another one a few hundred yards away was a dry hole.

Much has changed. More than one hundred years of exploring for oil and gas in the U.S., provides the experience and scientific theory on which modern exploration is based. Millions of wells have been drilled during the past century, resulting in the discovery of oil reserves in the U.S.; during 1994 these reserves were being produced at the rate of about 6.6 million barrels per day (down 35% from 8.9 million barrels per day ten years earlier in 1984).

The experienced explorationist understands and evaluates the risks involved in drilling a well, and manages them the same way the pedestrian manages to cross a busy thoroughfare. He makes estimates of the costs and the potential reserves (typically on a best-case, most-likely-case and worst-case basis). By analogy with other wells drilled under similar circumstances and in similar geologic conditions on the basis of similar data, he understands the risks involved, and compares them to the potential rewards.

A number of newsletters, periodicals, advisors and other experts provide rankings that categorize oil and gas companies as well as their investment programs, based on the accounting data oil and gas producing companies are required to disclose under securities laws. There are also a variety of statistics that are sometimes invoked in efforts to quantify the risk, or the probability of success, in drilling wells. Although these data may be useful within certain contexts, when they are taken to be 'scientific proof' or evidence of a particular tendency or trend, these types of statistics can be very misleading.

A good prospect is a good prospect, and the professional exploration geologist knows one when he sees one in a geologic environment or basin with which he is familiar.

If there is a key to successfully investing in oil and gas, it may as simple as ... *participating with good people ... who know what they are doing ...* and *who offer a fair deal.*

And then to *stay with them over the long term.*

Know the people you decide to invest with!

Sponsors of oil and gas investment programs typically incorporate wide-ranging discussion of 'risk' in their offering documents (as required under the SEC guidelines for full disclosure). Appendix E provides the discussion of "Risk Factors" from Five States Energy Company, kindly provided by Jim Gibbs, President of Five States.

To What Extent Can Oil & Gas Investments Risks Be Avoided, Controlled, or Minimized?

	"It is economically feasible to control or minimize negative effects by exercising due diligence, planning, and thoughtful preparation"	"Negative effects cannot be controlled or influenced beforehand"	"Negative effects can be hedged or insured against"
Stupid Mistakes	100%	0%	0%
Operator Fraud	95%	5%	0%
Drilling Cost Greater Than Projected	80%	20%	0%
Management / Administrative Errors	80%	20%	0%
Production Cost Greater Than Projected	70%	30%	0%
Changes in Tax Rates	50%	50%	0%
Blowout / Other Mechanical Disasters	30%	30%	40%
Product: Oil or Gas?	25%	75%	0%
Production Rate Lower Than Expected	10%	90%	0%
Reserves Less Than Expected	5%	95%	0%
"Fire, Flood, Other Natural Disasters"	5%	95%	0%
No Discovery (Dry Hole)	0%	100%	0%
Quality of Product	0%	100%	0%
Oil / Gas Price Fluctuations	0%	25%	75% *

* In his article "Portfolio Risk Management Protects Against Volatility" (The American Oil & Gas Reporter, December 1995, p 31-3.), David Chang makes an impressive case for the disciplines of 'risk management'.

In a presentation at IPAA meetings in November 1996, Jeffrey Mayer addressed "the risks of risk management".

So maybe the 75% figure is a bit high?

The idea for this chart comes from a chart created by Bob Wilson which appeared in the AIPN Newsletter, *Advisor*, March 1997. It is presented here courtesy of Bob Wilson, WRW Associates, Dallas.

Chapter 15

MEASURING PERFORMANCE

"A bird in the hand is worth two in the bush"

"Present Value" is the typical way alternative investment opportunities are evaluated. It amounts to little more than the idea that a dollar in your bank account today is worth more than the same dollar received at a year from now. If you question the concept, consider: would you be interested in putting your savings in a bank account that doesn't earn interest?

How much would you pay today, for a dollar to be received a year from today?

Suppose you have your today's dollars sitting in a bank account drawing 5% annual interest. Every $1.00 in your bank account today will become $1.05 a year from now.[106] An enlightening way of looking at the same thing is to say that every 95 cents in your bank account will become approximately

---

"...technology breakthroughs are bringing about a much higher ratio of successful exploration. Today maybe one in three wells; a dozen years ago it was on in 10."

George Gaspar, quoted in interview "Black Gold", BARRONS July 29, 1996

$1.00 a year from now. Without your having to do anything, your bank account money will grow at the rate of 5% per year.

Your stock broker might propose that you could get a better return if you were to take money out of your savings bank and buy stock, which he says could earn you 10% over the next year.

Suppose that your brother-in-law wants to induce you to withdraw some money from your bank account today, to invest in a project of his that (he says) will generate a dollar that you will receive a year from now. How much are you willing to pay to receive that dollar a year from now? You are already receiving 5% from your bank account (essentially 'risk-free'), so it will likely take some additional upside potential to induce you to withdraw funds to put in his scheme.

In the case of your stock broker's proposal, if you were willing to invest 90 cents today, for the opportunity to receive one dollar a year from today, you have effectively established a "discount rate" of 10%. In other words you have discounted the value of the dollar to be received next year, back to a value of 90 cents in today's money.

In the case of your bother-in-law's scheme, if it is a really well-thought-out one, with little risk involved, maybe a discount rate of 10% seems reasonable to you. If on the other hand, he is a really flaky dude, and everyone in the family has already lost money on his previous schemes, then you might be willing to invest much less today, in order to receive an expected dollar a year from now. Maybe you would only be willing to invest only 70 cents in today's money in order to receive an expected dollar a year from now. In this case you've established a discount rate of 30%.

Here is not the place to get any deeper into investment theory and analysis. The following discussions will simply address some of the measurements that are involved in oil and gas investment attractiveness (before investment is made) and performance (after the project has begun).

Physical Measurements - Reserve Estimates

The investment opportunities discussed in this book are interests in oil and gas reserves, acquired either by drilling, or purchasing. The value of the interests depends on the value of the reserves acquired. And this depends primarily on:

- the quantity of the reserves in the ground,
- the rates at which they can be produced, and
- the wellhead price that can be received for them when they are produced.

Reserve estimation takes into account each of these factors. (Of course the quality of the reserves, their geographic location, and many other factors are also significant.)

The appropriate reserve estimation method depends on the data available, the stage in the evolution of the production of the property, and the budget (time and money) available for making the estimation.

Analogy

Analogy is a method of reserve estimation that can be used when data are available from similar nearby fields (or wells) that are already producing from the same reservoir with the same drive mechanism, and the fields (wells) have been producing long enough to have provided a example of what can be expected.

This method is inexpensive. It can be done very quickly. And it can be done before drilling.[107] Resulting estimates can then be subjected to a range of probabilities to arrive at a risk-adjusted expected value.

Volumetric Calculations

In the volumetric method the 3-dimensional volume of the reservoir trap is estimated. Then reasonable geologic and engineering assumptions are made to arrive at the volume of oil or gas in the trap that is available to be recovered through production. Well data including wireline logs and core data allow an estimate of the (vertical) thickness of the pay zone and the porosity. Geological maps provide an estimate of the (horizontal) areal extent of the pay zone. Recovery factors and fluid properties are either estimated from production or assumed, by analogy, and can be significantly in error.

This method can be done early in the life of the property, and can be done quickly, but is prone to huge errors. (It requires assumptions about area and recovery factors, which when combined, can lead to estimates that may be in error by as much as 500% - 1,000% or more!)

Decline Curve Trend

Decline curve estimation requires production history data - monthly production volumes over a long period of time (at least a couple of years, and ideally, for a significant percentage of the life of the property). It doesn't involve any assumptions about size or reservoir, and is both fast and inexpensive to perform. It can be quite accurate under specific circumstances, and has the advantage of projecting future production over time. (This is probably the method most frequently used for a 'first-look' estimate of the value of a producing property.)

Material Balance

Material balance is based on the conservation of matter: "the volume produced = the volume originally in place, minus the volume remaining".

The objective here is to arrive at the estimated recoverable reserves (ERR).

Material balance estimates are based on production history, and require detailed data on both production history and bottom-hole pressure, as well as fluid properties and reservoir properties (relative permeability).

In the case of gas reservoirs, it is referred to as the "P over z" method, as a value derived from pressure and production measurements (P/z) is plotted on the y-axis, against 'cumulative gas produced' on the x-axis, to arrive at the amount of gas that will be ultimately be produced from the well, (where the curve crosses the x-axis).[108] It is particularly well suited to gas well estimation, except that it can lead to estimates too high in reservoirs under high pressure, and too low when the reservoir porosity/permeability are not homogeneous across the reservoir - for example, in tight gas sands which are naturally fractured.

This method requires measurements of bottom-hole pressure taken at intervals of about a year or more. These pressure measurements may not otherwise be recorded in the normal course of business.

They require that the well be shut-in long enough: 1) to lower a pressure-measuring device down into the well, and 2) to record the equilibrium bottom-hole pressure.[109] The time involved in this process depends somewhat on well depth, but commonly takes as much as 48 hours or more. Many very cost-conscious operators may simply choose to receive two days of production revenues (instead of the pressure data).

> Terror group warns of more attacks on oil sites
> "Two Saudi guards died while stopping threat ... at the Abqaiq plant in eastern Saudi Arabia..."
>
> *THE OKLAHOMAN, Sunday, Februany 26, 2006*

Reservoir Model Studies

Computer simulation of reservoirs (reservoir modeling) used to be available only to large companies and large reservoirs because of the time and cost in developing computer models of the physical environment of the reservoir. The models include reservoir-wide maps of many parameters of the reservoir, with the data coming from measurements in wells, production histories, well-log data, produced fluid properties, cores, etc. Once a model is created, it can be tweaked this way and that way until it can closely approximate the actual production history of the field. Then it can then be used to project future production and to guide the further development and exploitation of the reservoir.[110]

The accumulation of the data necessary for reservoir simulation remains a formidable task, but the computing power of currently available workstations and even some desktop computers put reservoir simulation models, of even rather small reservoirs, within the reach of modest sized companies.

Financial Measurements - Ratios

Excellent discussions of oil and gas company performance measures are presented in Daniel Johnston's 'Oil Company Financial Analysis in Non Technical Language' published by PennWell books, and in 'Oil & Gas Performance Measures' published by COPAS. Please refer to Recommended Resources.

Here follows a very brief mention of some of the commonly used methods of evaluating oil and gas investment opportunities.

Return on Investment (ROI)

ROI

You invest $1 in a drilling deal. Over the 5-year life of production, it is projected that you will receive $5 in production net revenues (after paying royalties and operating costs). You will receive these future revenues at the rate of $1 per year. This deal has an ROI of 4-to-1.

ROI =

(Net revenues - cost of the invest
ment)/ (cost of the investment).

DISCOUNTED ROI

All of the $5 dollars of revenue will be received in
the future. (From discussions above, we know that
dollars received in the future are worth less than
today's dollars.) If you discounted the $5 of future
net revenues at a discount rate of 10%, the present
value of the $5 of future net revenues would be in
the neighborhood of $4.50. This deal would be de-
scribed as having a Discounted ROI of approximately 3.5-to-1 (using a discount rate of 10%).

Discounted ROI =

(Present value of future net revenues - cost
of the investment)/(cost of the investment).

Payout

PAYOUT PERIOD

The Payout Period is the time it takes for you to
receive back in net revenues, the amount of your
investment. In the preceding example, there is a
big difference if:

A) you are to receive $5 in production net revenues over a productive well life of 5 years, or

B) you will receive those same $5 over a productive life of 25 years.

The ROI in both instances is the same 4-to-1; the payout period provides a measure for comparison on the basis of how quickly you will get your money back.

Discounted Payout

If you were to discount future net revenues that you will receive in the future, back to their present value, and then calculate when you will receive back in *today's* dollars the amount of your investment (which you made using *today's* dollars), you will arrive at the Discounted Payout Period. It will be longer than the (undiscounted) Payout Period.

Net Operating Income

Recall that throughout the payout period, you are receiving net revenues (gross revenues less royalties, severance tax, etc.) but you are still paying lease operating expenses.

Net Operating Income is the stream of net revenue reduced by ongoing operating costs. A useful measure might be the time it will take for you to receive back in net operating income, the amount of your initial investment; it will be longer than the discounted payout period.

Discounted Cash Flow Rate (DCFR)

This is a mathematical discipline by which future net cash flows are discounted back to the present at a specific discount rate. When the present value of the future net revenues discounted back to the present at a discount rate of 15% are equal to the investment, the investment is said to provide 'a 15% rate of return' (ROR) or 'a 15% internal rate of return' (IRR). It is a calculation not easily done with pencil and paper (but can easily be done on computers and even some hand-held calculators).

What is really involved here is solving mathematical equations to arrive at a single discount rate that will account for the present value of the cash flow to be received in the future. The equations for calculating the Internal Rate of Return automatically incorporate (mathematically assume or require) the reinvestment of revenues at the discount rate being used. This is a scenario which is often improbable.[111] Even more serious in the context of oil and gas investments, the equations used in IRR calculations are not able to handle negative cash flows (and negative cash flows are not an uncommon occurrence in the development of an oil well or oil field).

Reinvestment Rate of Return (RRR), also referred to as External Rate of Return (ERR), addresses the reinvestment problems of IRR, by artificially introducing a fixed period of time into the calculation.[112]

Growth Rate of Return (GRR) calculations address the problem of negative cash flows, by treating negative cash flows and positive cash flows separately and then combining the results to arrive at the GRR.[113] The end result of the GRR discipline might be described in terms along the lines of "...the projected after-tax adjusted rate of return on investment is 20%, using a safe 8% rate for negative cash flows and a reinvestment rate of 15% for positive cash flows". Many would prefer to think in simpler terms they can more easily relate to, like Return On Investment and Payout.

Expected Value (EV)
Expected Monetary Value (EMV)

The drilling of a well can result in any of a variety of diverse possible outcomes - ranging from a dry hole with zero return, to the discovery of a prolific new oil field.

'Expected Value' is the probability-weighted average of all possible outcomes. When it is quantified in terms of money, it become Expected Monetary Value - EMV.

Assume the drilling of a well on a turnkey basis will cost $100. According to the drilling history in this area, likely possible outcomes might be

    A) a successful well with a net present value of $1000,

    B) a successful well with net present value of $250, or

    C) a dry hole.

Based on the geologic understanding of the prospect and drilling experience in the area, the probability of these outcomes are quantified as below:

Outcome	Value	Prob- ability	Probability Weighted Value
successful well	NPV = $1000	10%	$100
successful well	NPV = $250	20%	$50
dry hole	NPV = $0	70%	$0
	EMV		$150

When looking at alternative prospects, the most attractive is the one with the highest EMV.

Profitability Index (PI)

'Risk-weighted profitability index' (PI) is computed as EMV / Expected Costs. It incorporates the expected cost of the investment as well as the expected value. Like EMV, Expected Cost is calculated as the probability-weighted average of all possible costs.[114] In the example, the drilling is on a turnkey basis, so the Expected Cost is the actual cost (no cost-overruns under a turnkey contract.)

In the previous example, the risk-weighted profitability index (PI):

$$PI = EMV/Expected\ Costs = \$150/\$100 = 1.5.$$

Rules of Thumb for market value indicators

Without discussion, here are some rules of thumb that are often invoked about oil and gas deals.

Drilling Deals

In the case of a drilling deal AFTER DRILLING, the actual ROI for *a single well* has been known to range as high as 10-to-1 or even 15-to-1 (but this is a rare occurrence and maybe accounts for only one or two wells, out of several hundred wells drilled). Such a high ROI is typically accompanied by a short payout period – occasionally 6 months or less.

During the past 10 years, on a *program basis* (a portfolio of drilling deals), an AFTER DRILLING

Ethanol Boom

"... the U.S. produced about 3.4 billion gallons of fuel ethanol in 2004."

by Garance Burke, AP Writer, The Oklahoman, Feb 23, 2006

ROI of 3-to-1 would probably be acceptable to most observers. An AFTER DRILLING actual payout period of 48 - 56 months would be also considered acceptable by many.

In the case of a drilling deal BEFORE DRILLING, a projected risked ROI of 3-to-1 or more, and an anticipated payout period of 36 months or less, would probably be required before many knowledgeable investors would want to participate in drilling the well.

There are a few exceptions, apparently, as in the case of horizontal wells drilled in the Austin Chalk, where the ROI may commonly be 2-to-1 or less.[115] Initial production in these wells is generally robust, and the payout period is short (or at least the time to, say, 80% of payout is short - maybe a year or less).

The productive life of the wells is also short.

Wall Street financial advisors and some operators seem very much enamored of these types of wells, but many old-timers in the industry seem to be maintaining a wait-and-see posture about this kind of drilling strategy; it involves a frantic pace of drilling, to find only rather modest reserves per well. Some liken this to riding a bicycle. (At the end of the day, you wind up with not very much in the way of reserves in the ground available for future production.) Quite a few companies prefer properties with a very long productive life, say, twenty years or more.

There seems to be a genuine difference in philosophy here, between some oil industry professionals on the one hand who tend to regard owning oil in the ground as a store of value, and most financial analysts on the other hand who tend to consider the value of reserves in the ground, strictly in terms of the cash flow generated when they are produced and sold. For a good discussion of the financial analyst view, see Bert Johnston and James Purser's article, "Financial capital value criteria examined".[116] (Please see Recommended Resources.)

Production Acquisition

In the case of purchasing producing properties, the question is always how much are the properties worth. Parameters that reflect the marketability of a property include the following:[117]

Dollars per barrel of reserves in the ground

> While the spot price of oil has ranged $15–$22, the value of reserves in the ground has been in the range of 1/3 of the spot market price.[118]

Anticipated ROI

> Commonly from 2-to-1 to 3-to-1.

Discounted ROI

> Fair market value might be in the range of 2/3 to 3/4 of the future net revenues discounted back to the present at a discount rate of the current cost of money (1-2% more than the prime interest rate).[119]

Anticipated Payout Period

> Commonly projected to range from 42 to 60 months.

Discounted Cash Flow Rate of Return (IRR)

> Commonly projected in the range of 18% - 30% (lower in 1999).

Discount Rates

> When calculating the present value of moneys to be received in the future, what is the rate at which the future revenues should be discounted? Common rules of thumb cited by Johnston:[120]
>
> - 1-2% above prime rate of interest,
> - after tax discount rate of 15% for mature production (lower in 1999),
> - before tax discount rate of 18-20%.

Chapter 16

NEW TECH

There's always a better way . . .

In the last five years, the oil and gas business has experienced a sea level change in technology. Many tightly run ships have not only weathered the changes, but also prospered; many more are working furiously to keep from being overwhelmed by successive waves of computerization, the changing nature of the work place, and inter-connectivity of computers, people, and disciplines.

It is probably fair to observe that there are so many new ways of doing things that no one can yet imagine the impact that all this will have on the oil and gas industry. Bear in mind, the petroleum industry continues to be one of the nation's largest and there are no economically viable substitutes for its products in the foreseeable future. For the companies that can adapt and master the technologies relevant to their day-to-day activities, there seems to be no limit to the upside potential for their business prospects.

> "Today the United States is one of only two oil-producing countries that are not increasing oil production. The other is Russia ..."
>
> *William F O'Keefe, Developing new US oil sources,*
> *THE JOURNAL OF COMMERCE, Monday, July 15, 1996*

Computerization / Information Technology

Certainly the proliferation of personal computers, desktop machines, and workstations accounts for many of the recent advances. For years, now, the drilling and production of wells has generated vastly greater quantities of data than could be analyzed and used ... or even stored and retrieved easily. Much of it is graphical (spatially-related in the form of maps and well logs); more is time-related in the form of well histories involving cost and production data spanning tens of years.

Computerization not only increases the ease of managing, analyzing, capturing these data. It is also provides the environment for huge changes in the way the work gets done. Work that formerly could only be done by a very few highly trained experts with access to very powerful computers, can now be performed by many more broadly-trained nonspecialists. The highly trained experts are still needed of course, but their special talents can be directed to many more projects, in the same way that attorney skills are leveraged through the use of paralegals.

It's like using the popular 'Quicken' software to keep track of your own personal banking and financial transactions. Even if you have little or no grounding in accounting, it allows you to perform many of the functions that used to require the services of a bookkeeper or accountant. Now you can do your own Federal and state income tax returns on income-tax preparation software, performing the functions you used to pay an outside accountant to do. This same phenomenon is transforming the educational and staffing requirements for all types of job functions throughout the oil industry.

Some of the new ways of doing business (categorized in alphabetical order):

Business

- expert systems (artificial intelligence) are being developed for applications in all aspects of E&P business.
- internet bulletin boards are used to provide location of specialized (mobile) rig equipment and supplies.

Drilling

- computerized drilling rigs! Although only a handful are in operation today, this looks like the way of the future (in areas where labor costs are high). One of the first sold is an electric rig, capable of drilling to 6,000 feet on land. Operated by a crew of only two, it has a small footprint, is easily transportable, and quiet. Stands of pipe are a single joint instead of the traditional three, making for a much smaller super-structure. Connections are made with mechanical 'robots'; the driller's console looks more like the cockpit of a 747, than the doghouse on a conventional rig. Still *very* expensive, but an exciting new development.
- planned perforating techniques oriented in the direction that the formation is most likely to fracture when hydraulic fracturing pressure is applied.
- hydraulic fracturing enhanced with combinations of both fiber and proppant to allow better flow back.
- materials technology such as:
  - reactive materials used to form plugs for blowout control.
  - polycrystalline diamond compact (PDC) bits whose design and material improve drilling performance and lower drilling cost.
  - synthetic drilling fluids (such as 'polyalphaolefin' mud) improve drilling rates and reduce cost by a) increasing

the stability of the borehole, especially in areas with shales consisting of water-reactive clay minerals smectite and illite - such as Gulf of Mexico, b) improved transportation of cuttings, c) reduction in torque and drag on the bit.

". . . a precipitous decline in production from Russia effectively concealed the upward trends developing in many areas of the world as technological advances were allowing increased profits despite a relatively flat trajectory for world oil prices."

OGJ SPECIAL-OIL & GAS JOURNAL Dec. 25, 1995
Non-OPEC Oil Supply Continues to Grow by David H. Knapp

Geologic Interpretation

- mapping and data base management programs on computer aided exploration (CAEX) workstations and desktop computers that integrate geologic, geophysical, geochemical, satellite imagery, land, drilling, production, and financial data.

Horizontal Drilling

- Measurement While Drilling (MWD) – allowing downhole measurements to be taken and transmitted back to the surface, without pulling the entire drill string out of the hole to run wireline logs and then running the drill string back into the hole (the round trip can take 24 - 36 hours or more in a deep well).

- 'bit steering from surface' capability is expanding as a result of borehole-orientation technology combined with measurement while drilling.
- multiple lateral borehole extensions from a single vertical well.
- tight radius turns (about radius of 60 feet or so).
- record extended reach more than 20,000 feet of lateral extension from a vertical borehole.
- air drilling and sophisticated under-balanced drilling techniques ; the latter , particularly, allow much faster rates of penetration, surface monitoring of downhole reservoir conditions including pressure changes and inflows while drilling, reduced skin damage to the borehole, longer life on bits, elimination of differential sticking problems, etc.
- coiled tubing drilling of new shallow wells, reentries through tubing, sidetracking, and depending of existing wells.
- cross-well tomography or connectivity mapping using the drilling bit as the energy source and acoustic receivers in nearby wells to record acoustic signals; allows a sort of seismic interpretation of the rock sections in between existing wells.

Logging

- magnetic resonance imaging log (MRIL) from the same technology used in medical

MRI scans; MRI log allows interpretations of reservoir porosity and water saturation that are independent of the clay and sand mineralogy of the reservoir (the log response of clays in some sand-shale sequences tends to obscure the presence of hydrocarbons).

- logging while tripping (LWT) - running a gamma ray and neutron log more quickly (50%) by sending a logging tool down inside the drill string to be pulled up to surface with the drill pipe, taking measurements through a log-transparent drill collar in the bottom hole assembly.
- borehole imaging technology (BIT) - using sound or electricity to image the borehole wall, as well as lowering a video camera down into the borehole for a first hand look at borehole wall conditions, etc.
- cased hole logging tools that can detect oil and gas pays behind pipe.
- pulsed echo logging tool (PET) that produces an ultrasonic bond log.
- widespread and inexpensive digitizing of old wireline logs that were recorded on paper and film.

Petroleum Engineering

- reservoir management, reservoir modeling, risk analysis, reserves estimation, production allocation, gas balancing, geological mapping, log analysis are now possible on desk top computers.
- advances in parallel computing allow vastly expanded reservoir flow simulation modeling.

3-D Seismic

- three dimensional visualization technology such as subsurface modeling, and then rotating and seeing through the geologic layers allow new ways to look at subsurface geology.
- refinements of seismic 'bright spot' interpretation through digital processing of seismic data amplitudes so that subtle relationships are quantified and can be statistically recognized, even though not visually apparent as 'bright spots' to the eye.
- improvement in exploration and production efficiency in some areas, in the range of 25%-30% - resulting in finding more oil with fewer wells, and at the same time, avoidance of drilling a significant number of dry holes.
- exploration projects that would not be economically justifiable with conventional 2-D seismic methods.
- seismic data capture and then transmission by radio frequency telemetry systems (radio signals) instead of the expensive process of laying cables out on the ground by hand.
- increased application of 3-D seismic data for sophisticated onshore stratigraphic inter-

Circa. 1987:

"A common seismic program these days consists of one or two short lines designed to locate a small fault and/or a drill site that is slightly higher than a promising show in a nearby well."

OIL & GAS JOURNAL May 11, 1987
Evaluating Subtle Subsurface Prospects by Joy J. Anneler

pretation (in the Williston Basin, for instance) whereas earlier applications were directed toward structural interpretation along the Gulf Coast and West Texas.

- expanded processing of seismic data and modeling, allowing more extensive studies of Amplitude Variation with Offset (AVO) and Maximum Coherency Seismic (MCS) velocities work - even by relatively small organizations with modest budgets.

- seismic inversion studies that allows a digital comparison of seismic response to reservoirs that are water-filled (dry holes) and those that are hydrocarbon-filled (oil or gas), especially useful in some Gulf of Mexico natural gas plays.

- 4-D (time-dependent) seismic mapping of producing reservoirs combined with reservoir engineering so that maps can monitor a reservoir over time as a field is producing.

- with 3-D seismic and subsurface modeling, up-front dollars can be risked on 3-D seismic, instead of on drilling (a cost-effective trade off, even though the drilling costs have tax benefits which, as of this writing, the 3-D seismic does not).

Surface / Airborne / Satellite Geochemical Exploration

- surface geochemical (iodine) prospecting - an indirect indicator of petroleum at depth; hydrocarbon seepage in contact with iodine compounds in presence of sunlight (ultraviolet light) form a particular type of chemical compound called iodine-organic ('iodorganics'); surface soil samples are taken and concentrations are mapped; in combination with 3D seismic maybe referred to as "3-D Geochemistry".

- surface and aerial gamma-ray spectroscopy measuring gamma radiation from potassium and uranium compounds; measurements are normalized and plotted; areas over hydrocarbons tend to show low potassium and high uranium normalized readings.

- ongoing work to improve the reliability of airborne 'hydrocarbon sniffer technology' (airborne detectors that can recognize even minute traces of natural gases in the air just above ground surface which are presumed to represent seepage from hydrocarbon accumulations at depth).

- use of directed microwave bursts to excite molecules in the air near ground level and record the resulting energy patterns - thereby identifying the presence of natural gas molecules (presumed to have leaked from underground reservoirs).

- synthetic aperture radar (SAR) imaging systems, which operate at wavelengths of 0.3 to 300 microns and can penetrate clouds, rain, fog (which visible light cannot); satellite uses its own source of energy (not dependent on sun light).

Teamwork

Each of these technical advances is significant in and of itself, but even the sum of these advances cannot explain the extraordinary transformation of the oil business over the recent 5-6 years. It seems that it is all happening so quickly and has such extensive ramifications that the basic unit of work effort has changed from individual man-hours to hours of teamwork. Various pieces of the puzzle have been available for some time, but now they are being brought together through new and evolving work-relationships. The reasons for an emphasis on 'teams' are several:

Cost-driven teams

- independent oil company partners with academic institutions to access massively parallel computing capability for use in exploration projects.
- operator and service company pool their abilities to make cost-effective completions on marginal wells that otherwise would have to be abandoned.

Complexity-driven teams

- The Department of Energy (DOE) disseminates new technologies to independent oil companies via the Petroleum Transfer Technology Council (PTTC).

- Gas Research Institute and gas companies develop dozens of Process Driven Alliances (PDA).

Information-driven teams

- the traditional vertical corporate hierarchy is flattened into a horizontal structure to accommodate vastly increased information and communication capabilities and at the same time cope with lower staffing levels.

Time-driven teams

- immediate solutions to real-time operational problems require participation of geologists, geophysicists, reservoir engineers, drilling engineers, well-design engineers working together to provide timely and more accurate response.

Chapter 17

WHAT ABOUT THE FUTURE?

The basic business of exploration and production companies is to find and produce reserves, making a profit in the process and do it in an ethical manner.[121]

Mineral owners on the other hand, want someone else to provide the technology and money that they lack, to produce more reserves from increased production in existing fields, and from new discoveries. This is as true of foreign governments as it is of farmers and ranchers in Oklahoma and the rest of the U.S.

Clearly the oil business in the U.S. and the oil business in the rest of the world are becoming more and more alike.

Controlling Cost

As everyone in the oil industry learned during the first quarter of 1986 (... and again in the fall of 2005!) participants in the domestic oil business have virtually no control over the price of the product. From 1986 through 2004, the only way to stay in business was to learn how to control costs.

Necessity really was the mother of invention. It might never have happened otherwise, but we now have new ways of doing business, new technologies, new concepts in partnering and sharing. The domestic U.S. oil business of 2006 is more cost efficient, more competitive, and arguably better staffed (staffed with better qualified personnel) than at any time in its history. There are companies with extraordinary success stories to tell in all aspects of the business. Some are the result of having been in the right place at the right time, with the right strategy. Others have struggled to overcome obstacles, survive, and prosper in the newly emerging business environment.

To most observers the message is clear. If you can compete successfully in the domestic U.S. exploration and production business in the 2000's, you can compete anywhere. The U.S. domestic industry has a unique service available for export. The overseas competition cannot begin to match domestic U.S. industry in terms of results, cost-efficiency, capability of staff, ethical business practice, or environmental preservation. Beginning in 1996, after decades of looking inward on itself and the political scene in Washington, the Independent Petroleum Association of America (IPAA), began to look outside the U.S. It created an International Committee, and then quickly organized delegations to Europe and South America.

> "The bottom line is the oil industry is going through a 'Great Depression' unmatched in severity by any other industry."
>
> *OIL & GAS JOURNAL July 13, 1992*

Asset Management - Mergers

Some call it rationalization of function, others call it strategic alliance-making, still others say it is old fashioned divestiture and merger activity. By what ever name, the trend of near future is clear. It will be a continuation of A) shedding non-profitable assets, B) contracting 'non-core' activities out to third parties who can do the job better and at lower cost, C) collaboration and sharing of operational responsibilities, and D) forming partnerships to reduce costs.

Spin-offs and liquidation of non-producing assets have been so popular that miscellaneous oil and gas interests have been traded at auctions, regularly for the past 15 years; the trend continues on a larger and larger scale, and today, online!

Looking back, Mobil agreed to sell its gas gathering, processing, and pipelines to Pan Energy Corporation, while Chevron merged its gas operations with NGC (Natural Gas Clearinghouse).

Amoco and Shell announced they would combine their producing properties in the Permian Basin of West Texas in a joint venture that would become the nation's third largest oil producer. The joint venture would allow for cost and operational efficiencies and synergistic creativity from the combined staffs.

And then the "mega mergers": ExxonMobil, BP-Amoco, Total-Fina-Elf, Chevron-Texaco, Conoco-Phillips, etc.

"Of 10 million barrels daily of new volume added since 1990. . . OPEC has accounted for less than 40%"
OPEC Hangs On, A Mere Shadow Of Its Former Self by Nicholas Moore.
THE JOURNAL OF COMMERCE, Monday, June 10,1996

These trends extend overseas to OPEC member countries, as well. There has been talk about a refining and marketing alliance between ARAMCO on the supply side and Shell on the marketing side. It would create the largest gasoline retailer in the U.S. accounting for about 15% of U.S. gasoline sales.[122]

Nigeria's finance minister announced plans to sell off its national petroleum assets including the government's share of half a dozen production-sharing joint ventures.[123] A Chinese-Government-controlled company makes an offer to acqurie Unocal, later withdrawn due to "political pressure".

Changes are also developing among big producing countries (Mexico, Russia, Kuwait, Venezuela, Iran) as well as among countries that hope to develop new production and become big producers.

Demand - Supply - Price

As many people have observed, the oil and gas business seems to run in cycles. It goes like this:

A   Demand for crude increases.

B   Since it takes time to find and produce new reserves, and to increase deliverability, there is a near-term 'shortage'.

C   Prices rise. (Conservation becomes the hot button.)

D   Oil companies and investors alike, rush to invest in E&P.

E   The results of E&P investment start to be felt 18 months or more later. Supplies increase.

F   Prices recede. Conservation is not on everyone's mind.

G   Eventually, demand increases. And the cycle starts all over again.

If this cyclic theory is valid, perhaps at the start of 1997, we were in phase F. (Many observers noted, that adjusted for inflation, oil was never as cheap as it was then, since 1973.) Now 2006 looks like phase D.

Recall, however that the U.S. government (indeed all industrialized governments) have a huge stake

Wind energy blows across state

"In the past three years … power from wind … has grown to nearly 475 megawatts enough to power 120,000 - 142,000 homes."

by Beverly Bryant, The Oklahoman Classified, March 5, 2006 in keeping crude oil prices low. As the U.S. currently imports 60% of consumption, there is a big difference in our balance of trade account between an oil price of $15 per barrel as compared to $60 per barrel.

In the next few years, we will witness a very complex interplay between contrasting developments in the areas of world supply and demand. Some analysts currently project oil prices of as much as $200 or more for brief periods; others (certainly a minority, these days!) expect oil prices as low as $10 or less. So what's new?

What's new is that the stakes are higher for both producers and consumers, alike.

Increasing demand? YES!

Long term fundamentals point to vastly greater demand as the newly developing economies increase their per capita consumption of crude oil. China's market for motorcycles was increasing at 50% per years in the 1990's.[124]

Assume that population growth in China and India continues on current trends. If per capita consumption in (just) China and India were to increase to the current level of per capita consumption in, say, Mexico, the increase in world demand could range to as much as an *additional* 60 million barrels a day. World production in 2006 is about 84 million barrels a day.[125]

U.S. automobile fuel efficiency trends have remained stagnant for years. Until the recent introduction of 'hybrid' cars, fuel efficient cars weren't selling. For the past ten years, the popular items have been sport utility vehicles (SUV) and mini-vans which are classed as light trucks; the increase in the market share of these vehicles (to more than 40% of all new vehicle sales)[127] means that U.S. drivers have been using as much as 10-20% more gasoline than would be consumed (for the same amount of travel) in more fuel efficient luxury sedans. Considering that in many cases these SUVs are driven more miles and at higher speeds, the impact on gasoline consumption may have been even greater.[128]

U.S. oil imports are projected to increase, unabated. The origin of imports is projected to continue to diversify away from Middle East producers toward North America (Canada), and Latin/ South America (Venezuela, Columbia, Brazil, Mexico, etc.). Middle East crude is more likely to be redirected to the booming economies of SE Asia.[129]

> "In 1993-1994 ... the American affiliate of the German conglomerate Metallgesellshaft AG suffered losses of $1.3 billion assoicated with its derivatives trading activities ..."
> *The Use of Derivatives in The Energy Industry   by Vinko Barcot, Ronna Edwards,Wesley Sherer, USAEE Dialogue, April 1998*

Increasing supply? PROBABLY!

Some observors project that long term fundamentals will greatly increase the availability of reserves to be produced. New technologies make it possible to find oil and gas more cost-effectively, and to get more oil out of the ground, and to do it more quickly. Some suggest that as these new technologies become more refined and integrated, it may eventually be possible to recover as much as 2/3 of the original oil in place[130] ... up from the 1/3 recovery, long considered the industry average. Although this will not happen overnight, on a world-wide basis, it would ultimatley translate into additional potential recovery of as much as all the oil as has ever produced.

About half of world production (Saudi Arabia, Iran, Iraq, Kuwait, Mexico, Venezuela, Russia, China, etc.) has not yet enjoyed any significant benefit from the progress and new technologies developed over the recent 10 years.[131]

Application of these and other new and still-to-be-developed technologies to OPEC oil fields where investment in production has been minimal for years, will certainly increase recoverable reserves.

Reduction of government subsidies for domestic consumption in producing countries (such as Saudi Arabia, Russia, Mexico) and consuming countries (such as the Ukraine; where a 4-day standoff developed in 2006 between the Ukraine and Russia, its main supplier of natural gas) should result in increased energy efficiencies in all aspects of energy consumption. Replacement of crude oil by natural gas and LNG consumption (which is rapidly developing in the U.S. and around the world) should also contribute to a net increase in crude oil supply.

Many see the primary obstacle to accelerated development of existing fields as being host-government-related. They cite reliance on inefficient national oil companies (think in terms of the US

Postal System, or FEMA during Hurricane Katrina), severely regressive tax schemes in exploration and producing contracts, internal subsidies, etc. As such obstacles are removed, increased exploration and development can be expected.

Venezuela took the early lead in opening more and more of its producing areas, first to 'reactivation' service contracts, and then to true exploration contracts. In 1996, two of the exploration contracts awarded each received high bids of more than $100,000,000. (The fact that the next highest bidders offered less than half of the wining bids, is clear evidence that even major international oil companies had vastly differing perspectives on the value of these properties.)

Emotional price projections

These factors and many more can be (and are being) studied and quantified on local, regional, and worldwide scale. The many critical assumptions required in these quantification efforts are so extensive, as to often make the value of the resulting projections to be questionable, at best.

The head of Arab Center for Oil Studies in Abu Dhabi believed that OPEC countries lost more than $200 billion in revenues as a result of their price war in the 1980's.[132] What are the chances that they would intentionally do the same thing again? (Or was it even intentional, the first time?)

Some observers predict on-going proliferation of religion-based war in the Middle East, continued brush fire wars in the important producing regions of the former Soviet Union (FSU), etc. There is no limit to the number and diversity of possible doomsday scenarios - and they make great headline news. All sorts of unforeseen catastrophic events are possible - and some, perhaps are even likely. Is anyone betting today in 2006, that peace will soom breakout in the Middle East?

The one thing that catastrophic events tend to do - even if only for the short term - is to stimulate an increase in oil prices. Take the Gulf War, for example.

In August 1990, before the invasion, a poll of 21 knowledgeable entities (oil companies, banks, analysts, and securities firms) predicted a 1995 price of $26.42 per barrel for WTI (the highest prediction was $31.65 per barrel and the lowest prediction was $22.00.)[133] Actual average spot price for WTI during 1995 was $18.43!

Here is not the place to embarrass the oil price prognosticators. Let's just agree that no one can know what the future trends of supply and demand will be, much less, how those trends will translate into crude oil prices. There may be a trend of increasing oil prices or a trend of decreasing prices, but in all probability there will continue to be wild volatility in spot price, responding to the emotions of the oil-and-gas futures marketplace.

Economics controls production

Increases in production depend more on the economics than on the availability of resources.

Throughout the 1990's, in an environment of a) low real prices, b) substantial gains in energy efficiency c) nearly 20 years of conservation, and d) unrestrained consumption, the price of oil was above cost, making it economically profitable (although barely! for many producers) to find more reserves.[134]

The measurable result has been increased crude oil reserves. Between 1970 and 2005, world crude oil production increased from 46 million BOPD to 84 million BOPD. During the same period, world crude oil reserves, increased from 555 billion BO to 1,188 billion BO. Think about this for a moment. It amounts to an annual increase in production of of 3.3 million BOPD, and an annual increase in world oil reserves of 25.3 billlion BO. And at no time during this time frame (until the end of 2005) did oil prices even begin to approach $50. per barrel. Now is the time for you to re-visit the graph on page 116, where you can see for yourself that higher oil prices translate into increased reserves (the area under the long tail of the decline curve).

Consider the economics of supply and demand on a world basis, and it becomes common-sense to expect crude oil reserves to grow very substantially in the future, as long as oil prices remain high and as more and more E&P investment is allocated to non-OPEC countries and non-producing countries.

The International Scene

Sooner or later, every oil field development project becomes an unavoidable tug-of-war between diminishing returns and increasing knowledge .[135]

U.S. independent oil companies have more experience with this scenario than any other group in the world. They have the knowledge base, and the know-how developed over the past 130 years, that no other country possesses. The E&P sectors of OPEC member countries have traditionally been run by state-owned national oil companies. (Again think in terms of the FEMA response to hurricane Katrina.) These governments are quickly coming around to recognize the value of efficient operations. Kuwait and Venezuela were early adapters. Mexico, the FSU countries, recently Libya (and other countries with state-owned oil companies) are following suit.

Many major oil companies still generate much of their net income from giant oil and gas fields discovered decades ago. Some suggest that they are so desperate to find big new reserves, that they seem to be spending more and more on exploring for new reserves, while producing less and less. By nearly all measures, it was generally believed that some major oil companies paid too much for deals in Venezuela's exploration round in 1996. But from the persepctive of $60 oil in 2006, maybe they got a real bargain! In essence, the major oil companies appear to be following three strategies simultaneously:

1) investment in technology,

2) substitution of natural gas for crude oil, and

3) the acquisition of reserves (by purchasing reserves or entire companies that own reserves) the time-tested strategy the majors have used for decades.[136]

In The U.S.

Environmental Concerns

API reported that in 1994, the oil and gas industry spent more than $10 billion on environmental protection. This amounts to more than twice as much as was spent on domestic exploration and production in the U.S. in the same period, and was equal to about 2/3 of the U.S. profits of the 300 oil and gas companies in the country.[137]

Oil and Gas diverge / Gas and Electric converge

At a time when the oil and natural gas businesses seem to be diverging from the wellhead, downstream, there is little question that the very downstream activities of the natural gas and electric businesses are converging.

But we just can't seem to change our ways ...

Everyone involved in and around this business wonders from time to time: "Will oil and gas prices will increase?" or "Prices will decline?".

Conflicting predictions have become commonplace among editors and business writers. Many are hypothesized by world renowned experts; the facts enlisted to support the different views are impressive; the reasoned arguments are persuasive. But which scenario is correct?

Almost certainly, both! Prices will increase and prices will decline. Whether we will witness a sea-level change in prices such we had in the 1970's and again in the first quarter of 1986 and again in the fall of 2005 remains to be seen .

What is not controversial is this prediction:

You and I will rely on petroleum-based energy for at least the next 50 years. Our well-being, life style, culture, indeed world civilization is based on energy and products derived from petroleum.

Just how pervasive is our dependence on oil?

To paraphrase the TV credit card commercial of a few years back:

You _can't_ leave home without it!

Think about it.

Appendix A

Oil Terms • Severance Tax • Basins

LIQUID PETROLEUM

Crude Oil .... is liquid petroleum
Sour Crude .... contains sulfur or sulfur compounds
Sweet Crude .... is free of sulfur
Tar .... is heavy, viscous crude oil

GASEOUS PETROLEUM

Natural Gas............................. is gaseous petroleum

In the reservoir:
Wet Gas .... contains liquid hydrocarbons
Associated Gas .... occurs naturally along with crude oil
Solution Gas .... is dissolved in crude oil
Gas Cap .... an accumulation of free gas, above an oil
accumulation already saturated with solution gas
Dry Gas .... is devoid of liquid hydrocarbons
Unassociated Gas ..... occurs naturally without crude oil present

At the Surface:
Casinghead Gas .... is gas separated from the
oil produced from an oil well
Dry Gas .... gas from which liquids have been separated
Sour Gas .... contains sulfur or sulfur compounds
Sweet Gas .... is free of sulfur

CONDENSATE
is a gas in the reservoir. Due to changes in pressure
and temperatures, it becomes a liquid at the surface. Also called 'natural gas condensate'.

Oil and condensate are measured in barrels (42 U.S. gallons), sometimes referred to as stock tank barrels (STB).

Gas is typically measured in thousands of cubic feet (MCF).

In the United States, amounts of oil, gas, and condensate are normally measured by volume, at surface temperature and pressure.

In certain overseas areas, oil, gas, and condensate are measured either by volume or by weight (according to the metric system):

1 Barrel	=	159 Liters
1 MCF	=	28.32 Cubic Meters
1 Metric Ton	=	6.297 Bbls (of water @ 60° F)

In the case of oil, conversion depends on the density (API gravity) of the oil:

25° API	=	6.96 barrels / metric ton
40° API	=	7.62 barrels / metric ton.

Severance/Production Taxes by State

STATE	OIL	GAS	Notes:
Alabama	8%	8%	4% for qualified wells *
Alaska	15%	10%	*
Arizona	3.125%	3.125%	
Arkansas	5%		Gas: $.003/mcfg; Stripper oil: 4% *
California	Determined annually. 1990 rate: $0.026136 per bo or per 10 mcfg.		
Colorado	2-5%	2-5%	*
Florida	8%	5%	*
Idaho			Oil: 5 mills per bo; gas: 5 mills per 50 mcfg. *
Illinois	None	None	
Indiana	1%	1%	
Kansas	8%	8%	*
Kentucky	4.5%	4.5%	
Louisiana	12.5%		Gas: $0.07 per mcfg *
Maryland			Allegany County gas - 7% *
Michigan	6.6%	5%	Stripper oil: 4% *
Mississippi	6%	6%	*
Missouri	None	None	
Montana	5%	2.65%	*
Nebraska	3%	3%	Stripper oil/gas: 2% *
Nevada			50 mills per bo or per 50 mcfg
New Hampshire			Oil: 1/10 of 1%*
New Mexico	3.75%	3.75%	*
New York	None	None	*Oil/gas is a factor in real property tax.
North Dakota	5%	5%	*
Ohio			Oil: $0.10 per bo gas: $0.025/mcfg.
Oklahoma	7.085%	7.085%	*
Oregon	6%	6%	First $3,000 sales each quarter, exempt.
Pennsylvania	None		None
South Dakota	4.5%	4.5%	*
Tennessee	3%	3%	
Texas	4.6%	7.5%	*
Utah	4%	4%	*
Virginia			Oil: 1/2 of 1%; Gas: ≤1%*
West Virginia	5%	5%	New gas wells after 7/87: 5%
Wyoming	6%	6%	*Stripper oil: 4%; Ad valorem tax ranges 6.5-7%

* Additional Taxes May Be Applicable:
Individual states may also assess 'Conservation Tax', 'Gas Processor's Tax', 'Oil Museum Tax', 'Oil & Brine Tax', 'Resource Tax', 'School Tax', 'Ad Valorem Tax', 'Property Tax', and other taxes in connection with oil and gas production. Rates in this table may not be precise and are subject to qualifications and change, in any case. Please verify with appropriate state agencies.

Source: "State Oil And Gas Severance/Production And Conservation Taxes", TC-10, American Petroleum Institute, 1220 L Street NW, Wash D.C. 20005, Interstate Oil Compact Commission Publications, and other sources.

Tax structures change all the time. Please be sure to check with appropriate state regulating agencies for the latest definitive information on tax rates (and possible tax incentives) in your state.

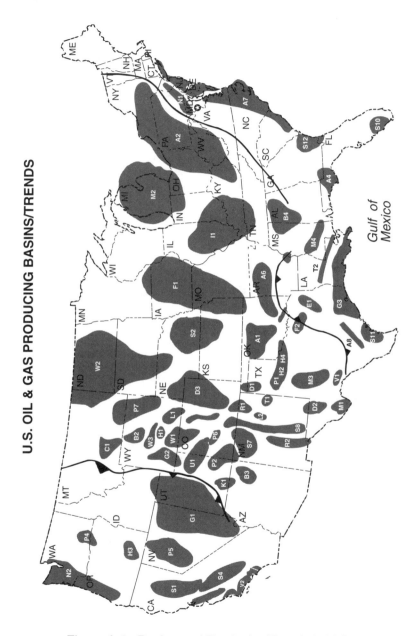

Figure A.1. Basins and Producing Trends in U.S.

Major basins and geologic trends that are significant in terms of U.S. oil and gas exploration and production. Many of these features are also known locally by other names.

Locations and orientations of these geologic features are interpretive and vary somewhat from geologist to geologist.

Code	Name	Location
A1	Anadarko Basin	Ok, Tx
A2	Appalachian Basin	Ky, NY, Oh, Pa, WV
A3	Appalachian Overthrust Belt	
A4	Apalachicola Basin	Fl
A5	Ardmore Basin	Ok, Tx
A6	Arkoma Basin	Ar, Ok
A7	Atlantic Coastal Basin	
A8	Austin Chalk Trend	Tx
B1	Bass Island Trend	NY
B2	Big Horn Basin	Wy
B3	Black Mesa Basin	Az
B4	Black Warrior Basin	Al, Ms
B5	Bull Mtn Basin	Mt
C1	Crazy Mtn Basin	Mt
D1	Dalhart Basin	Tx
D2	Delaware Basin	NM, Tx
D3	Denver-Juleburg (D-J) Bas.	Co, Ne, Wy
D4	Desha Basin	Al, Ar
E1	East Texas Basin	Tx
F1	Forest City Basin	Iw, Ks, Mo
F2	Fort Worth Basin	Tx
G1	Great Basin	Nv, Ut
G2	Green River Basin	Wy
G3	Gulf Coast Salt Dome Basin	La, Tx
H1	Hannah Basin	Wy
H2	Hardeman Basin	Tx
H3	Harney Basin	Or
H4	Hollis Basin	Tx
I1	Illinois Basin	Il, In
K1	Kaiparowitz Basin	Ut
L1	Laramie Basin	Wy
L2	Las Vegas	NM
L3	Los Angeles Basin	Ca
M1	Marfa Basin	Tx
M2	Michigan Basin	Mi
M3	Midland Basin	Tx
M4	Mississippi Salt Dome Basin	Ms
N1	Newark Basin	NJ, Pa
N2	Northwest Coastal Basin	Or, Wa
O1	Ouachita Overthrust Belt	Tx
P1	Palo Duro Basin	Tx
P2	Paradox Basin	Co, Ut
P3	Parks Basins (N-S)	Co
P4	Pasco Basin	Or, Wa
P5	Permo Triassic Basin	Nv
P6	Piceance Basin	Co
P7	Powder River Basin	Mt, Wy
R1	Raton Basin	Co
R2	Rio Grande Low	NM
R3	Rocky Mtn Overthrust Belt	
S1	Sacramento Basin	Ca
S2	Salina Basin	Ks, Ne
S3	Salinas Basin	Ca
S4	San Fernando	Ca
S5	San Gabriel	Ca
S6	San Joaquin Basin	Ca
S7	San Juan Basin	NM
S8	San Luis Basin	NM
S9	Santa Maria Basin	Ca
S10	South Florida Basin	Fl
S11	South Texas Salt Basin	Tx
S12	Southwest Georgia Embayment	Ga
T1	Tucumcari Basin	NM
T2	Tuscaloosa Trend	La
U1	Uinta Basin	Co, Ut
V1	Val Verde Basin	Tx
V2	Ventura Basin	Ca
W1	Washakie Basin	Co, Wy
W2	Williston Basin	Mt, ND, SD
W3	Wind River Basin	Mt, Wy

U.S. Crude Oil Imports 2004

12,100,000 Barrels Oil Per Day (BOPD)

= 60% of Total U.S. Consumption
(20,700,000 BOPD in 2004)

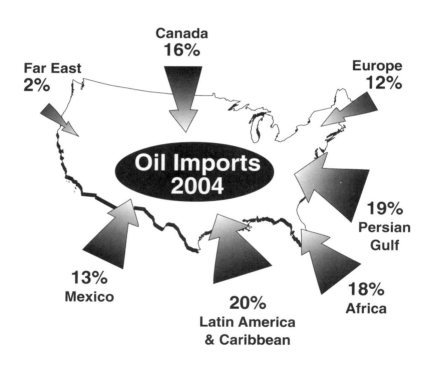

Canada
16%

Far East
2%

Europe
12%

Oil Imports 2004

19%
Persian Gulf

13%
Mexico

20%
Latin America & Caribbean

18%
Africa

Source: DOE-EIA 2006

Appendix B

Authorization for Expenditure
(AFE)

The following data were provided courtesy of
John Kerr, Woods Petroleum Corporation
Oklahoma City

Well A   is a 10,760 foot producing oil well drilled in the fourth quarter of 1981, under a day-work contract.

Well B   is a 10,709 foot producing oil well drilled in the third quarter of 1983, under a footage contract.

	A	**B**
Well:	Pine Tree Unit #5-31	Pine Tree Unit #28-66
Total Depth:	10,760 feet	10,709 feet
Spud Date:	11-27-81	08-15-83
Rig Released:	12-28-81	09-07-83
State:	Wyoming	Wyoming
Cost:	$1,533,940	$886,573 (-43%)

Both wells are in the same field in Wyoming. The following pages compare the actual costs incurred in the drilling of these two wells, and the percentage by which actual drilling and completion costs changed during a period of less than 2 years.

Both wells were operated by Woods Petroleum Corporation.

Authorization For Expenditure *(AFE - after drilling costs)* —Actual Costs Incurred—	Dec 1981 **Well A** 10,760 ft	Sep 1983 **Well B** 10,709 ft	% Change

Drilling INTANGIBLES (BCP)

Before Casing Point

103	Administrative overhead	9,978	5,718	-43%
107	Oper Extra Expense Ins		13,313	
121	Company labor	8,974	9,672	8%
130	Conductor pipe	5,757	2,240	
131	Location, roads & damages	26,651	31,294	17%
132	Footage		101,103	
133	Daywork	316,732	11,479	
134	Cement and Service	38,267	30,287	-21%
135	Dst and coring			
136	Logging	27,249	17,759	-35%
137	Geological supervision			
138	Engineering services – contract	200		
139	Mud materials	42,549	29,243	-31%
140	Fuel	64,002		
141	Water	20,455	29,224	43%
142	Drill bits	16,965		
143	Rental tools & equipment	38,594	3,036	-92%
144	Trucking	13,438	12,063	-10%
145	Plugging and abandonment			
146	Rig move-in & move-out	9,559		
150	Casing crews	26,382	8,053	-69%
158	Pipe inspection	5,011	4,640	-7%
172	Miscellaneous unforeseen	48,636	17,312	-64%
	DRILLING Intangibles BCP	719,399	326,436	-55%

Completion INTANGIBLES (ACP)	Well A	Well B	% Change
After Casing Point			
221 Company labor	5,596	5,561	-1%
231 Location, roads & damages	15,561	16,266	5%
234 Cement and Services	6,859		
235 Perforating	10,632	9,443	-11%
236 Logging	2,163		
244 Trucking	10,752	2,694	-75%
250 Casing crews			
253 Rental tools & equipment	27,174	8,630	-68%
260 Frac/formation treating	185,486	148,286	-20%
272 Miscellaneous	48,883	12,547	-74%
276 Completion unit	<u>84,592</u>	<u>18,364</u>	<u>-78%</u>
COMPLETION Intangibles ACP	397,698	221,791	-44%
TOTAL INTANGIBLES	**1,117,097**	**548,227**	**-51%**
EQUIPMENT (ACP, except as noted)			
400 Tubing	88,642	57,993	-35%
500 Casing ACP/BCP	129,452	105,398	-19%
600 Surface pipe BCP	30,743	40,389	31%
700 Wellhead equipment ACP/BCP	52,742	23,518	-55%
800 Rods	16,360	16,046	-2%
825 Bottom-hole pump	2,640	750	-72%
850 Centralizers, Scratchers, etc	261	209	-20%
875 Tank battery	15,150	4,693	-69%
900 Separators			
925 Heaters	11,301	6,802	-40%
950 Gas production unit			
960 Pumping Unit and engine	64,721	62,436	-4%
970 Compressor			
975 Dehydrator			
980 Flow lines	5,685	2,472	-57%
985 Miscellaneous	94		
990 Trucking	5,031	4,734	-6%
995 Installation	13,171	12,906	-2%
999 Salvage			
TOTAL EQUIPMENT	**436,843**	**338,346**	**-23%**
TOTAL WELL COST	**1,553,940**	**886,573**	**-43%**

MONEY IN THE GROUND

SUMMARY

Well A	BCP	ACP	Total	
Intangible Costs	719,399	397,698	1,117,097	(72%)
Equipment Costs	37,854	398,989	436,843	(28%)
Total	757,253	796,687	1,553,940	(100%)
	(49%)	(51%)	(100%)	

Well B	BCP	ACP	Total	
Intangible Costs	326,436	221,791	548,227	(62%)
Equipment Costs	50,079	288,267	338,346	(38%)
Total	376,515	510,058	886,573	(100%)
	(42%)	(58%)	(100%)	

Appendix C

Tax & Securities Law: Influence On Oil Deals

Investment vehicles for oil and gas exploration ventures include four main categories of entities:

JOINT VENTURES
PARTNERSHIPS
    General Partnerships
    Limited Partnerships
CORPORATIONS
    C-Corporations
    S-Corporations
LIMITED LIABILITY COMPANIES.

Each has it's own particular characteristics. Huge libraries are devoted to the many aspects of these types of business structures. The purpose of the following discussion (with apologies to professional oil and gas attorneys and accountants) is to provide a few of the many concepts which are important in well-structured oil & gas ventures, and how they may relate to these various business structures.

Some characteristics of traditional oil industry deals have substantially influenced the structure of oil and gas investment schemes. As a starting point, the concept of carried interests and back-in interests are described, followed by some discussion about various the business entities.

Carried Interests / Back-in Interests

In a typical oil industry (joint venture) deal (among 4 parties), the party who generates a prospect, leases the exploration rights, and drills the well (as operator of the joint venture), retains a carried working interest to the casing point. This carried party assigns 100% of the working interest to the three carrying parties (referred to here as investors–whether they are 'partners' from within the oil industry or 'investors' from outside the industry).

The effect of the carried interest is to transfer tax advantages available through the casing point (intangible drilling costs - IDC) to the investors, thereby inducing them to participate in the drilling of the well. (As owners of 75% of the working interest during the complete payout period, they are entitled to currently expense 75% of the IDC before the casing point; they must capitalize the remaining 25%.) From the casing point (or other specified point of carry) onward, the carried party's working interest converts from a carry (numerically a zero working interest) to a full working interest, the carrying parties' working interests are correspondingly reduced, and future costs and revenues will be shared according to each party's fractional working interest in the property.

The concept "full payout period" has been established by precedent set by IRS rulings: a party may deduct intangible drilling and development costs only to the extent of his fractional working interest during the full payout period.

When the prospect generator retains a back-in interest after payout, a similar result can be achieved. The investors pay all of the costs of drilling and completing the well, and producing it (during the complete payout period), to receive 100% of the associated tax advantages (which, as of this writing, include current deduction of intangible drilling costs - IDC, and depreciation of equipment costs). Furthermore, during the payout period, they also enjoy the tax benefit of the depletion allowance. The effect of the back-in interest after payout is to transfer all tax benefits to the investors through the drilling and completion of the well, and through the payout period of established production, thereby inducing them to participate in the deal.

Perhaps the deal structure most attractive to all parties involved, is when the prospect generator retains an overriding royalty, convertible to a full working interest at payout. The override gives the prospect generator a stream of income during the payout period. (Please see discussion of sale and sublease transactions in Glossary.) Meanwhile, the investors own 100% of the working interest during the complete payout period entitling them to currently expense (deduct) 100% of the intangible drilling and development costs.

Business Organizational Structures as Oil & Gas Investment Vehicles

Joint Ventures

The typical oil deal among oilmen is a joint venture. By acquiring a fractional working interest in an oil and gas property, each participant becomes a co-owner. Under the joint operating agreement, one of the co-owners (the operator) manages the project for the group. Each co-owner is billed his proportionate share of costs, by the operator (through a system of 'joint interest billing' - JIB). Each co-owner is potentially liable for all of the venturers. By carrying insurance to cover blowouts, loss of well control, pollution, public liability, workmen's compensation, and other possible eventualities, some of the liability risk is lowered. Still, knowledgeable participants in the oil industry tend to be very particular about whom they will joint venture with, and can be even more particular about which participant is selected to be the operator of the venture.

Under the Federal income tax system, a joint venture will normally be classified as a tax partnership ("partnership for tax purposes"). If improperly structured however, a joint venture (or even a legally registered partnership) could be classified as an "association taxable as a corporation" with the attendant problems of double taxation. Please see Appendix D.

If the joint venture qualifies as a "partnership for tax purposes", there is an election specifically designed for ventures in the mining industry (which include oil and gas ventures). It is called a "mining partnership". Using this special structure, an oil and gas joint venture may elect to be excluded from the application of subchapter K of the tax code (which deals with partnership taxation). To be eligible for this election, the purpose of joint venture must be "for the joint production, extraction, or use of property, but not for the purpose of selling services or property produced or extracted". The election requires that each *participant:*

- must be able to compute his own income separately from the other participants,
- must reserve the right to take his share of produced oil and gas in kind (rather than only in cash), and
- must not sell his oil and gas jointly with the other participants in the ventures, for a duration of more than one year.

In other words, the joint venture can be considered a partnership having a limited purpose. That limited purpose is the drilling of a well up through the point of establishing commercial production.

Once production is established, each participant is on his own, in terms of selling his production, etc., (even though the operational maintenance of the well continues to be managed and administered according to the joint operating agreement - JOA).

The significance of this type system is that if the venture were to be formally established as a legal partnership (instead of as a joint venture electing to be treated for tax purposes as a "mining partnership"), it could potentially be subject to a variety of Federal and state tax and tax and securities laws.

By not being a formal legal partnership, a joint venture is a convenient and relatively inexpensive vehicle, well suited for oil and gas deals among participants from within the oil industry. It may not be suitable for most investors who are not, themselves, professionals within the oil and gas industry, due to their unlimited liability for joint venture operations. From the point of view of a potential sponsor, a joint venture is often a more desirable vehicle for oil ventures than a partnership because 1) it avoids a number of accounting considerations which affect partnerships, 2) costs of formation can be much less, and 3) it may exist for a much shorter term.

Partnerships

Partnerships (notably limited partnerships) have become a common vehicle for oil and gas ventures. When structured as a 'tax partnership', the partnership, itself, is not a taxable entity. Tax advantages available to the partnership, as well as revenues and other accounting items, are passed through ('flow-thru') the partnership and are distributed to the investors (the individual partners).

In the case of a general partnership, there is one class of partners, and each is individually liable for the activities of the partnership.

In the case of a limited partnership, there are two classes of partners the general partner is individually liable for the activities of the partnership, but the limited partners are liable only to the extent of their cash contribution to the limited partnership (as specified in the limited partnership agreement). Costs, revenues, and various tax items can be allocated between general and limited partners according to the sharing arrangement of the partnership agreement.

Fractional working interests, royalties, and overriding royalties are relatively illiquid assets. They can be reserved, or assigned by deed. Depending on the amount and quality of attributable reserves, location, and other factors, they can be bought and sold (and the proceeds treated as taxable capital gain or deductible loss). An interest in proved developed producing reserves, might be accepted by a bank, as collateral for a loan.

Interests in a limited partnership (which itself owns fractional working interests, royalties, and overriding royalties) are less liquid. Three types of dispositions may *potentially* be available to the limited partner investor.

'**Right of Presentment**' is a standard clause in the limited partnership agreement, which allows the sale of a limited partners interest, to the general partner (without obligation on the part of the general partner to purchase such interest). Any such sale is burdened with partnership limitations and restrictions, which often make it an unattractive option. Furthermore, proceeds of such sale are subject to capital gains taxation plus recapture of tax items (deductions and tax credits). Other clauses in the partnership agreement may allow sale of a limited partnership interest to the partnership itself, or individually to other limited partners. Typically, sales of a limited partners interest in the partnership, to parties unrelated to the partnership, may theoretically be possible (but typically only with the consent of the general partner, or of the partnership itself).

A 'Roll-Up' of a limited partnership occurs when interests in one or more limited partnerships are exchanged for ('rolled into') shares of stock in a newly formed corporation. The (former) limited partners now become shareholders in the new corporation. The transaction may be structured as a nontaxable exchange. The shares of stock can subsequently be traded (with some restrictions) like the stock of any other corporation. The sale would be subject to capital gains, and recapture of tax items. A number of new publicly owned independent oil companies were created by this mechanism.

A 'Master Limited Partnership' (MLP) is a vehicle created when interests in limited partnerships sponsored by the same general partner over a number of years, are merged into one ('master') limited partnership. The general partner offers to make a (nontaxable) exchange of units of interest in the new master limited partnership, for units of interest in the various individual limited partnerships; units in the master limited partnership subsequently may become tradable on a public securities exchange.

If a general partner makes such an offer, and it is acceptable to a sufficient number of limited partners, and the master limited partnership is formed, and it is listed on a public securities exchange, then liquidity may become available to those limited partners who accepted the exchange offer. Proceeds from the sale of the tradable units are subject to capital gains taxation and recapture.

A number of master limited partnerships have been formed. Theoretically, both the limited partners and the general partner stood to gain from the transaction. The limited partner gained liquidity and diversification (from the oil and gas properties owned by his original limited partnership, to *all* oil and gas properties owned by *all* limited partnership interests included in the master limited partnership). More importantly, the MLP scenario avoided corporate tax on profits that would have been imposed if the limited partnership interests had been exchanged for shares of stock in a corporation (as in the Roll-Up scenario.) Also, a substantial part of the cash distributions may be able to be treated as a return of capital, and as such would not be taxed as ordinary income (please refer to 'cash distributions' in the Glossary).

In concept, the general partner stood to gain the advantage of simplified accounting and bookkeeping (for a single master limited partnership, instead of for multiple individual limited partnerships). Still, accounting for a master limited partnership whose units are traded daily on public securities markets is bound to be a formidable task.[139] (The evolution of the MLP, however fundamentally amounted to the liquidation of the properties held, with the final projection that if the MLP were to persist through the life of the properties held by the MLP, the general partner would eventually be the general partner of completely depleted properties, or in other words, of nothing.)

Eventually, the Tax Reform Act of 1986 changed the landscape for MLP's, as it did for limited partnerships. Both were deemed passive investments, and any losses generated in the (early) drilling stages of the activity could no longer offset ordinary income from other sources, they could only offset taxable income from other passive investments.

Limited Partnerships and Joint Ventures

In many instances, a limited partnership is, itself, a joint venturer in an oil and gas deal. This allows potentially greater flexibility in the sharing of costs and revenues (between the general partner, commonly a corporation with its attendant limited liability, and the limited partners in the partnership). As a co-owner in a property, the partnership is billed its share of the costs of exploring and developing a property, by the operator. The partnership, in turn, passes these costs (and attendant tax benefits) on to its general and limited partners according to the sharing arrangements of the limited partnership agreement. Each use the resulting tax deductions to reduce their own gross passive income. Revenues to the partnership (as a co-owner in the joint venture) are similarly passed through to the limited and general partner(s) according to the sharing arrangements of the limited partnership agreement.

The sharing arrangement in a limited partnership agreement will not be allowed by the IRS if the purpose is simply for avoidance of Federal income tax. The sharing arrangement must have "substantial economic effect", as measured by a partner's entitlement to the proceeds (in the event of) liquidation of the partnership. This is typically handled by establishing and maintaining capital accounts for each partner and basing any potential liquidations on them.

Corporations

There are two categories of corporations. The normal type of corporation with which most stock exchange investors are familiar (often referred to as a "C" corporation, to distinguish it from a more specialized form known as an "S" or sometimes 'Sub-Chapter S' corporation). The name derives from Sub Chapter S of the Federal Tax Code.

In terms of oil and gas investment, a "C" corporation poses a major disadvantage: it is a taxable entity. This sets up a situation of 'double taxation'. At the corporate level, the corporation is taxed on it's income, then at the shareholder level, the individual shareholder is taxed on any cash dividends which may be distributed to him out of the corporation's after-tax net profits. Perhaps more significant, because a "C" corporation is a taxable entity, any tax advantages resulting from oil and gas drilling (such as current deducibility of intangible drilling costs) are available to the corporation, but not to it's shareholders (investors). For these reasons, a corporation is generally considered to be not a very attractive (or common) vehicle for participating in oil and gas ventures.

An "S" corporation is something like a cross between a corporation and a limited partnership. An "S" corporation has the option of electing to be treated as a Subchapter S corporation during its first tax year. This allows tax obligations to flow through the "S" corporation to the individual shareholders. There are a number of limitations and restrictions however. For example, the number of shareholders is limited to not more than 35 and until recently, none of them could be a corporation. The dual benefits of limited liability and flow-through taxation would seem to make "S" corporations an attractive vehicle for oil and gas ventures. Drilling is very capital-intensive, however. The restriction on the number (and nature) of shareholders creates a practical obstacle to the formation of capital adequate to fund the drilling of even a single deep well (which might cost several million dollars) not to mention, an entire drilling program which might own interests in dozens of such wells. Accordingly, "S" corporations are not a particularly common vehicle for oil and gas ventures.

Limited Liability Companies

As discussed earlier in Chapter 12, the concept of the limited liability company has been gaining momentum in the past few years. The concept has been around for quite some time in certain Central and South American and Western European countries where it is known as a 'limitada'. The Panamanian form of limitada has sometimes been used to undertake high-risk ventures, because under Panamanian law, none of the members of the limitada has any liability for debts of the limitada, other than the extent of their capital contributions. This is in contrast to a U.S. limited partnership, for example, in which the general partner(s) have unlimited liability.[140] Limited liability company (LLC) structures include a number of features that may be attractive for structuring an oil and gas venture, in comparison to limited partnerships and other more traditional structures. Among them:

1 Limited Liability

In a 'C' or 'S' corporation, shareholders enjoy limited liability

In a limited partnership, the limited partners enjoy limited liability, but the general partner does not. (In a general partnership each partner is liable for debts and obligations of the partnership - in other words, no limitation on liability. Upon dissolution or death of a general partnership, the general partners are obliged to fund partnership debts.) If in a limited partnership, a limited partner were to actively participate in the management of the limited partnership, under some legal jurisdictions, the limited partnership might be regarded as a general partnership, in which case, the limitations on the limited partners liability would be lost.

In a limited liability company, *all* members enjoy limited liability - limited to the amount of their respective capital investments. Upon dissolution, members of the LLC are not obliged to fund any debts of the LLC. This limited liability is not affected by participation in the management of the venture.[141]

2 Flow through tax treatment

In a 'C' corporation, there is the problem of 'double taxation'.

- At the corporate level, the corporation pays tax on its income.
- At the shareholder level, the individual pays tax on any cash dividends he may have received as dividends (distributed to shareholders out of the corporation's after-tax net profits).

In the case of 'S' corporations there is no taxpaying obligation at the S-corporation level. Instead the taxpaying obligation 'flows through' to the S-corporation's individual shareholders.

In the case of limited partnerships there is no taxpaying obligation at the partnership level. Instead the taxpaying obligation 'flows through' to the limited partnerships individual partners (both general and limited).

In a limited liability company, there is no taxpaying obligation at the company level. Taxpaying obligations flow through to the individual members of the LLC.[142]

3   Flexibility in venture structure

A. Number and nature of participants

In a 'C' corporation there are no significant restrictions on the nature or number of individual shareholders.

In an 'S' corporation, the number of shareholders is limited to 35, and among other restrictions, none can be foreign corporations, or holding companies etc.

In a limited liability company, there are no restrictions on the nature or number of members (although it would seem likely there may develop some practical limits to the number of members that can be comfortably included - especially in view of an LLC's operating agreement calling for dissolution of the LLC upon the bankruptcy, death or withdrawal of a member ...)[143]

B. Allocation of profits, losses, tax benefits, etc.

In a 'C' corporation several classes of stock (such as common and preferred) can be issued, but there is no flexibility in the sharing or allocation of losses and tax benefits among classes of shareholders.

In an 'S' corporation, only one class of stock can be issued, and there is no flexibility in the sharing or allocation of losses and tax benefits among classes of shareholders.

In a general partnership or limited partnership the allocation of profits, losses, tax benefits is flexible, and partnership interests can be acquired through the contribution of services or property, in addition to cash.

In a limited liability company, LLC interests can be acquired through the contribution of cash, property, or services, and there are virtually no restrictions on the allocation of profits, losses or tax benefits. In fact, revenues interests can be assigned to other LLC members, or even to nonmembers.

Appendix D

Corporation / Partnership Classification for Federal Income Tax Purposes

The following discussion includes material provided courtesy of Stephen A. Zrenda, Jr., Partner, Bright Nichols Zrenda & Dunn.

A corporation is a business entity organized under state law. In the (Federal) Internal Revenue Code, one section requires that every "corporation" must pay income tax, but does not actually define what is a "corporation". Another section of the Code uses the term "corporation" to include "associations, joint-stock companies, and insurance companies". An organization which, under state charter is a corporation, is likely to be classified as a corporation for Federal income tax purposes. An organization which under state charter is *not* a corporation, however, *might* be classified as a corporation for Federal income tax purposes, and this has far reaching effect on the structuring of oil and gas (and many other) business ventures.

Under current law, oil and gas exploration provides several tax benefits including 1) the current deduction of intangible drilling and development costs (subject to passive/active income classification of the Tax Reform Act of 1986) and 2) the depletion allowance in the event of oil or gas production. In order to induce an investor to participate in oil and gas exploration, the investment vehicle must be properly structured so that these tax advantages will, indeed, be available to the investor.

For the purposes of Federal income tax treatment, most oil and gas ventures must fit one of three classifications, either:

- "a partnership for tax purposes",
- "an association taxable as a corporation", or
- a joint venture which has elected not to be treated as a partnership under the special subchapter K election available for mining (oil and gas) ventures.

Joint ventures are discussed in Appendix C.

A 'partnership for tax purposes' or 'tax partnership' essentially means that the partnership, itself will not be a taxpayer; instead, the taxpaying obligations 'flow through' the partnership to the individual partners, themselves.

A corporation or "an association taxable as a corporation" is the least desirable classification for two main reasons: (1) income is taxed twice, and (2) the corporation is a taxable entity in itself (meaning that any tax benefits accrue to the corporation itself, not to the shareholders).

Unless certain tests are met, it is possible that a partnership or limited partnership legally organized under applicable state securities law, could be classified, under Federal income tax law, as "an association taxable as a corporation." If this were to happen to a limited partnership designed to provide items (of partnership revenues, deductions, etc.) to (limited partner) investors, the economic results for the investors could be disastrous.

Corporations - Partnerships

Corporations and partnerships share certain similar characteristics in common: each has one or more associates, and its associates are joined in the common goal of realizing a profit. Four characteristics of a corporation are held to distinguish it from a partnership:

1. continuity of life
2. centralization of management
3. liability for organization debts limited to organization itself, and
4. free transferability of interest in the organization.

These characteristics can be regarded as "tests" of possessing corporate characteristics. On the basis of court rulings, the Internal Revenue Service (IRS) will classify an organization as "an association taxable as a corporation", if it possesses 2 or more of these characteristics. (In other words, to be classified as a "partnership for tax purposes", an organization must fail to meet 2 or more of these tests.)

If a limited partnership is structured so that (contrary to item 1 above) it will cease to exist upon the incapacity (death, retirement, insanity, etc.) of the general partner, and (contrary to item 4 above) transferability of limited partner interests is restricted, then the limited partnership would probably not be classified as "an association taxable as a corporation". This probability, however, may not provide adequate assurance to induce a prospective investor to become a limited partner.

Under the IRS system, it is possible to request an advance ruling from the IRS on the classification of a limited partnership as a "partnership for Federal income tax purposes", *before* the offering of limited partnership interests to prospective investors. The IRS has established guidelines which must be met before a favorable advance ruling will be issued. They relate primarily to (item 3 above) establishing the general partner's liability (a characteristic of a limited partnership that distinguishes it from a corporation):

1. Corporate general partner(s) of a limited partnership must have minimum aggregate net worth(s) equalling 10%-15% of the total contributions to all limited partnerships of which the corporation(s) are general partners.

2. If the partnership has a sole corporate general partner, the limited partner must not own (in the aggregate) more than 20% of the stock of the corporate general partner.

3. The general partner's interest in a limited partnership must equal at least 1% of each item of partnership income, gain, loss, deduction or credit.

4. The aggregate deductions claimed by the partners, as their distributive share of partnership losses for the first 2 years of operation, must not exceed the amount of equity invested in the partnership.

5. No creditor making a nonrecourse loan to the partnership will have or acquire, at any time as a result of such loan, any direct or indirect interest in the profits, capital or property of the partnership other than as a secured creditor.

Avoiding classification of an oil and gas investment vehicle as "an association taxable as a corporation" is critical in providing to an investor, the tax benefits for which he likely participated in the deal in the first place. Please see Appendix C for some discussion of oil and gas investment vehicles.

A look back in time ...

Protecting the Gulf (circa 1997)

The number of U.S. soldiers, sailors, airmen, and Marines stationed in the Persian Gulf fluctuates as ships, air wings and brigades rotate in and out, but the total usually is around 20,000. About 200 aircraft fly roughly 200 sorties daily over southern Iraq.

Land forces in Gulf region:

Saudi Arabia	Prince Sultan Air Base	5,500
	Riyadh HQ complex staff	500
Bahrain	U.S. Fifth fleet HQ staff	400
Kuwait	Operational exercises	2,000
Qatar	Air Expeditionary Force	1,000

Ships in Gulf:

Aircraft Carriers	1
Guided Missile Cruisers	1
Destroyers	4
Frigates	1
Attack Submarines	1
Counter-Mine Ships	2
Combat Support Ship	1
Supply Ships	4

Source: U.S. Central Command, Navy and Air Force public affairs, as reported by The Associated Press, THE DAILY OKLAHOMAN, Monday

jihad (2003)

Some Arab volunteers returning home, disillusioned by jihad in Iraq

by Tanalee Smith, Associated Press Writer

"We volunteered to defend Baghdad," said Firas Ali Abdullah, who returned to Syria with seven other Syrians and Lebanese on Wednesday. "Instead of giving us weapons to fight, they used us as human shields."

San Francisco Chronicle SFGate.com, Thursday, April 10, 2003

Appendix E

Risk Factors

The following discussion of risk factors has been excerpted verbatim from offering documents accompanying Five States Energy Company's Limited Partnership Drilling Programs, with permission of Jim Gibbs, Five States' president.

This discussion is included to provide a perspective on the many different risks which can potentially affect the success of drilling activities.

Reserve Estimates. Reserve estimates of producing oil and gas properties are based on available geological and engineering data, the extent, quality and reliability of which will vary.

Petroleum engineering is not an exact science. Estimates of economically recoverable oil and gas reserves and of the future net revenues therefrom are based upon a number of variable factors and assumptions, such as historical production of the properties, the assumed effects of regulation by governmental agencies, assumptions concerning future oil and gas prices and future operating costs, production curtailments, severance and excise taxes, development costs and workover and remedial costs, all of which may in fact vary considerably from actual results. All such estimates are to some degree speculative, and classifications of reserves are only attempts to define the degree of speculation involved. For these reasons, estimates of the economically recoverable reserves of oil and gas attributable to any particular group of properties, the classification of such reserves and estimates of the future net revenues expected therefrom, prepared by different engineers or by the same engineers at different times, may not occur as estimated.

Estimates with respect to proved developed non-producing reserves that have been acquired by the Partnerships are based upon volumetric calculations and upon analogy to similar types of production rather than upon actual production history. These methods are not as reliable as actual production history in estimating reserves. Later studies of the same reserves based upon production history will result in variations in the estimated reserves.

Non-Operation of Properties. The Partnerships have not acquired 100% of the Working Interest in most Properties, and do not serve as operator of most purchased Property. As a result, costs and revenues from the Properties are shared with third parties, and the Partnerships may have little, if any, control over the third parties that serve as operator of a particular Property.

Mechanical Problems/Workovers. Wells may develop mechanical problems which require substantial repair expenses. In some cases the estimated expenses of repairs or equipment replacement may exceed the value of remaining oil and gas reserves, and the well must be plugged and abandoned before all the reserves can be produced and sold. Unforeseen mechanical problems cause unbudgeted expenditures which reduce net income available for Partnerships distributions.

Participation with Other Operators. Additional financial risks are inherent in operations wherein the cost of operating wells may be shared by more than one party. For example, the Partnerships may be required to pay expenses attributable to one or more co-owners of Properties who do not pay their pro rata share. In certain situations, the Partnerships may suffer the loss of a portion or all of its interest or be forced to farmout its ownership interest due to limited capital available for some operational cost.

Environmental Matters. The activities of the Partnerships may expose them to potential liability for pollution and other damages under existing statutes and regulations related to environmental matters. Compliance with these statutes and regulations may cause delays and increased costs in producing oil and gas from properties and may prevent the Partnerships from acquiring or developing otherwise desirable properties. Certain regulations impose penalties for damage to the environment, whether or not caused by negligence. Governmental regulations relating to environmental matters could also require operators of Partnership Properties to cease operations in certain areas. If a Partnership is determined to be in violation of environmental statutes and regulations, a Partnership could lose any oil and gas production from the Property and be liable for costs in excess of the purchase price of the impacted Property or Properties.

Indemnification. Sellers of properties purchased have often required that the purchaser indemnify them against all future claims for damages, whatever the cause. Such purchased properties may at some future date result in litigation expense and an award against a Partnership for damages which might result in possible loss of the Property and/or revenue.

Risk of Leverage. Partnerships beginning with Five States 1993-C (Leverage), Ltd, and all partnerships thereafter have borrowed monies from commercial lenders to finance the purchase of the oil and gas reserves. The loans are secured by pledges of the Properties. This debt leverage increases the risk of loss. If a Partnership fails to timely pay any of its obligations, including its note payments with respect to the Properties, the Partnership may lose by way of foreclosure proceedings all rights to, and interests in, the Properties, and each Partner may lose his entire Capital Contribution.

Legal Fees for Operations. Operating agreements generally allow Working Interest owners to be compensated for damages arising from willful neglect or mismanagement by the operator of a Property. Payment of legal fees by an operator, arising from the defense against such charges by other Working Interest owners, regardless of the merits of such charges, are normally charged to the Working Interest owners not joining in the action against the operator.

Increasingly, federal, state and local agencies are citing operators for alleged infraction of laws and regulations relating to oil and gas property operations. Legal fees and related expenses may greatly exceed the normal operating expenses anticipated for a Property.

Plugging Obligations. Every producing well eventually reaches its "economic limit," the point at which taxes and the expenses of operations equal or exceed revenue obtained from the sale of oil and gas. State and federal statutes and regulations mandate that depleted wells be plugged and abandoned. The purchase of producing wells includes the obligation to ultimately plug the wells. In most instances the value of equipment salvaged from a plugged well is equal to or greater than the cost of plugging. In some instances, however, the cost of plugging can exceed, by a wide margin, the value of equipment salvaged. There can be no assurance that in the future equipment salvaged from plugged wells can be sold. If plugging requirements become more stringent, the costs of plugging wells in the future may be even greater than they are currently.

Risks of Interruption of Cash Distributions. The acquisition of producing oil and gas properties is intended to provide funds for cash distributions to Partners. The date any such distributions, or their subsequent timing or amount, cannot be accurately predicted. The Partnerships may acquire producing properties from which oil and gas is not currently being sold, or which is being sold either on a spot basis or under a short-term contract. Sales of natural gas in some markets are subject to a contractual condition which allows the purchaser to impose a moratorium on such purchases for lengthy periods of time. Gas purchasers may also fail to make contractually required purchases of gas due to current market conditions. The cessation of production from a substantial number of Partnerships properties or the necessity for reworking of wells could curtail or delay cash distributions for a significant period of time.

Overproduction. The partnerships may have acquired Working Interests in gas properties in which the acquired interest may be "overproduced." This can occur when one Working Interest owner has delivered for sale a disproportionately larger share of gas from the well than have other Working Interest owners. Operating agreements generally contain "gas balancing" clauses which specify the terms by which other Working Interest owners receive either production or compensation from the overproduced interest owner. In acquiring overproduced Working Interests of properties whose operating agreements do not contain "gas balancing" clauses, assumptions must be made as to when and how compensation to other Working Interest owners is accomplished. Such assumptions may prove to be incorrect.

Drilling Activities. It is anticipated that the production Partnerships will not engage in a significant amount of drilling activities. This policy serves to diminish the risks (and concomitantly the potential profits and tax benefits) traditionally associated with oil and gas exploration and development programs.

However, situations may occur when, in the judgment of the General Partner, participation in drilling may be prudent despite the risk of loss to protect or enhance Partnerships assets (as could result if an operator of an adjacent tract drills a well sufficiently near the Partnerships' Property to "drain" a portion of the Partnerships' assets away. A well drilled on the Partnerships' Property near the mutual boundary might then be warranted.) Likewise, geologic and engineering studies may suggest that the value of the Partnerships' Property could be enhanced by infill drilling, waterflooding, or completing in zones deeper or more shallow than zones currently being produced. In such situations the General Partner will determine Partnerships' participation in such wells after review of geological, economic and risk factors.

Leasehold Defects. The Partnerships obtained interests in Properties without general warranty of title. Although the General Partner had the title to currently producing acreage examined prior to acquisition in those cases in which the economic significance of the acreage justified the cost, there can be no assurance that losses will not result from title defects or from defects in the assignment of leasehold rights. In many instances, title opinions were not obtained if in the General Partner's discretion it would be uneconomical or impractical to do so. This increases the possible risk of loss and could result in total loss of Properties purchased. Furthermore, in certain instances the General Partner, may have determined to purchase properties even though certain technical title defects existed, if it believed it to be in the best interests of the Partnerships.

Dependence on the General Partner. The Partnerships are entirely dependent upon the oil and gas experience of James A. Gibbs, a Manager of the General Partner, for the direction of its business. Mr. Malouf and Mr. Budge, other Managers of the General Partner, do not have oil and gas production experience. The General Partner will seek to obtain the services of additional operating personnel as required. There can be no assurance that the General Partner will be able to successfully obtain the services of additional operating personnel if and when required.

Competition, Markets and Regulation. Competition for acquisition of economically desirable producing properties is intense and, accordingly, it may be difficult for the Partnerships to obtain suitable Properties. The Partnerships will be competing with a number of potential purchasers, many of which may have substantially greater financial resources than the Partnerships and substantially larger staff then the General Partner.

The purchase price for interests in oil and gas Properties acquired by the Partnerships will be based in part on anticipated future prices for crude oil and natural gas and on anticipated production rates. The price obtained for any oil and gas produced by the Partnerships will depend upon numerous factors which cannot be foreseen, including the extent of domestic production and foreign imports of oil and gas, market demand, domestic and foreign economic conditions in general and government regulations and tax laws. Thus, assumptions concerning the prices at which oil and gas will sell in the future may prove incorrect. Significant price declines may result in the Partnerships being unable to pay its monthly note payments. In such event the Properties could be lost by the lender taking them through foreclosure. From time to time there may be significant oversupplies of crude oil and gas inventories which stem from recessionary economic conditions, energy conservation efforts, world crude oil production levels and other factors. Oil and gas prices have fluctuated in recent years and there can be no assurance that oil and gas prices will not decline in the years ahead.

Since 1973, the worldwide price of crude oil, and to a lesser degree the price of natural gas, have been determined largely by the policies and actions of the Organization of Petroleum Exporting Countries ("OPEC"). Within OPEC, Saudi Arabia has been most influential in setting prices and production levels. More recently, however, Saudi Arabia has met with resistance in its efforts to maintain stable pricing for crude oil. At the present time, the relationship of Saudi Arabia and OPEC with the United States is regarded as neutral to friendly, but some OPEC countries which are not friendly to the United States are among those which have resisted OPEC's production quotas. Significant changes in attitude of OPEC or any of its members to the United States or to other nations or groups of nations could result in sudden changes in worldwide crude oil supplies and prices.

OPEC's ability to establish world oil prices appears to be waning. Known world crude oil reserves have increased to more than 1 trillion barrels from 600 billion barrels within the last decade, much of which is non-OPEC countries. Meanwhile, OPEC excess production capacity decreased to less than 2,000,000 barrels per day from a high of 18,000,000 barrels per day between 1983 and 1993.

Oil prices continue to fluctuate. Factors exist which could cause prices to decline in months and years ahead, such as production increases from Nigeria, Kuwait, Colombia, the North Sea, and other areas; resumption of petroleum exports from Iraq; and success in developing and exporting oil from China and the former Soviet Union countries.

The oil and gas business is subject to comprehensive governmental regulations which presently influence prices and other matters affecting Partnerships activities. The activities of the Partnerships are subject to statutes and regulations related to environmental matters which could delay or prevent the Partnerships from acquiring or producing from otherwise desirable properties or which could substantially increase drilling and operational costs. The price of natural gas is subject to competitive pressures which sometimes results in lower prices. Existing and future government regulation may further restrict the benefits to the Partnerships of any future oil and gas price increases.

Armed Conflict. Armed conflict and other instability in oil exporting areas in the Middle East can cause significant price changes in sales worldwide of crude oil. The lack of stability in crude oil prices could significantly impact the income the Partnerships will receive for its oil sales. If the price for crude oil drops significantly the Partnerships revenues will be materially affected.

Waterflood Project. The Partnerships may invest in properties which are involved in secondary recovery programs, such as a waterflood. A waterflood project is a program involving pressurized injection of water through selected wells into the oil-bearing reservoir. Many unanticipated delays may be encountered in a waterflood project. Also, mechanical problems and geologic conditions may result in a secondary recovery program recovering less oil and gas than anticipated.

294

Appendix F

New Technology

These lists come from "The Potential for Natural Gas in the United States", published by the National Petroleum Council, 1992, and are reprinted here with the permission of Marshall Nichols, Executive Director, National Petroleum Council.

Please note that this National Petroleum Council natural gas study is an extraordinary compilation of the best available information about the U.S. gas business and is strongly recommended to anyone with an interest in the subject.

Existing Technologies Which are Still Developing

2D-3D Seismic Processing (Signal Processing)
Acid Frac Stimulation
Advanced Drill String Measure System
Air Drilling
Amplitude Versus Offset (AVO) - Exploration
Analytical Instrumentation
Automation Technology
Barium Sulfate and NORM - Containing Scale Technology
Basin Analysis
Bright Spot - Exploration
CAT Scanning Cores
Clastic & Carbonate Geological Models
Co-production
Coalbed Methane Production Technology
Conversion of Drilling Mud to a Cementitious Material
Cross-Well Tomography - Exploration
Directional Drilling
Downhole Instrumentation
Environmental Compliance
Formation Damage Control
Fracture Models
Fracturing
Geochemical/Acidizing Model
Geopressured Gas Reserves Prediction
Geostatistic Fractal Geometry
Gravel Pack Tech
H_2S Cleanup
High Temperature Cementing Technology
Higher Prop Concentration
Horizontal Drilling
Horizontal Well Completions
Improved Downhole Sources for Cross-Well Seismology
Improved Fracture Fluids
Improved Logging Tools
Logging Tools
Low Density Cementing Technology
Magnetic Resonance Imaging (MRI)
Massive Hydraulic Fracturing

Material Tech - Sour Environment
Measurements-While-Drilling (MWD) Technology
Monitoring While Drilling (MWD) Tech
Natural Fracture Detection
Nuclear Magnetic Resonance (NMR)
Perforating Tech
Polycrystalline-Diamond-Compact (PDC) Drill Bits
Polymer Based Drilling Fluid
Produced Water Cleanup
Production Chemistry
Production Data Handling
Propellant Fracturing
Reservoir State Core Analysis
Satellite Remote Sensing
Seismic Data Acquisition and Interpretation
Slimhole Drilling
Source Rock Geochemistry
Source Rocks as a Reservoir Rock
Steerable Drill Bits
Sub-Sea Well Completions
Tectonics
Tension-Leg Well Platforms (TLWP)
Top Drive Drilling
Vertical Seismic Profile (VSP)
Well Cleanup
Workovers

Future Technologies - To Become Available

3 Phase Flow Meter
Advanced Geophysics
Bio-Technology for Waste Disposal
Bio-Technology Operating on Heavy Oil
Cheaper Directional Drilling
Coiled Tube/Casing Drilling
Compressor Technology: Low Cost in Field, Low Noise
Computer Based Training & Technology Access
Computerized Data Integration
Corrosion Resistant Alloys for Deep, Hot, Sour Gas Wells
Deep Gas Requirements

Disposable Drill Bits
Downhole Fluid Flow Measurements
Drill without Waste
Efficient Non-Damaging Frac Treatment
Enhanced Coalbed Methane Recovery
Enhanced Gas Recovery in Conventional Resources
Expert Systems/Artificial Intelligence
Fully 3-D Frac Model - Real Time Control
Gas Drag Reduction
Geographic Information Systems
High Temperature Acidizing Techniques & Computer Models
High Temperature, non-oil-based Drilling Fluid
Horizontal Well Stimulation
Hydraulic Fracture Diagnostics - Geometry Measurement
Improved 3-D Seismic
Improved Downhole Source for Tomography
Improved Downhole Sources for Cross-Well Seismology
Improved Flow Measurement & Transmission of Data
Improved Logging Tools
Improved Understanding of Reservoir Geometry
Log Interpretation in Horizontal Wells
Multi-Component Seismology
Multiphase Pumps - Pressure Boosting for Production Streams
NORM Disposal Techniques
Porosity Prediction Reliability
Real Gas Content Log for Shale and Coal
Real Permeability Logging
Safety - More Remote and Automatic Operations
Sensor Technology
Separation of Dissolved Organics from Produced Water
Separation Technology
Separation Technology for CO_2 & N_2
Short Radius Drilling Techniques
Three Phase Metering - Production Stream Monitoring
Through Casing Pressure Detector
Vertical Permeability Measurements
Water Shut-Off Using Polymers

Notes

1   A Price Waterhouse study, quoted in editorial, "Vital information", Oil & Gas Journal, June 15, 1992, p. 19.
2   The Journal Record, January 22, 1996, p.1.
3   Personal communication, Feb, 2006.
4   Personal communication, Mar, 2006.
5   "API details loss of jobs in U.S. petroleum industry", Oil & Gas Journal, June 19, 1995, p. 25.
6   The Oklahoman,Feb 24, 2006, p.2B.
7   Role of futures expands, Oil & Gas Journal, Jan 23, 1989, p. 11.
8   USAEE Dialogue, April, 1998, p. 14.
9   Schweizer, Peter, Victory, The Atlantic Monthly Press, 1994.
10 Schweizer, Peter, Victory, The Atlantic Monthly Press, 1994.
11 The Journal Record, Oct 1, 1996, p.9.
12 Riva, Joseph A., Oil distribution and production potential, Oil & Gas Journal, Jan 18, 1988, p. 58.
13 New pools boost reserves in China's Karamay oil field, Oil & Gas Journal, May 26,1986,p.34.
14 Moore, Leonard V., Significance, classification of asphaltic material in petroleum exploration, Oil & Gas Journal, Oct 8,1984, pp. 109-11.
15 Roadifer, R. E. How heavy oil occurs worldwide, Oil & Gas Journal, May 3, 1986, pp. 111-5.
16 Big heavy oil recovery seen in U.S., Oil & Gas Journal, July 4, 1988, pp. 16-7.
17 Barker, Colin and Takach, Nicholas E., Prediction of Natural Gas Composition in Ultradeep Sandstone Reservoir", AAPG Bulletin, V.76 No.12, December 1993, pp 1859-1873.
18 Chui, Glennda, Swedish Methane Find Could Mean Theories on Energy All Wrong", Knight-Rider Newspapers, The Daily Oklahoman, August 2, 1992.
19 Pratt, Wallace R., Toward a Philosophy of Oil Finding, AAPG Bulletin, Tulsa OK, Dec 1952, p. 2236.
20 AAPG Explorer, American Association of Petroleum Geologists, Tulsa, OK, 1993.
21 Bruce, Clemont H., Smectite Dehydration – Its Relation to Structural Development and Hydrocarbon Accumulation in Northern Gulf of Mexico Basin, Bulletin of American Association of Petroleum Geologists, June 1984, pp 673-83.
22 How Much Oil and Gas?, Exxon, Exxon Background Series, New York, NY, May 1982, p 7.
23 How Much Oil and Gas?, Exxon, Exxon Background Series, New York, NY, May 1982, p 7.
24 Levorsen, A.I., 1954, Geology of Petroleum, W.H. Freeman, San Francisco, CA, p 110.
25 Skinner, D.R., Introduction to Petroleum Production - Volume II, Gulf Publishing Company, Houston, TX, 1981, p. 11.
26 American Association of Petroleum Landmen, Fort Worth, TX, 1994.
27 Burk, Joan, 1983, Petroleum Lands and Leasing, PennWell Books, Tulsa, OK, pp 11,15.
28 Wheeler, R.R. and Whited, M., 1981, Oil From Prospect to Pipeline, Gulf Publishing, Houston, TX, p 69.
29 Van Zandt, F.K., 1976, Boundaries of the United States and the Several States, US Geological Survey Professional Paper 909, US Govt Printing Office, p. 83. Also: Wilford, J.N., 1981, The Mapmakers, Alfred A. Knopf, New York, NY.
30 Fundamentals of Petroleum, 1981, Petroleum Extension Service, University of Texas at Austin, Austin, TX, pp 55-7.
31 Burk, Joan, 1983, Petroleum Lands and Leasing, PennWell Books, Tulsa, OK, pp 12-3.
32 Burke, F.M. and Bowhay, R.W., 1984, 1984 Income Taxation of Natural Resources, Prentice Hall, Englewood Cliffs, NJ, para 2.02.
33 Industry Briefs, Oil & Gas Journal, Feb 6, 1995, p. 44.
34 Stafford, Jim, 1981, Look Before You Lease, ROAR Press, Ada, OK pp 3-6.
35 Burke, F.M. and Bowhay, R.W., 1984, 1984 Income Taxation of Natural Resources, Prentice Hall, Englewood Cliffs, NJ, para 14.04.

36 Burke, F.M. and Bowhay, R.W., 1984, 1984 Income Taxation of Natural Resources, Prentice Hall, Englewood Cliffs, NJ, para 14.04.

37 Society of Petroleum Engineers, 1994

38 Burke, F.M. and Bowhay, R.W., 1984, 1984 Income Taxation of Natural Resources, Prentice Hall, Englewood Cliffs, NJ, para 14.04.

39 Improved Oil Recovery, Exxon, Exxon Background Series, New York, NY, Dec 1982, p 2.

40 Burke, F.M. and Bowhay, R.W., 1984, 1984 Income Taxation of Natural Resources, Prentice Hall, Englewood Cliffs, NJ, para 14.14.

41 Constantino, Thomas, Strategies Let Producers 'Make' Price, The American Oil & Gas Reporter, February 1996, p. 104.

42 National Petroleum Council, 1992, The Potential For Natural Gas, Vol II Source and Supply, pp. 200-216.

43 Fundamentals of Petroleum, 1981, Petroleum Extension Service, University of Texas at Austin, Austin, TX, pp 167-70.

44 Fundamentals of Petroleum, 1981, Petroleum Extension Service, University of Texas at Austin, Austin, TX, pp 140-73.

45 Vandewater, Bob, Oil Field Theft Defies Proof, Official Say and Well Meters Gather Dust at Agency, The Daily Oklahoman, June 18, 1989, Section C, p. 1-2

46 Burke, F.M. and Bowhay, R.W., 1984, 1984 Income Taxation of Natural Resources, Prentice Hall, Englewood Cliffs, NJ, para 1.09.

47 Summary of State Statutes and Regulations for Oil and Gas Production, Interstate Oil Compact Commission, Oklahoma City, OK, June 1984.

48 National Petroleum Council, The Potential For Natural Gas in the United States, December 1992, Vol IV, p. 14.

49 Bittker, B.I., 1981, 1984, Federal Taxation of Income, Estates, and Gifts, Warren Gorham & Lamont, Boston, MA, para 1.1.6.

50 Paxton, John, 1985, The Statesman's Yearbook 1984-1985, St. Martin's Press, New York, NY, p 1389.

51 Bittker, B.I., 1981, 1984, Federal Taxation of Income, Estates, and Gifts, Warren Gorham & Lamont, Boston, MA, para 1.1.6.

52 The United States Government Manual 1984/85, Office of the Federal Register, General Services Administration, Washington D.C., p 445.

53 The United States Government Manual 1984/85, Office of the Federal Register, General Services Administration, Washington D.C., pp 68-9.

54 Pessin, Alan H. and Ross, Joseph H., Words of Wall Street, Dow Jones-Irwin, Homewood IL, 1983, p. 260.

55 Bittker, B.I., 1981, 1984, Federal Taxation of Income, Estates, and Gifts, Warren Gorham & Lamont, Boston, MA, para 4.3.2.

56 Bittker, B.I., 1981, 1984, Federal Taxation of Income, Estates, and Gifts, Warren Gorham & Lamont, Boston, MA, para 2.1.4.

57 Meyer, R. Running For Shelter, Ralph Nader Group Public Citizen, reported by UPI in Oklahoma City Journal Record, Feb 12, 1985.

58 Bittker, B.I., 1981, 1984, Federal Taxation of Income, Estates, and Gifts, Warren Gorham & Lamont, Boston, MA, para 105.1.7.

59 Thor Power Tool Co v. CIR, cited in Bittker, B.I., 1981, 1984, Federal Taxation of Income, Estates, and Gifts, Warren Gorham & Lamont, Boston, MA, para 105.1.7.

60 Bittker, B.I., 1981, 1984, Federal Taxation of Income, Estates, and Gifts, Warren Gorham & Lamont, Boston, MA, para 20.1.1.

61 Burke, F.M. and Bowhay, R.W., 1984, 1984 Income Taxation of Natural Resources, Prentice Hall, Englewood Cliffs, NJ, para 14.12.

62 Burke, F.M. and Bowhay, R.W., 1984, 1984 Income Taxation of Natural Resources, Prentice Hall, Englewood Cliffs, NJ, para 14.02.

63 Burke, F.M. and Bowhay, R.W., 1984, 1984 Income Taxation of Natural Resources, Prentice Hall, Englewood Cliffs, NJ, para 14.12.

64 Burke, F.M. and Bowhay, R.W., 1984, 1984 Income Taxation of Natural Resources, Prentice Hall, Englewood Cliffs, NJ, para 14.12.
65 Mosburg, L.G. Jr., 1983, Structuring Exploration Deals, Energy Textbooks International Inc., Oklahoma City, OK, p 45.
66 Mosburg, L.G. Jr., 1983, Structuring Exploration Deals, Energy Textbooks International Inc., Oklahoma City, OK, p 46.
67 Coopers & Lybrand, An Introduction to U.S. Oil and Gas Taxation, Solution for Small Business, May 1992, p. 28.
68 Coopers & Lybrand, An Introduction to U.S. Oil and Gas Taxation, Solution for Small Business, May 1992, p. 30.
69 Edmunds, Mark A. et al, Tax Advantages of Drilling vs Acquisition of Oil & Gas Properties, Deloitte & Touche, Nov 5, 1993.
70 Edmunds, Mrak A. et al, Tax Advantages of Drilling vs Acquisition of Oil & Gas Properties, Deloitte & Touche, Nov 5, 1993.
71 Coshow, Dick, KPMG Peat Marwick LLP, Oklahoma City, private communication Nov 2, 1995.
72 Mann, Billy, Federal Taxation of Oil and Gas Operations, Unpublished, Excerpted from Andersen, Arthur, Oil and Gas Federal Income Tax Manual, 1982, Arthur Andersen, Chicago, IL, p 5.
73 Mann, Billy, Federal Taxation of Oil and Gas Operations, Unpublished, Excerpted from Andersen, Arthur, Oil and Gas Federal Income Tax Manual, 1982, Arthur Andersen, Chicago, IL, p 5.
74 Burke, F.M. and Bowhay, R.W., 1984, 1984 Income Taxation of Natural Resources, Prentice Hall, Englewood Cliffs, NJ, para 2.08.
75 Burke, F.M. and Bowhay, R.W., 1984, 1984 Income Taxation of Natural Resources, Prentice Hall, Englewood Cliffs, NJ, para 2.07.
76 Burke, F.M. and Bowhay, R.W., 1984, 1984 Income Taxation of Natural Resources, Prentice Hall, Englewood Cliffs, NJ, para 2.06.
77 Garber, Robert, 1983, 1974, The Only Tax Book You'll Ever Need, Harmony Books, New York, NY, pp 122-4.
78 Bagget, M.R., et al, 1980, Anatomy of a Drilling Fund, Coopers & Lybrand, pp 11-12.
79 Bittker, B.I., 1981, 1984, Federal Taxation of Income, Estates, and Gifts, Warren Gorham & Lamont, Boston, MA, para 86.1.3.
80 Bittker, B.I., 1981, 1984, Federal Taxation of Income, Estates, and Gifts, Warren Gorham & Lamont, Boston, MA, para 86.1.3.
81 Bittker, B.I., 1981, 1984, Federal Taxation of Income, Estates, and Gifts, Warren Gorham & Lamont, Boston, MA, para 86.2.2.
82 Bittker, B.I., 1981, 1984, Federal Taxation of Income, Estates, and Gifts, Warren Gorham & Lamont, Boston, MA, para 86.4.
83 Bittker, B.I., 1981, 1984, Federal Taxation of Income, Estates, and Gifts, Warren Gorham & Lamont, Boston, MA, para 86.2.3.
84 Bittker, B.I., 1981, 1984, Federal Taxation of Income, Estates, and Gifts, Warren Gorham & Lamont, Boston, MA, para 86.2.3.
85 Johnston, Daniel, Oil Company Financial Analysis in Nontechnical Language, PennWell Publishing Company, Tulsa, OK 1992, p. 189.
86 Johnston, Daniel, Oil Company Financial Analysis in Nontechnical Language, PennWell Publishing Company, Tulsa, OK 1992, p. 190.
87 Johnston, Daniel, Oil Company Financial Analysis in Nontechnical Language, PennWell Publishing Company, Tulsa, OK 1992, p. 189.
88 Boras, Alan, Analysts Say Interest in Royalty Trusts in Canada Likely Will Remain Strong, The Oil Daily, September 4, 1996, p. 4.
89 Wolf-Smith, Risa Lynn, Independents Can Benefit from Limited Liability Company Structure, Oil & Gas Journal, Nov 14, 1994, pp. 67-71.
90 Wolf-Smith, Risa Lynn, Independents Can Benefit from Limited Liability Company Structure, Oil & Gas Journal, Nov 14, 1994, pp. 67-71.
91 Oklahoma Statutes Title 18, Corporations, Chapter 32.
92 Burke, Frank M. Jr., and Dole, Richard D., Business Aspects of Petroleum Exploration in Non-

Traditional Areas, BMC Inc., 1991, p. 129.

93 Galbraith, J.K., 1980, The Great Crash 1929, Andre Deutsh, London.

94 The U.S. Code, Title 15 – Commerce and Trade, Chapter 2A, Subchapter I, para 77 b (1) Definitions, 1983, U.S. Government Printing Office, Washington D.C., p 216.

95 Fox, Grayson Cecil, 1983, Oil and Gas Drilling Funds, State Bar of Texas, Austin, TX, para 5.02.

96 Andersen, Arthur, Oil and Gas Reserve Disclosures 1980-83, Summary Edition, p S-3.

97 Coopers & Lybrand Energy Newsletter, Issue # 23, May 290, 1992, p. 15.

98 Johnston, Daniel, Oil Company Financial Analysis in Nontechnical Language, PennWell Publishing, Tulsa, OK 1992, p. 51.

99 Johnston, Daniel, Oil Company Financial Analysis in Nontechnical Language, PennWell Publishing, Tulsa, OK 1992, p. 56.

100 Statement of Financial Accounting Standards, No. 69, Financial Accounting Standards Board, Stamford, CT, November 1982, p.9.

101 Schweizer, Peter, Victory, The Atlantic Monthly Press, 1994.

102 Edmunds, Mark A, and Dauber, Christopher S., Tax Advantages of Drilling vs. Acquisition of Oil and Gas Properties, Deloitte & Touche, Dallas, TX, November, 1993.

103 Pratt, Wallace, Toward a Philosophy of Finding Oil, AAPG Bulletin, December 1952, p 223.

104 IPAA estimates.

105 Cooper, R.G., A Matter of Life and Debt, The Oil and Gas Investor, Hart Publications, Denver, CO, Jan, 1985.

106 Lankford, Stephen M. et al, Estimating value of producing properties, Oil & Gas Journal, Mar 16, 1987, p.69-72.

107 Thompson, Robert S., and Wright, John D., Oil Property Evaluation, Thompson-Wright Associates, Golden, CO, 1984, p. 4-13.

108 Thompson, Robert S., and Wright, John D., Oil Property Evaluation, Thompson-Wright Associates, Golden, CO, 1984, p. 4-11.

109 Hudson, E.J. and Neuse, Stephen, H., Depletion stage determines most effective methods for reserve-estimate integrity, Oil & Gas Journal, Apr 1, 1985, p. 80-91

110 Thompson, Robert S., and Wright, John D., Oil Property Evaluation, Thompson-Wright Associates, Golden, CO, 1984, p. 4-12.

111 Roebuck, Field, Minimum-interest rate of return optimizes ROI, Oil & Gas Journal, Feb 20, 1984, p 69-70.

112 Starks, Laura, Economic performance of oil projects evaluated by modified IRR, Oil & Gas Journal, Apr 22, 1985, p 72.

113 Buck, Neal, Here are two better methods of pricing oil properties with obligations, Oil & Gas Journal, June 15, 1987, p 50-54.

114 Schuyler, John R., Modeling an exploration program: Insensitivity to prospect ranking criteria, Oil & Gas Journal, Dec 25, 1989, p. 140.

115 Union Pacific press Austin chalk development, Oil & Gas Journal, June 26, 1995, p 29.

116 Johnston, Bert E. and Purser, James, Financial capital value criteria examined, Oil & Gas Journal, Sept 9, 1985, p. 158-165.

117 Beninger, Wayne A. and Arndt, David C., Guidelines can improve property-acquisition results, Oil & Gas Journal, Oct 12, 1987, p. 39-44.

118 Johnston, Daniel, Rules help evaluate oil or gas acquisitions, Oil & Gas Journal, Feb 20, 1989, p. 49.

119 Beninger, Wayne A. and Arndt, David C., Guidelines can improve property-acquisition results, Oil & Gas Journal, Oct 12, 1987, p. 39-44.

120 Johnson, Daniel, Oil Company Financial Analysis in Non technical Language, PennWell Publishing Company, Tulsa, OK, 1992, p. 46.

121 Fletcher, Sam, Ideal Latin American Oil Projects Benefit Firms and Countries, Maxus Official Says, The Oil Daily, March 6, 1996.

122 Wheatley, Richard, Shell, Texaco, Aramco eye R&M alliance, Oil & Gas Journal, Oct. 14, 1996, p. 29.

123 Bearman, Jonathon and Katsouris, Christina, Nigerian Minister Reveals 5-Year Plan To Sell off

Country's Petroleum Assets, Oil Daily, October 3, 1996.

124 Teitelbaum, Richard, Your Last Big Play in Oil, Fortune, Oct 30, 1995.

125 Simmons, Matthew R., The Case For Crude Is Water Tight, The Oil & Gas Investor, Dec 1995, P. 39.

126 Simmons, Matthew R., The Case For Crude Is Water Tight, The Oil & Gas Investor, Dec 1995, P. 39.

127 Baltimore, Chris, Oil Will Hold its Own in U.S. Over Next 10 Years, New Study Says, The Oil Daily, June 11, 1996.

128 Hebert, H. Josef, Motorists' love of gas guzzlers drive environmentalists crazy, The Journal Record, Oct 1, 1996, P.9.

129 Baltimore, Chris, Oil Will Hold its Own in U.S. Over Next 10 Years, New Study Says, The Oil Daily, June 11, 1996.

130 Corzine, Robert, quoting Schlumberger CEO Euan Baird in New Technology 'to bring big rise in output', Financial Times, Apr 9, 1996.

131 Masseron, Jean, and Cueille, Jean Phillipe, Evolution and Outlook for Fossil Fuel Production Costs, International Association of Energy Economists Newsletter, Fall, 1996, p.24.

132 OPEC Loss Set At $200 Billion, The Daily Oklahoman, March 30, 1990, p. 19.

133 Analysts scurry to revise oil price forecasts amid Middle East crisis, Oil & Gas Journal, Aug 20, 1990, p. 28.

134 Masseron, Jean, and Cueille, Jean Phillipe, Evolution and Outlook for Fossil Fuel Production Costs, International Association of Energy Economists Newsletter, Fall, 1996, p. 6-7.

135 Adelman, Morris A., No OPEC, International Association of Energy Economists Newsletter, Winter, 1997, p. 14.

136 From major to minor, The Economist, May 18th, 1996, p. 64.

137 Smith, C.M. An Assessment of Oklahoma's Oil & Gas Industry, Shale Shaker, Nov-Dec 1996, p.55.

138 The 'lectric Game, Oil & Gas Investor, December, 1995, p. 49.

139 Ted Harms, Ted and Gutierrez, Johnny , "Oil and Gas Master Limited Partnerships", Journal of Petroleum Accounting, Fall-Winter 1985.

140 Burke, Frank M. Jr., and Dole, Richard D., Business Aspects of Petroleum Exploration in Non-Traditional Areas, BMC Inc., 1991, p. 128.

141 Wolf-Smith, Risa Lynn, Independents Can Benefit From Limited Liability Company Structure, Oil & Gas Journal, Nov. 14, 1994, p. 67-71.

142 Wolf-Smith, Risa Lynn, Independents Can Benefit From Limited Liability Company Structure, Oil & Gas Journal, Nov. 14, 1994, p. 67-71.

143 Wolf-Smith, Risa Lynn, Independents Can Benefit From Limited Liability Company Structure, Oil & Gas Journal, Nov. 14, 1994, p. 67-71.

144 The Potential For Natural Gas In The U.S., National Petroluem Council, December 1992, Volume II, p. J-16.

145 Energy Information Sheet, DOE/EIA0578(91), p 41.

146 Russell, C.W. Income Taxation of Natural Resources 1995, Research Institute of America, NY, p 1425.

147 Russell, C.W. Income Taxation of Natural Resources 1995, Research Institute of America, NY, p 1424-5.

148 Russell, C.W. Income Taxation of Natural Resources 1995, Research Institute of America, NY, p 1424.

149 Cline, Scott B. and Stanley, Brian J., Unitization formulas need scrutiny, Oil & Gas Journal, Sept 13, 1993, p. 73.

"I can't remember not being a John Wayne fan . . . He shot people in the heart, and drank whiskey, and treated his horse like a horse. In fact, he treated his women like he treated his horse. He seemed real because he reminded me of men in my neighborhood.

I never went to a John Wayne movie to find a philosophy to live by or to absorb a profound message. I went for the simple pleasure of spending a couple of hours seeing the bad guys lose."

Mike Royko
Syndicated Columnist of the Chicago Tribune
Chicago Sun-Times, June 13, 1979

Recommended Resources

References

Petroleum Industry - General

FUNDAMENTALS OF THE PETROLEUM INDUSTRY, R.O. Anderson, University of Oklahoma Press, Norman, OK 1984.

Petroleum Geology

GEOLOGY OF PETROLEUM, A.I. Levorsen, W.H. Freeman and Company, San Francisco, 1954.

POWER FROM THE EARTH: Deep Earth Gas - Energy For the Future, Thomas Gold, J.M. Dent & Sons, London, 1977. For readable review, see Reviews, AAPG Bulletin, 1991, pp 191-2.

Oilwell Drilling, Completion and Production

A PRIMER OF OILWELL DRILLING, Third Edition, Petroleum Extension Service, The University of Texas at Austin in cooperation with International Association of Drilling Contractors and Texas Education Agency, Austin Texas.

FUNDAMENTALS OF PETROLEUM, Second Edition, Petroleum Extension Service, The University of Texas at Austin, 1981.

HOW MUCH OIL?, Exxon Background Series, Public Affairs Department, Exon Corporation, New York, NY 1982.

INTRODUCTION TO OILWELL DRILLING AND SERVICING, Canadian Association of Oilwell Drilling Contractors, Gulf Publishing, Houston, 1982.

OIL FROM PROSPECT TO PIPELINE, Tobert E. Wheeler and Maurine Whited, Gulf Publishing, Houston, TX, 1982.

Land and Leasing

LOOK BEFORE YOU LEASE, Jim Stafford, ROAR Press, Ada Oklahoma, 1981.

THE MAPMAKERS, John Noble Wilford, Alfred A Knopf, New York, 1981.

PETROLEUM LANDS and LEASING, Joan Burk, PennWell Books, Tulsa, 1983.

STRUCTURING EXPLORATION DEALS, Lewis G. Mosburg, Energy Textbooks International, Inc, Oklahoma City, 1983.

LAND AND LEASING, Judith Eubank, Petroleum Extension Service Division of Continuing Education, The University of Texas, Austin, 1984.

WHO'S MINDING YOUR MINERALS, A. Meeh, Minding Your Minerals, Inc., Oklahoma City, 1996.

Federal Income Taxation - General

FEDERAL TAXATION OF INCOME, ESTATES AND GIFTS, Boris I. Bittker, Warren Gorham & Lamont, Inc., Boston, 1981, 1984.

Federal Income Taxation - Oil & Gas

AN INTRODUCTION T0 U.S. OIL AND GAS TAXATION, Coopers & Lybrand, LLP., 1995

INCOME TAXATION OF NATURAL RESOURCES 1995, C.W. Russell, Research Institute of America, New York, 1995. (Published annually by partners of KPMG PEAT MARWICK.)

OIL AND GAS FEDERAL INCOME TAX MANUAL, Eleventh Edition - 1982, J. R. Jones Editor, Arthur Anderson & Co., Chicago, 1982.

Arthur Young's OIL & GAS FEDERAL INCOME TAXATION 1984 Edition, James L. Houghton Editor, Commercial Clearinghouse Inc., Chicago, IL, 1982.

Oil and Gas Economics

DETERMINATION OF OIL AND GAS RESERVES, Petroleum Society Monograph No. 1, The Petroleum Society of the Canadian Institute of Mining, Metallurgy, and Petroleum, , Calgary, 1994.

ECONOMIC EVALUATION AND INVESTMENT DECISION METHODS, Stermole, Franklin J. and Stermole, John M., Investment Evaluations Corporation, Golden, CO 1993.

MARGINAL OIL AND GAS: FUEL FOR ECONOMIC GROWTH 1996 EDITION, Interstate Oil and Gas Compact Commission, Oklahoma City, 1996.

OIL & GAS PERFORMANCE MEASURES, Second Edition 1993-1994, COPAS Research Project, Council of Petroleum Accounting Societies (COPAS), Dennison, TX.

OIL & GAS RESERVE DISCLOSURES, Arthur Andersen & Co. (published annually).

OIL COMPANY FINANCIALS IN NONTECHNICAL LANGUAGE, Daniel Johnston, PennWell Publishing Company, Tulsa, 1992.

OIL PROPERTY EVALUATION, Thompson, Robert S. and Wright, John D., Wright-Thompson Associates, Golden, CO, 1984.

PETROLEUM ECONOMICS, Jean Masserson, Institut Francais du Petrole Publications, Paris, 1990.

PROVED RESERVE DEFINITIONS, Society of Petroleum Engineers, Dallas.

Oil and Gas Tax Shelters / Limited Partnerships

ACCOUNTING STANDARDS AND REGULATIONS FOR OIL AND GAS PRODUCERS, C.H. Moore & J.C. Grier, Prentice-Hall Inc., Englewood Cliffs, New Jersey, 1983.

ANATOMY OF A DRILLING FUND, M.R. Baggett, R.D. Dole, and J.E. Short, Coopers Lybrand, 1980.

INVESTING IN OIL AND GAS FUNDS, Coopers & Lybrand, 1982. (Also published a Second Edition, 1983)

OIL & GAS LIMITED PARTNERSHIPS, K.M. Burke & F.L. Durand, Professional Development Institute, Denton, Texas, 1984.

OIL & GAS PROGRAMS, Touche Ross & Co., 1983.

TAX SHELTERS - THE BASICS, Arthur Anderson & Co., Harper & Row, Cambridge, 1983.

THE ONLY TAX BOOK YOU'LL EVER NEED, Robert Garber, Harmony Books, New York, NY, 1983, 1984.

Oil and Gas – Securities Law

MANUAL OF OIL & GAS TERMS, H.R. Williams & C.J. Meyers, Mathew Bender, 1981.

OIL AND GAS DRILLING FUNDS A Primer For Attorneys and Investors, Grayson Cecil Fox, State Bar of Texas Professional Development Program, Austin, 1983.

STARTING A LIMITED LIABILITY COMPANY, Martin M. Shenkman, et al, John Wiley & Sons, Inc., New York, 1996

HOW TO LIMIT TAX CONSEQUENCES OF SELLING AN OIL, GAS PROPERTY, R.D. Robason, D.R. Jackson, THE OIL & GAS JOURNAL, Oct 31, 1983, p 114-6.

QUALITY OF RESERVE ESTIMATE, E.J. Hudson & S. H. Neuse, THE OIL & GAS JOURNAL: Part 1 - Cutting through the mysteries of reserve estimates, Mar 25, 1985 p 103-106; Part 2 - Depletion stage determines most effective methods for reserve-estimate integrity, Apr 1, 1985, p 80-91.

QUESTIONS FACING THE INDEPENDENT OPERATOR, A.M. Schiemenz, THE OIL & GAS JOURNAL, Mar 4, 1985, pp 146-9.

REGULATION D - Rules Governing the Limited Offer and Sale of   Securities Under the Securities Act of 1933, Securities Exchange Commission; Also: Interpretive Release on Regulation D, 17 CFR Part 231 [Release No. 33-6455], publication of SEC staff interpretations.

STATISTICAL ANALYSIS SHOWS CRUDE-OIL RECOVERY, Todd M. Doscher, THE OIL & GAS JOURNAL, Oct 29, 1984, p 61-63.

The Natural Gas Business

THE POTENTIAL FOR NATURAL GAS IN THE UNITED STATES, The National Petroleum Council, Washington D.C., December 1992.

THE GAS SELLER'S COMPANION, William D. Watson, PennWell Publishing Company, Tulsa, 1992.

Associations

AAPG	American Association of Petroleum Geologists
	Box 979
	Tulsa, Ok 74101
	(918) 584-2555 *800/364-2274* < www.aapg.org>
AAPL	American Association of Petroleum Landmen
	4100 Fossil Creek Blvd.
	Ft. Worth, TX 76137
	(817) 847-7700 *< www.landman.org >*
AGA	American Gas Association
	1515 Wilson Blvd
	Arlington, VA 22209
	(202) 824-7000 *< www.aga.org >*
API	American Petroleum Institute
	1220 L Street N.W.
	Washington, DC 20005
	(202) 682-8000 *< www.api.org >*
COPAS	Council of Petroleum Accounting Societies
	PO Box 1190
	Denison, TX 75201-1190
	(903) 463-5473 *877/992-6727* <*www.copas.org*>
EIA-DOE	Energy Information Agency of U.S. Dept. of Energy
	Forrestal Building, Room 1F-048
	1000 Independence Avenue
	Washington, DC 20585
	(202) 586-8800 < *www.eia.doe.gov* >
GTI	Gas Technology Institute
	1700 South Mount Pleasant Road
	Des Plaines, IL 60018-1804
	(847) 768-0500 *< www.gti.org >*
International Society of the Energy Advocates	
	1437 South Boulder Ave. Suite 160
	Tulsa, OK 74119-3622
	(918) 599-7767 *< www.energyadvocates.org >*

IOGCC	Interstate Oil & Gas Compact Commission 900 NE 23rd Street Oklahoma City, OK 73105 (405) 525-3556 < *www.iogcc.state.ok.us* >
IPAA	Independent Petroleum Association of America 1201 15th Street N.W. Suite 300 Washington, DC 20036 (202) 857-4722 < *www.ipaa.org* >
NARO	National Association of Royalty Owners P.O. Box 21888 Oklahoma City, OK 73156 (405) 286-9400 / (800)-558-0557 < *www.naro-us.org* >
NPC	National Petroleum Council 1625 K Street NW Washington, DC 20006 (202) 393-6100 < *www.npc.org* >
OIPA	Oklahoma Indpendent Petroleum Association 3555 NW 58th Street Suite 400 Oklahoma City, OK 73112 (405) 942-2334 < *www.oipa.com* >
PDI	Professional Development Institute (oil & gas acctg) 2207 I-35 E. North Denton, TX 76205 (940) 565-2483 < *www.pdi.org* >
SEG	Society of Exploration Geophysicists P.O. Box 702740 Tulsa, OK 74170 (918) 497-5500 < *www.seg.org* >
SPE	Society of Petroleum Engineers 222 Palisades Creek Dr. Richardson, TX 75080 (972) 952-9393 *800/456-6863* < *www.spe.org* >
TIPRO	Texas Independent Producers and Royalty Owners Association 515 Congress Avenue Austin, TX 78701 (512) 477-4452 < *www.tipro.org* >

Periodicals

American Oil & Gas Reporter   1326 E. 79 Street So
(316) 788-6271   Wichita, KS 67233
< www.aogr.com >

Daily Oil News Service   The Independent Oil & Gas Service
(316) 263-8281 *800/536-8281*   226 North Emporia
< www.iogsi.com >   Wichita, KS 67201

Energy Daily, The   1325 G Street N.W.
(202) 638-4260   Washington, D. C. 20005
< www.kingpublishing.com >

Michigan Oil & Gas News   206 W. Michigan, Ste. 200
(989) 772-5181   P.O. Box 250
Mount Pleasant, MI 48804-0250
< www.michiganoilandgasassociation.org >

Oil Daily, The   1401 New York Ave. NW #500
(202) 662-0700   Washington, D.C. 20005
< www.energyintel.com >

Oil & Gas Journal   PennWell Publishing Co.
(713) 621-9720   1700 West Loop So # 1000
< www.ogj.pennnet.net>   Houston, TX 77251

Petroleum Accounting and Financial Management Journal
Institute of Petroleum Accounting Univ of North Texas
(940) 565-3170   P.O. Box 305460
< www.unt.edu/ipa >   Denton, TX 76203-5460

Petroleum Economist   Petroleum Press Bureau Ltd.
011 44 207 831 5588   P.O. Box 105
Baird House 15/17 St. Cross Street, EC1N 8UN London
< www.petroleum-economist.com >   England

Petroleum Finance Weekly   3 East 37th Street, 5th Flr
(212) 941-5500   New York, NY 10016-2807
< www.energyintel.com >

Platt's Oilgram News   333 Clay Street # 3800
(713) 658-9261   Houston, TX 77002
< www.platts.com>

Rocky Mountain Oil Journal 303/778-8661 < www.rmoj.com >	906 South Pearl Denver, CO 80209
Roughnecker 618/676-1220	318 South 10th St SW Clay City, IL 62824
S & H Drilling Reports (432) 682-1704	P.O. Box 3858 Midland, TX 79702
Southeastern Oil Review (601) 353-6213	Oil Review Publishing Co. P.O. Box 145 Jackson, MS 39205
The Shale Shaker (405) 235-3648 < www.ocgs.org/shaleshaker.asp >	Oklahoma City Geological Society, Inc. 120 N. Robinson # 900 Ctr. Okc, OK 73102
Upstream 713/626-3113 < www.nhst.no/english/upsinfo.jsp >	5151 San Felipe # 1380 Houston, TX 77056
World Oil (713) 529-4301 < www.worldoil.com >	Gulf Publishing Co. Box 2608 Houston, TX 77252

*Whenever you may have occasion to
contact these companies,
please tell them you heard about them in*
MONEY IN THE GROUND
*published by Meridian Press, Oklahoma City.
Thanks!*

Bookstores

Brown Book Shop   < *www.brownbookshop.com* >
    1517 San Jacinto
    Houston, TX 77002
    (713) 652-3937, (800) 423-1825

The Tattered Cover Bookstore   < *www.tatteredcover.com* >
    2955 East First Avenue
    Denver, CO 80206
    (303) 322-7727, (800) 833-9327

Catalogs

Kraftbilt   < *www.kraftbiltoilandgas.com* >
    P.O. Box 800
    Tulsa, OK 74101
    (800) 331-7290

Museums

Drake Well Museum and environs (plan to spend 1 full day)
    202 Museum La., **Titusville, PA** 16354   **(814) 827-2797**
    < *www.drakewell.org* >

East Texas Oil Museum (plan to spend 1 half-day)
    Kilgore College, Highway 259 Ross
    Kilgore, TX 75226   **(903) 983-8295**
    < *www.easttexasoilmuseum.com* >

Houston Museum of Natural Science (spend 2 half-days)
    Weiss Energy Hall, Hermann Park, 1 Hermann Circle Dr.
    Houston, TX 77030   **(713) 639-4600**
    < *www.hmns.org* >

Permian Basin Petroleum Museum (plan to spend 1 half-day)
    1500 Interstate 20 West
    Midland, TX 79701-2041   **(432) 683-4403**
    < *www.petroleummuseum.org* >

Here is the section, township and range system used to identify legal land descriptions in most states west of the Mississippi River. (See also Fig 3.2 on page 50.)

Use this page to map out
your prospect and your land position!

Prospect Name: _____

State & County: _____

Township & Range: _____

MONEY IN THE GROUND - Insider's Guide to Oil Deals

ISBN 0-9615776-6-5

Meridian Press, Okla. City, OK

36	31	32	33	34	35	36	31
1	6	5	4	3	2	1	6
12	7	8	9	10	11	12	7
13	18	17	16	15	14	13	18
24	19	20	21	22	23	24	19
25	30	29	28	27	26	25	30
36	31	32	33	34	35	36	31
1	6	5	4	3	2	1	6

Hydrocarbons & Natural Gas Terminologies

PHASE	Hydro-carbon	Chemical Structure	Approx Boiling Point *	
GASES	Methane	CH_4	$-260\,^oF$	**LNG**
	Ethane	C_2H_6	$-125\,^oF$	
	Propane	C_3H_8	$-50\,^oF$	**LPG**
	Butane	C_4H_{10}	$30\,^oF$	
LIQUIDS	Pentane	C_5H_{12}	$100\,^oF$	
	Hexane	C_6H_{14}	$160\,^oF$	**NGL**
	Heptane	C_7H_{16}	$210\,^oF$	
	Octane	C_8H_{18}	$258\,^oF$	
	Paraffins C_9 thru C_{17}			
	Aromatics C_{6+}			
	etc.			
SOLIDS	C_{18} thru C_{50+}			

LNG	Liquefied natural Gas
LPG	Liquefied Petroleum Gas
NGL	Natural Gas Liquids
Condensate	More or less the same usage as NGL

* Water has a boiling point of 212°F; below this temperature: liquid; above this temperature: gas (at atmopsheric pressure).

Glossary

Italicized terms are defined in the Glossary

ABANDON - To stop production from a well. A well is permanently *plugged* and abandoned if it is drilled and found to be a dry hole, or in the case of a producing well, if it ceases to be economically productive.

ABANDONMENT LOSS COSTS - *Lease* acquisition costs on *leases* that are abandoned, and non-salvageable equipment costs on dry holes, which provide *deductions* against *gross income.* In oil and gas partnerships, they are generally allocated between the *general partner* and *limited partners* according to who paid the costs.

ABSTRACT OF TITLE - A chronological history of the ownership of a tract of land. It may consist of all recorded legal documents affecting the title of ownership of a tract of land, from one owner to another, dating back to when the land was originally homesteaded or granted by the government, or it may be abbreviated to some degree. (Generally, 'recorded' means recorded at the courthouse of the county in which the land is located).

ACIDIZING - Pumping acid (usually hydrochloric acid) into a *reservoir*. As the acid dissolves *calcite*, the naturally occurring holes in the rock are opened and enlarged, facilitating increased flow from the *reservoir*. *Limestones* are frequently treated with acid. *Sandstones* may be treated with acid if they contain calcite. (The acid does not affect the quartz grains making up the *sandstone*.) See also *fracturing*.

ACRE - The most common unit of land measure in the United States. A square 210 feet on a side (44,100 sq ft) would be a bit larger than an *acre* (43,560 sq ft). There are 640 acres in a square mile.

ACRE-FOOT - In the U.S., the thickness of a *pay zone* is measured in feet, and the area of the *reservoir* is measured in *acres*. An acre-foot is a volume of *reservoir* rock that is one *acre* in area and one foot thick. Estimates of recoverable oil or gas from a particular *reservoir* are generally expressed in *barrels* of oil per acre-foot, or in *MCF* (thousands of cubic feet of gas) per acre-foot. Commercial oil recoveries typically range from about 50 to 500 barrels per acre-foot, gas recoveries range from about 10 to 1000 MCF (thousands of cubic feet) per acre-foot.

ADJUSTED BASIS - The *basis* (or cost) of property increased (for *capital improvements*) or decreased (for investment *tax credits* and *depreciation allowance* adjustments to gross income) used in computing gain or loss, for income tax purposes. See *basis*.

AFE - See *Authorization For Expenditure*.

AIR DRILLING - Drilling in which the circulated drilling fluid is air, rather than liquid mud. Uses an 'air hammer' that pulverizes rock cuttings to the point that they are just about useless to a geologist in analyzing the penetrated section, but the drilling cost is much less than drilling with liquid mud because mud is not required, and also air drilling is often faster. It is more risky than drilling with mud, due to reduced well control options in the event of encountering unexpected pressurized zones. Also zones of lost circulation cause problems. Cost savings for drilling a well on air, compared with drilling the same well with mud, depend on the depth of the well, but can range as much as $25,000 or more per well. [144]

ALLOWABLE - The maximum amount of oil or gas a well or field is permitted to produce per day. It is typically set by state regulating agencies, after considering the economic market for the product, the *maximum efficient rate* (MER), and other factors.

ALTERNATIVE MINIMUM TAX - A tax imposed when an individual's *tax preference* items exceed: his regular tax plus his regular minimum tax liability.

AMI - Area of Mutual Interest. An area outlined on a map, that may accompany an exploration, drilling, or farmout agreement. It provides each party to the agreement, the right of first refusal on leases acquired by another party to the agreement. It may also provide for the sharing of interests that may be obtained by a party to the agreement.

AMORTIZE - To pay off a sum of money due, over a period of time, in installments. Also to *write-off* the cost of properties, typically by the unit-of-production method.

AMORTIZABLE (Tax Usage) - The tax accounting procedure by which the costs of qualified *capital expenditures* are (allowed to be) recovered, in the form of scheduled annual *deductions* from *gross income* (in Federal income tax calculations). See *depreciation allowance.*

ANNULUS - The donut-shaped space around the outside of the *drill pipe* in an open *borehole.* A *cased well* has two annular spaces: one between the *drill pipe* and the *casing,* the other between the *casing* and the *borehole.*

ANTICLINE - The 'textbook' type of (structural) oil or gas *trap.* It consists of layers of rock that have been *folded* into a domal shape, that would look like an inverted soup plate. Oil or gas can be trapped in an anticline, the way air might be trapped inside an overturned rowboat.

API - American Petroleum Institute, a petroleum industry association that sets standards for oil field equipment and operations. See *oil gravity.*

ARTIFICIAL LIFT - The application of power (energy) to lift oil to the surface in a producing well. In the typical case, artificial lift is required after the natural reservoir pressure has declined to the point that oil will no longer flow to the surface. Examples include surface pumps, submersible pumps, and gas lift. See *lifting costs.*

ASSESSMENTS - Additional capital *contributions* that may become required of the *limited partners* during the course of the partnership's existence, after capital formation of a *limited partnership.* The amount and circumstances (voluntary, mandatory, etc), relating to assessments are addressed in the partnership agreement. Although an assessment may be called 'voluntary' or 'optional', the *limited partnership* agreement may state that the investor will suffer a penalty if he does not pay it.

ASSET - Any physical property or legal right that is owned, can be legally transferred to another party, and has a monetary value.

ASSIGNMENT (ASSIGN) - Legal document transferring an interest in a property from one party to another. The receiving party is the 'assignee'; the transferring party is the 'assignor'.

ASSOCIATED GAS - *Natural gas* that naturally occurs in a *reservoir* along with ('associated' with) *oil*, in a *gas cap*, or dissolved in the oil.

ASSOCIATION FOR TAX PURPOSES - When two or more taxpayers are engaged (associated) in a common undertaking, if their association resembles a corporation (even though it may not be one), the association might be taxed as a corporation.

AT-RISK LIMITATION - The amount of (tax) losses *deductible* from *gross income* is limited to the amount the taxpayer has invested (in cash, property, or recourse debt for which he is liable) that is at *risk* of being lost.

AUTHORIZATION FOR EXPENDITURE (AFE) - An estimate of the costs of drilling and completing a proposed well, which the operator provides to each *working-interest* owner before the well is commenced. Various categories of costs are typically listed as 'dry hole' costs (the costs to drill to the *casing* point; these are costs that would be incurred if no indications of *hydrocarbons* are found), *completion* costs (the additional costs to complete the well), and the total cost. Please dee Appendix B for examples.

BACK-IN - A type of interest in a well or property that becomes effective at a specified time in the future, or on the occurrence of a specified future event. See *reversionary interest.*

BACKWARDATION - The situation when the current (spot market) price of a commodity is greater than the forward (futures) price. This scenario characterized the price of oil during periods of 1996, when traders were anticipating the return of Iraqi oil to the world market. The influx of Iraqi crude would be expected to lower oil prices; related to this anticipation, crude oil inventories in the U.S. were (intentionally kept) low, as no one wanted to be holding large inventories of crude oil that would have a lower market value in the future than at the time it was purchased (if and when the Iraqi crude came on the market).

BARREL (BBL) - The standard unit of oil measurement in the U.S. oil industry. A barrel equals 42 U.S. gallons, or 159 liters. [In some countries oil is measured using the metric system: volumes in liters, or weights in metric tons.] Please see Appendix A.

BASEMENT - (Usually) non-sedimentary rock in which oil is not likely to be found. It underlies the various layers of *sedimentary rock.*

BASIN - A natural depression on the earth's surface, in which (usually waterborne) sediments accumulate over millions of years. The Gulf of Mexico is an example. About 600 sedimentary basins have been identified around the world.

BASIS (tax usage) - The cost of property that is used in computing gain or loss, for Federal income tax purposes.

BASIS DIFFERENTIAL - The difference between quoted prices for a commodity as a result of differences in location, quality, grade, or timing of delivery.

In the natural gas industry, it has the very significant geographical component of where the natural gas is produced and where the physical delivery is to be taken. Originally it was assumed to represent the cost incurred in moving natural gas from one geographical basin to another area, but in reality, when distribution pipelines are full (or nearly full) to capacity, it becomes virtually impossible to ship gas from one producing area to a distant market, regardless of price. When this happens, as it has to natural gas producers in the Rocky Mountain areas, a very large differential develops between the value (price) of a quantity of natural gas in the producing region limited pipeline access, as compared to the same quantity available in the consuming region or region with abundant pipeline access. By way of example, during the first half of 1996, the price paid for natural gas available in the Gulf Coast ($2.65/MCF) was substantially more than twice the price paid for the same amount of gas available in the Rocky Mountains ($1.14/MCF).

Interestingly on the international front during 1996, Iran attempted (so far, unsuccessfully) to persuade South Africa to store vast quantities of Iranian crude oil in South Africa. Presumably this ploy would be to mitigate 'basis differential' risk. (In the event of supply interruptions in the Persian Gulf, the value of crude located in the Middle East would likely be priced at a substantial discount to crude located elsewhere.)

BASIS RISK - The risk that the commodity whose price is being hedged may be different from the commodity on which the futures and options contracts are based.

BCF - Billions of cubic feet (of gas). In the U.S. oil and gas industry, the cubic foot is the standard unit of measurement of gas at atmospheric pressure. Billion is 1,000 million (10^9).

BED - A layer of rock.

BEHIND PIPE - If a well drills through several *pay zones* and is *completed* in the deepest productive *reservoir, casing* is set all the way down to the producing *zone*. Viewed from (a perspective) inside the *borehole, reserves* in the shallower *pay zones* up the hole are **behind** the *casing* (**pipe**).

BIOMASS FUELS - Combustible material of current vegetable and animal material. By way of example, some buses in Szechuan province of China have been fitted with huge flexible rubber bladders (on the roof of the bus) which are filled with decomposing vegetable, matter, manure, etc. The methane gas that is generated from this biomass is captured in the bladder and piped to the engine, which it fuels. In this case, methane is a renewable energy source.

BLIND POOL - Refers to an oil and gas *limited partnership* which has not committed to specific *prospects, leases*, or properties at the time of capital formation (*subscription* by the *limited partners*).

BLOWOUT - A sudden uncontrolled flow from a well into the atmosphere (of oil, gas, water, or mud). It can occur when a *borehole* is drilled into a rock-layer in which natural pressures are greater than that exerted by the column of drilling *mud* in the borehole. The force of the uncontrolled flow from a blowout is dangerous enough; if gas is present, there is the additional danger of explosion and fire.

BLOWOUT INSURANCE - An insurance policy that protects the insured party (*working-interest* owner) from liabilities which might arise from a *blowout* during the drilling, completion, or production of a well.

BLOWOUT PREVENTERS - Heavy-duty equipment installed at the wellhead during drilling and completion operations, to prevent the possibility of a *blowout*, by sealing the *annular* space between the *drill pipe* and the *casing*. Pipe rams, shear rams, or blind rams may be activated to choke off flow from the *borehole*.

BLUE SKY LAWS - State regulations governing an offering to sell *securities* within that state (analogous to Securities Exchange Commission registration requirements at the Federal level). The expression originated with the first state securities laws enacted in the U.S. (Kansas, in 1911), intended to protect state residents from being sold *securities* as lacking in substance, 'as the blue sky'.

BOILER ROOM - Nowadays it might be called a 'telemarketing' operation. The term refers to a phone room manned by sales pros, who call prospective investors and try to interest them in oil and gas deals. Since *securities* regulations place restrictions on the distribution of offering documents (especially in the case of a *private placement*), the initial approach is often made by phone.

BONUS - Cash paid to the *mineral-rights* owner (lessor) for an oil and gas *lease*. The bonus is a negotiable provision of the *lease*. See *lease*.

BOREHOLE - The hole created by the drilling (boring) of a well.

BS&W - Bottom sediment and water that accumulates in the bottom of an oil tank (see illustration, Chapter 5). More generally in oil field conversation, anything that has no value and is a nuisance to dispose of.

BOTTOM-HOLE - An adjective referring to the deepest part of a borehole.

BOTTOM-HOLE AGREEMENT - A contract in which one party (the operator of an offsetting location, OLIVER) agrees to pay a sum of money to the operator of a well about to be drilled (DARRYL), provided that the well is drilled to specific depth or that it penetrates a specific geologic formation. The agreement may have nothing to do with whether the well is a producer or a dry hole. OLIVER proposes the agreement to induce DARRYL to drill to a specific depth or horizon and to share the resulting subsurface information with OLIVER; or DARRYL proposes the agreement to try to get OLIVER to help pay some of the cost of the well.

BOTTOM-HOLE PRESSURE - The pressure in a well, measured by an instrument that is lowered into the bore hole on a *wireline*. It may be measured under flowing or *shut-in* conditions.

BOTTOMS-UP - A temporary interruption in drilling (several hours in a deep well) to allow *cutting* samples to be *circulated* from the bottom of the hole up to the surface. The purpose is to allow the geologist at the wellsite to inspect the cutting samples before giving permission to resume drilling. If the cuttings contain *shows* of oil or gas, special procedures such as *coring* or *drill stem testing* may be desirable before drilling is resumed. See *drilling break*.

Btu - British thermal unit, a unit of heat energy, used to describe the amount of heat that can be generated by burning oil or gas. The heat generated from lighting a kitchen match is about 1 Btu; the heat needed to make a cup of coffee would be about 60 Btu. The average single family household in the U.S. consumes about 98 million Btu per year, or just under 2 million Btu per week. (1 Btu is the energy required to raise the temperature of 1 pound of water, 1 degree Fahrenheit.) [145] Very large quantities of energy are commonly measured in millions, trillions, and quadrillion Btu's ('quads'). One quadrillion is a 1 with 15 zeros after it.

CALCITE - The mineral calcium carbonate, $CaCO_3$. It is the primary ingredient of *limestone*, and is also present in dolomite, and often in *sandstone*.

CALIPER LOG - A *wireline log* that graphically indicates variations in the diameter of the borehole, displayed versus depth. See *logs*.

CAPITAL - Funds invested in a business for use in conducting the operations of the business.

CAPITAL ASSET - An *asset* acquired as an investment, for the purpose of creating a product or service intended to be used in the activities or operations of a business. (Not an *asset* intended for resale). A *royalty interest* held for investment would be a capital asset.

CAPITAL COSTS (Oil & Gas Tax Usage) - For Federal income tax purposes, the costs of *capital expenditures* which may be recovered by *deduction* against income (through *depreciation* and *depletion*).

CAPITAL EXPENDITURE - An expenditure intended to benefit the future activities of a business, usually by adding to the *assets* of a business, or by improving an existing *asset.* Such an expenditure is treated like an investment expected to generate future income for the business.

CAPITALIZE - To treat certain expenditures as capital expenditures for Federal income tax computations

CARRIED INTEREST - A fractional *working interest* in an oil and gas *lease* that comes about through an arrangement between co-owners of a *working interest.*

The owner of a carried interest is not liable for certain development and operating costs. The co-owner(s), who assumes these obligations and advances the cost of them, may or may not recoup his advances out of the carried party's share of production revenues (if any), according to the carrying arrangement.

In the case of a single well, the carry most typically includes all costs incurred in drilling to the *casing point,* but it could include any or all phases of the drilling, *completion,* and flowline hookup of a well. In the case of an oil well, the most extended carry would be a "carry through the tanks"; the comparable case for a gas well would be a "carry through the meter plus gathering costs".

In the case of *lease*d property, the carry can include costs incurred in any or all phases of exploration and development: from *prospect* generation and *lease* acquisition, through drilling the initial well on a *prospect*, through drilling a specified number of wells on a *prospect*, through the life of the *leased* property.

At the point of carry, the carried party's interest typically converts to a full *working interest*, although many other possibilities could be specified in a carrying arrangement. Details of the carried party's entitlement to revenue can vary considerably: starting from initial production, or not starting until the carrying party has recouped out of production, the costs he advanced, or some other arrangement.

Abercrombie-type, Herndon-type, and Monahan-type are types of carried-interest arrangements (named after parties involved in court decisions of the same name). They are discussed at length in "Income Taxation of Natural Resources 1995"; see Recommended Resources.

CARVED OUT INTEREST - A fractional portion of a revenue interest transferred (conveyed) to another party, by the original owner of the whole revenue interest. See *retained interest.*

CASED HOLE - A *borehole* in which *casing* has been run. If *casing* does not extend from the surface all the way to *total depth* (the bottom of the hole), the deeper uncased portion is *open hole.*

CASH DISTRIBUTIONS - Moneys paid by an oil and gas partnership to its partners according to the terms of the partnership agreement. They are net of state *severance* tax, etc.

Up to the amount of a partner's tax *basis* in the partnership, such distributions are generally held to be a return of capital investment (hence, not income). They are not taxable to the recipient until their (cumulative) total exceeds the partner's tax basis in the partnership. Thereafter, the distributions represent true income, and the receiving partner must pay income tax on distributions received.

CASING - Large diameter steel pipe placed in a *borehole* to support the sides or walls of the hole and to prevent them from caving in. It not only prevents the loss (flow) of drilling fluids from the *borehole* into porous rocks penetrated by the *borehole*, but also prevents rock fluids from flowing into the *borehole*.

Individual sections are usually about 30 feet long, and are screwed together as they are lowered (or 'run') into the hole. Once casing is run in the hole, it is *cemented* in place by pumping a slurry of *cement* into the space between the outside of the casing and the walls of the *borehole* (the *annulus*).

Casing run from the surface is called surface casing. One or more additional strings of 'intermediate casing' may be required during the drilling of the well. Production casing is run, in order to *complete* a well.

CASINGHEAD - A fitting attached to the top ('head') of the *casing* in a producing oil or gas well (usually at, or just above, ground level). It regulates the flow of oil or gas, helps separate oil from gas, allows the pumping of oil from an oil well, and facilitates periodic cleaning out of the well. See *Christmas tree*.

CASINGHEAD GAS - *Natural gas* produced along with oil from an oil well (as distinguished from gas produced from a gas well). CASINGHEAD OIL is oil produced from a gas well.

CAVINGS - Rock fragments that break off from the walls of a borehole and fall into the borehole during drilling operations

CEMENT - Fluid cement is mixed at the surface, pumped to the bottom of a *cased* well, forced to flow around the lower end of the *casing* and up into the space between the *casing* and the *borehole*. When the cement solidifies (sets), it holds the casing in place, and provides support.

CHOKE - A device placed in a flowline to restrict the flow of fluids; commonly used in measuring flow rates in producing wells. Various flow rates measured during initial testing of a well might be reported as '125 bopd on a 1/4" choke'.

CHRISTMAS TREE - A complex assemblage of valves/controls, fittings, gauges, and pipe connections at the top of the *casing* of a flowing oil well. It controls the flow of oil and gas from the well. A silhouette of this assemblage might be vaguely reminiscent of a heavily decorated Christmas tree, hence the name.

CIRCULATION - The continuous pumping of drilling fluid (*'mud'*) from *mud* tanks at the surface: down through the *drill pipe*, out the nozzles in the *drill bit*, and back up to the surface through the space between the *drill pipe* and the *borehole*. The flow of *mud* moves the rock *cuttings* (and *cavings*) away from the *drill bit*, and carries them up to the surface, where they are strained out of the *mud* system, by the *shale shaker*.

'Lost circulation' occurs when drilling fluid escapes from an uncased borehole into porous zones, or holes such as fractures or caverns that occur naturally in the penetrated rocks. Various plugging or clogging materials may be added to the *mud* in hope of stopping its loss. (As one might inject gummy fluid into an automobile tire to stop a leak.) Difficult (and often costly) mechanical operations may be required to drill through a *zone* of lost circulation. If an attempt to drill through zones of lost circulation are unsuccessful, a well might have to be *abandoned*.

CNG - Compressed Natural Gas.

COGENERATION - A process of obtaining more efficient use of fuel. The energy produced is used not only to generate electric or mechanical energy, but also to provide useful thermal energy (such as heat and steam), for use in industrial, commercial, heating or cooling processes.

A topping cycle is when the fuel is first used to generate electric or mechanical power, and the by-product (reject heat) is then used to provide thermal energy.

A bottoming cycle is when the fuel is first used to provide useful thermal energy, and the by-product (reject heat) is then used to generate electric or mechanical power.

COMMISSIONS - Payments to qualified agents of the sponsor of a *limited partnership,* for selling interests in it to investors. The agents typically include officers and directors of the sponsor, underwriters, securities dealers, and other qualified third parties. Commissions may take the form of a percent of partnership interests sold, an oil and gas interest, or stock in the sponsor's company. The costs of the commissions are not *deductible expenses;* they are non-*amortizable capital expenditures.*

COMMON LAW - Social customs and behavior patterns established in the past, that have come to be regarded and accepted as law (on the basis of court decisions and precedent, rather than legislative action). Also referred to as case law. Applicable in most of the U.S.

COMPLETION (COMPLETE A WELL) - After the drilling of a successful well, the 'completion' includes all the work required to make the well ready for commercial production.

CONDENSATE - *Hydrocarbons* naturally occurring in the gaseous phase in the *reservoir* that condense to become a liquid at the surface (due to the change in pressure and temperature).

CONTRIBUTION - In oil and gas *limited partnerships*: the payment of money, property, or services by which an investor becomes a *limited partner* in the partnership.

CONVERTIBLE INTEREST - An interest (usually a non-cost-bearing interest) that may, at the option of the owner or on the occurrence of a specified event, be changed into another type of interest (usually a cost-bearing interest). Example: a 5% *overriding royalty* convertible to a 1/8 (= 12.5%) *working interest* after *payout*.

CONVEY (CONVEYANCE) - Legal term for transferring the title of a property from one party to another, typically by *deed* (or bill of sale, etc.).

CORE - A cylindrical column of rock usually 4 to 6 inches in diameter cut in lengths of about 30 feet by a special *drill bit.* (The operation is a bit like removing the core from an apple). After the core has been brought to the surface, it is examined by the geologist for *shows* of *hydrocarbons.* Because of the time and high costs cost involved, only the most critical intervals are cored in the U.S. (In China, however, it is not uncommon to core an exploratory well from grass-roots to granite.)

CORRELATIVE RIGHTS - A *mineral-rights* owner is entitled to 'capture' oil and gas from an accumulation which exists beneath his property, even though the accumulation extends beyond his property line. He has the ('correlative') right to drill a well on his property, and produce oil and gas which might otherwise flow toward wells (drilled on adjacent land owned by others), that produce from the same oil and gas accumulation.

"CREEK-OLOGY" - Refers to locating the next well, not strictly on the basis of science and geology, but also in part, on the basis of gross natural features on the surface of the land. (The bend in a creek, for example, may represent the surface expression of a fault or a structural trap deep beneath the surface). A large corporation might never admit it to its shareholders, but even after all the scientific data are collected and analyzed (at considerable expense) often the results are still not conclusive; the final decision on where to drill has many times included a good measure of "creek-ology".

CRUDE OIL - A naturally occurring mixture of liquid *hydrocarbons* as it comes out of the ground (before or after any dissolved gas has been separated from it, but prior to any process of distilling or refining). Greenish crude is usually high in paraffin (wax) content; blackish oil is more likely to be asphaltic. Different types of *source rock* generate different types of crude oils.

CURE (Title) - To correct any things about the title that might potentially make ownership subject to being contested in court.

334

CURRENT - refers to the present (tax or fiscal) year.

CUTTINGS - Small chips of rock (usually about fingernail size) produced by the grinding motion of the *drill bit* during drilling. The drilling *mud* carries (*'circulates'*) them to the surface where they are strained out of the *mud* system by the *shale shaker.* Cuttings are examined under a microscope for direct observation of *porosity.* When placed under ultraviolet light, any *hydrocarbons* contained in the pore spaces of the cuttings will give off a distinctive glow (*'fluorescence'*). This fluorescence is recorded as a *show* of oil.

DARCY - See *reservoir.*

"DE-CONTRACTING" - A situation that is now developing as a direct result of the FERC Rule 636. Briefly: in the past, contracts by which natural gas utilities purchased natural gas were long-term contracts (10-30 years or more). Utilities also entered in to long-term contracts for the transportation of the gas. Some will expire in the next few years. As these long term transportation contracts expire, there is the very good likelihood (in the current era of increasing competition) that these transportation contracts will not be renewed. In other words, huge volumes of natural gas pipeline capacity are likely to become 'de-contracted' and hence available in the marketplace under terms that will be subject to short-term demand and supply. This will have serious implications for certain pipelines, and potentially for the price of natural gas, in certain regions of the country.

DEDUCTIONS - Tax items which may be subtracted from *gross income* to arrive at *taxable income* in Federal income tax computations. See *taxes due.*

335

DEED - A written document (legal 'instrument') by which the title to a property (real estate) is transferred (*conveyed*) from one party (the grantor) to another (the grantee). It is signed by the grantor and delivered to the grantee.

DEGREE-DAYS - There are 2 varieties:

Cooling degree days: the number of degrees (°F) per day that the average daily temperature is above 65°F. (Average daily temperature is the mean of the maximum and minimum temperatures for the 24-hour day.)

Heating degree days: the number of degrees (°F) per day that the average daily temperature is below 65°F. (Average daily temperature is the mean of the maximum and minimum temperatures for the 24-hour day.)

DELAY RENTAL - Periodic cash payments to the *mineral-rights* owner (lessor), by the *working-interest* owner (lessee), for the privilege of postponing the commencement of drilling operations on the *leased* property. (Delay rentals are usually specified as an annual payment per *acre* of land covered by the *lease*). A 'paid up *lease*' means that all the delay rentals were paid up-front. Delay rentals are a negotiable provision of an oil and gas *lease*.

DEPLETION - The value of a naturally occurring mineral deposit is a function of (1) the market value of the mineral, and (2) the concentration of the mineral in the mineral deposit. Physical depletion is the exhaustion of a mineral deposit through production of the mineral. Economic depletion is the reduction in the value of the mineral deposit as it becomes exhausted (less concentrated) through production.

DEPLETION ALLOWANCE - Income tax *deduction* allowed for the exhaustion of a natural resource.

DEPRECIATION - A tax accounting method in which the value of an *asset* (starting with its acquisition cost) is reduced each year. Scheduled annual (noncash) amounts are charged against the asset, representing the gradual loss of value, as it wears out, deteriorates, or becomes obsolete. (Theoretically such charged amounts accumulate over time, providing funds that could be used to replace the worn out *asset.*)

DEPRECIATION ALLOWANCE - In the computation of taxable income: a *deduction* from *gross income* allowed during the useful life of an *asset* (in recognition of its wear and tear, and eventual obsolescence). Different types of property (*assets*) have different years of useful life. This determines the methods (schedules) for calculating the deduction (straight line, declining balance, sum-of-the years-digits, etc).

DETERMINABLE FEE - A subset of 'fee ownership', in which ownership depends on the occurrence of a specified event. Under some conditions an oil and gas lease might be regarded as a determinable fee in land (real estate).

DIP - The angle that a rock layer happens to be inclined (at a specific location), measured relative to a horizontal plane (in degrees).

DIPMETER LOG - A wireline log that tells the angle and direction of the *dip* of rock-layers penetrated by the *borehole.*

DIRECTIONAL DRILLING - When a drilling rig cannot be positioned directly over a prospect, because of natural or man-made obstacles on the surface (buildings, a park, a swamp, a lake, etc.), it may be positioned off to one side. A *borehole* can be drilled at an angle (a 'slant hole') to reach the subsurface objective. See *whipstock*.

DIVISION ORDER - A contract for the sale of oil or gas, by the holder of a revenue interest (*royalty, overriding royalty, working interest,* etc.) in a well or property, to the purchaser. Based on the division order *title opinion,* it lists the names of revenue interest owners of a producible oil or gas well, along with their respective shares of production revenues, and directs the purchaser to distribute the proceeds of production sales, accordingly.

DOE - U.S. (Federal) Department of Energy.

DOODLEBUGGER - A *geophysicist* who interprets *seismic data.* 'Doodlebug' originally referred to any device (such as a divining rod or forked stick used to search for water) applied to the search for oil. Although it came to include any new method used in the direct detection of oil and gas accumulations, now it generally refers to the field of *seismic* interpretation.

"DOODLEBUG-OLOGY" - Can refer to any new and unproven method or technology (electrical, chemical, magnetic, etc.) used to search for oil and gas accumulations.

DOWNHOLE - Refers to equipment or mechanical operations that take place, **down** inside a bore**hole** (as contrasted with those at the surface).

DOWN TIME - **Time** lost during drilling, usually as a result of equipment break**down**.

DRAINAGE - The situation that may occur when hydrocarbons (originally static) under one tract of land (migrate) and are produced from a well on an offsetting lease. The working interest being drained has the correlative right to drill a well on his own tract to protect himself from such drainage.

DRILL BIT - A tool with very tough steel or diamond teeth that grind rock into small chips during drilling. The diameter of the bits used to drill a well may range from more than 22 inches at the upper part of the hole, to less than four inches at *total depth.*

DRILL PIPE - A special grade of extra-strong steel pipe threaded on both ends that comes in lengths of about 30 feet and diameters from about 6 1/2 to 2 1/2 inches. See *drill string.*

DRILL-STEM TEST (DST) - When a well is drilled into a potential *pay zone,* it may be desirable to try to make the zone flow, before continuing to drill ahead. To 'test' the zone, drilling is halted, and the string of *drill pipe* is pulled out of the *borehole.* The *drill bit* is removed and a special testing device is attached to the end of the *drill string* which is lowered back into the *borehole.*
A system of blocking devices (*packers*) allow rock fluids to flow from the reservoir directly into the drill pipe (drill stem). The quality and amount of formation fluids recovered, along with the pressures recorded during the drill stem test indicate whether the *zone* could be commercially produced.
(An alternative to drill stem testing is to continue drilling to the planned *total depth,* and then *log* the hole. If the *logs* suggest a good *zone, casing* may be set. Then the *zone* can be tested through *perforations* made in the *casing.* Although this is often a more conservative procedure than taking a drill-stem test during drilling, it is much more expensive.)

339

DRILL STRING - The entire assemblage of joints of drill pipe that are screwed together and lowered into a borehole. The drill string runs from the Kelly on the drilling rig to the drill bit at the bottom of the borehole.

DSU (Drilling and Spacing Unit) See *Spacing Unit*.

DRILLING BREAK - A sudden increase in the rate of drilling. Usually it indicates that the *drill bit* is penetrating 'weaker' rock. The 'weakness' of the rock is presumed to result from increased *porosity* (which might contain hydrocarbons). See *bottoms up*.

DRILLING RIG - The surface equipment used to drill for oil or gas. It consists of a TOWER framework (derrick) which supports the WINCH (pulley system) used to lift and lower *drill pipe*, a ROTARY TABLE that turns the *drill string* (and *drill bit* connected to the *drill string*), ENGINES to drive the winch and rotary table, and PUMPS to control the flow of the drilling *mud*.

DRILLING REPORT - Daily (morning) report from the wellsite to the operator's headquarters that details drilling progress and activities operations undertaken during the preceding 24 hours. A week of daily reports (or more) may be aggregated by the operator before being forwarded on to the other working interest owners.

DRY GAS - *Natural gas* that contains no appreciable liquid *hydrocarbons*. It may occur naturally, or may result from passing natural gas (that originally contained liquids) through standard separator equipment installed at a producing well.

DRY HOLE AGREEMENT - An agreement (contract) for the payment of money if a well is completed as a dry hole, typically in exchange for subsurface information that was obtained by the drilling of the well. It represents a subset of the concept, bottomhole agreement.

DUAL COMPLETION - When a borehole has encountered two or more widely separated *pay zones,* the *operator* has several options: (1) *complete* the well in the deepest *zone* and produce that *zone* until it is *depleted* (which might be several years), then come up the hole to the next shallower *pay zone* and complete in it; (2) *complete* in the deepest *pay zone* and drill a second well down to the shallower *pay zone* and *complete* the second well in this shallower *zone;* (3) make a dual completion by *completing* the original well in both *pay zones* so that each can be produced simultaneously through separate strings of *tubing.*

DUE DILIGENCE - In an offering of *securities,* certain parties who are responsible for the accuracy of the offering document, have an obligation to perform a 'due diligence' examination of the issuer: issuer's counsel, underwriter of the security, brokerage firm handling the sale of the security. Due diligence refers to the degree of prudence that might properly be expected from a reasonable man, on the basis of the significant facts which relate to a specific case (in other words, not measured by any absolute standard).

'EBITDA' - Earnings before interest, taxes, and depreciation and amortization.

ECONOMIC INTEREST - An interest in oil and gas in the ground. It entitles the owner to a *deduction* from *gross income* derived from production of that oil or gas (*depletion allowance*). As specified in

Federal income tax regulations, "an economic interest is possessed in every case in which the taxpayer has acquired by investment any interest in minerals in place or standing timber and secures, by any form of relationship, income derived from the extraction of the mineral or severance of the timber, to which he must look for a return of his capital."

ECONOMIC LIMIT (of a well) - A calculated amount of daily production (expressed as cash revenue, barrels of oil, or MCF gas), below which it becomes not profitable to operate the well. The economic limit is a function of the wellhead price received for the product, and the cost of operating the well. It can change with changes in the market for product, or the introduction of new technology or cost-efficiencies in operations, changes in the tax structure, etc. The economic limit of a particular well might be very different for different operators - depending on the respective cost-efficiency of their operations, the market price they can receive for the product, access to pipeline transportation, pipeline costs, etc.

ENHANCED OIL RECOVERY (EOR) - Various methods of increasing the recovery of oil and gas from a *reservoir*, (usually) after *primary recovery* has pretty much run its course. The procedure is to introduce an artificial drive and/or displacement system in the reservoir, to produce oil which has become unrecoverable as the natural energy (pressure) in the reservoir is depleted. In the case of certain (low-pressure) *reservoirs*, or (highly *viscous*) oils, some of these techniques (waterflooding, for example) may be necessary, right from the beginning of production. See *flooding, gas injection, primary recovery, secondary recovery.*

In recent years, the term "improved oil recovery"
has become preferred due to wider applicability.
Improved oil recovery is broad and general and
does not necessarily imply great cost or the latest
technology. It is simply the matter of doing whatever works best to increase recovery (production). Enhanced oil recovery could be considered
as a subset of improved oil recovery.

EOR - *Enhanced oil recovery.*

EQUIPMENT COSTS - Oil/gas well expenses which are
recoverable through depreciation, including those
for the likes of: casing, tubing, transportation of
casing and tubing to well site, stabilizers and other
downhole equipment, the Christmas tree, salt water
disposal equipment including cost of drilling the
disposal well and pipeline connections, etc., surface
equipment including pump jack, treaters, separators,
storage tanks, compressors, recycling equipment,
flowlines, earthwork for tank battery and maintenance roads, installation and labor costs for surface
oil storage tanks, flowlines, etc.[146]

ERTS - Earth Resource Technology Satellite. As
commonly used, ERTS refers to satellite images
of the earth's surface, digitally-recorded at various non-visible wavelengths (in the infrared part
of the spectrum).

Image enhancement by computer processing yields
'false-color images' that can reveal subtle features
on the earth's surface which cannot be observed
from the ground, or even on aerial photographs.
Some of these features might be interpreted as the
surface expression of geologic structures at depths
of thousands of feet below the ground (which
could contain oil or gas). See *trap.*

ET ... - Latin meaning 'and': et al (and others), et ux
(and wife), et vir (and husband). Sometimes

corrupted in oil deal usage: "The et als account for the other 7% of the interest in the Jones well."

EUR - Expected (or estimated) Ultimate Reserves. An estimate of the cumulative volume of *reserves* that will ultimately be recovered (from a specified *reservoir*) over the life of a well, field, or property.

EXPENSES (Tax Usage) - Expenditures for business items that have no future life (such as rent, utilities, or wages) and are incurred in conducting normal business activities. In computing Federal income *tax due*, expenses may be deducted from *gross income* to arrive at *taxable income*. See *taxable income*.

FARMOUT AGREEMENT - An arrangement (technically, a tax partnership) in which the responsibility for exploration and development for a specific work program is shifted (by assignment) from the working interest owner BEAVER, to another party ANTELOPE. BEAVER contributes his working interest (but retains a revenue interest), and Antelope contributes the costs of drilling a well.

ANTELOPE wants to drill a well on BEAVER's property. Under the farmout agreement: ANTELOPE is obligated to perform a specified exploration and drilling program to earn a working interest in BEAVER's property; BEAVER retains an interest in the net proceeds of future oil or gas production (if any) from the property.

In this case, ANTELOPE FARMED into BEAVER's property; BEAVER farmed out his interest to ANTELOPE. ANTELOPE is the 'farmee'; BEAVER is the 'farmor'.

FAULT - A crack or fracture in the earth's crust, along which the rocks on one side have moved relative to the rocks on the opposite side. The movement could be sideways or up and down, and can range from a few inches to tens (or even hundreds) of miles. A fault can juxtapose a non-porous layer of rock against an oil-bearing reservoir (sometimes thereby forming a *trap*).

FEE OWNERSHIP - The ownership of full right, *title*, and interest to the surface of a tract of land and to all minerals beneath it, as well as the air space above it.

FEE SIMPLE OWNERSHIP (FEE SIMPLE ABSOLUTE) - fee ownership without any limitation or restriction as to future transfer of the ownership.

FEET OF PAY - The thickness of the *pay zone* penetrated in a well. In the case of an *oil column* floating on water, it is the thickness of the layer of oil ('the *oil column*') above the *oil-water contact*.

FERC - Federal Energy Regulatory Commission.

FIELD (as in OIL FIELD or GAS FIELD) - A commercial oil or gas accumulation (or the land area above it). The size of an oil field can range from a few *acres*, to the Ghawhar oil field in Saudi Arabia (the world's largest) which is over 100 miles long and up to a dozen miles wide.

FINDING COSTS - A computed value that commonly means different things to different people. Depending on lots and lots of variables including company strategy, budget, and time period, etc., the 'finding cost' for development wells could easily range from say $2 to $40 per barrel of producible oil; the 'finding cost' for exploration wells could just as easily range from $10 to $1000 per barrel. The problem arises when these two activities are combined to arrive at a single 'overall' average finding cost that really doesn't mean very much.

FISHING - The procedure of locating and attempting to retrieve any object (a 'fish') that has accidentally fallen into, or been left in the *borehole*, and must be retrieved before mechanical operations (drilling, *logging, completion*, etc) can be resumed.

FLOODING - One of the methods of *enhanced oil recovery*. Water flooding or gas flooding might be considered *secondary recovery* methods; miscible flooding or chemical flooding, tertiary recovery methods.

The general procedure involves pumping (injecting) a fluid (commonly water) into the reservoir, through wells located around the perimeter of an oil field (peripheral drive). The 'pressure front' that is created, flushes oil toward the central part of the field, resulting in increased production.

'FLOW THROUGH' CONCEPT - In ventures structured as partnerships (or S corporations), certain items of tax significance (profit, loss, etc.) are passed on to the partners (or S corporation shareholders) in the venture. In a 'C' corporation, the responsible taxpaying party would be the corporation itself (not its shareholders).

FLUORESCENCE - An optical property of some materials: they glow emitting visible light when they absorb radiation from an ultraviolet source. Liquid *crude oils* fluoresce with colors that range from brown to yellow to green to blue. The color may give some indication of the density of the oil and its chemical characteristics.

FOLDING - The bending of layers of rock, which occurs naturally, in response to pressures and stresses in the earth's crust.

346

FORCED POOLING - The situation when a state regulating authority directs the pooling of contiguous leased tracts of acreage. It can be thought of as government-mandated cooperation among the interest owners of a drilling and spacing unit, after a legal court hearing at which all affected parties have the opportunity to present their various perspectives of the situation. A normal course of events in Oklahoma and Arkansas which have statutes that specifically provide for 'forced pooling'.

FORMATION - A layer of rock having characteristics that are distinct and recognizable. The rock layer is thus mappable, even among other layers of similar rocks. The thickness can range from a few feet to hundreds of feet. Distinctive features might include mineral composition, texture, diagnostic plant or animal remains (fossils) contained in it, etc.

FRACTURING - A procedure undertaken to attempt to increase the flow of oil or gas from a well. A fluid (usually crude oil, diesel oil, or water) is pumped into the *reservoir,* with such great force that the *reservoir* rock is physically broken and split open. Usually the 'frac fluid' carries small pellets or beads mixed in with it; the idea is for them to get caught in the fractures and prop them open (the beads or pellets are called the propping agent or *proppant*).

As the pumping pressures are gradually released at the surface, the natural *reservoir* pressures will force the 'frac fluid' out of the *reservoir,* and back into the well as the well begins to flow. The *proppant* remains behind, holding the fractures open, thereby increasing the flow of oil or gas from the reservoir into the well. This procedure is also

called hydraulic fracturing. 'To frac a well' means
to hydraulically fracture a reservoir in a well.

FRONT-END COSTS - Costs that are paid out of
initial investment in a venture, first, before the
venture activities actually begin. In a *limited
partnership*, these costs might include *syndication expenses*, legal fees, accounting fees, *management fees*, etc.

Front-end costs reduce the net amount available for
investment (for the drilling of wells, purchase of
producing properties, purchase of royalties, etc.)

FUEL OIL - A processed petroleum product (commonly a residue of distillation process, or sometimes a blend of distillate fractions) that is
burned for the production of electric power,
heat, or in industrial furnaces.

FUTURE NET REVENUES - Net revenues that will
be received in the future. After discounting back
to the present value of such revenues, the
amount is often expressed as the "present value
of future net revenues".

FUTURES PRICES - Refers to the New York Mercantile Exchange (NYMEX) which introduced futures
contracts for *crude oil* in 1985 and *natural gas* in
1990. A futures contract is an obligation to buy or
sell a specified quantity at a specified price in some
future month (as far as 18 months in the future).

An oil futures contract is for 1,000 barrels of *West
Texas Intermediate* (*WTI*) *crude oil* to be delivered at Cushing Oklahoma; price is quoted in dollars
per barrel. WTI is the domestic light, sweet crude
that is most widely traded in the *spot market*. See
API, sour crude, WTI.

A gas futures contract is for 10,000 MM *Btu* of gas to
be delivered during the calendar delivery month, at

the "Henry Hub" near Erath, Louisiana; price is quoted in dollars per MM *Btu.* (MM= 1,000,000.)

GAS BALANCING - The accounting process of adjusting the physical amount of gas taken or delivered (gas sales) to agree with what should have been taken or delivered. The imbalance results when one working interest owner who has a right to specific portion of the gas production from a well, has sold either more, or less, than his proportionate share of production from the well. The specific procedures for handling this situation may be specified in the joint operating agreement or in a side letter gas balancing agreement.

GAS CAP - In a *reservoir,* the accumulation of natural gas, above a layer of *saturated* liquid *hydrocarbons.*

GAS COLUMN - The vertical height of a gas accumulation above the gas-oil or gas-water contact. In commercial gas fields, a gas column can range from several feet to (rarely!) more than a thousand feet. See *oil column.*

GAS CONDENSATE - See *condensate.*

GAS DRIVE - When a well drills into an oil accumulation (which is under considerable natural *reservoir* pressure), free gas in the *gas cap* above the oil *zone,* expands. This forces the oil to flow into the wellbore, and up the surface (*'gas-cap drive'*); at the same time, *solution gas* dissolved in the oil comes out of solution, and it too expands, helping to force oil to flow into the wellbore and up to the surface (*'solution gas drive'*). See *water drive.*

GAS INJECTION - A method of *secondary recovery* in which a gas (usually dry *natural gas* or carbon dioxide) is injected into an oil *reservoir* to increase *reservoir* pressure around the injection well. Some of the gas dissolves in the oil, increasing the oil's ability to flow. The increased pressure and flowing ability of the oil result in increased production from the nearby production wells.

GAS LIFT - A method of artificial lift that is similar to the *secondary recovery* method of gas *injection,* except that the injection well and the production well are both the same well.

Dry natural gas is pumped: down through the (*annular*) space between the *casing* and the production *tubing,* and into the *reservoir.* Gas dissolves in oil increasing the oil's ability to flow. As pressure is bled off at the surface, the oil-and-gas mixture (which is lighter and less viscous than the oil by itself) expands, and flows from the *reservoir,* into the production *tubing* in the well, and up to the surface. The procedure of injecting gas and then flowing the oil-and-gas mixture can be carried on intermittently ('huff and puff') or continuously. The gas is separated from the mixture at the surface, where it is stored for reinjection. (Alternatively, the gas might be injected through the tubing and the oil produced through the annulus.)

GAS-OIL RATIO (GOR) - The volume of gas produced along with the oil from an oil well, usually described in *MCF* (thousands of cubic feet of gas) per *barrel* of oil. In the most general sense, an oil and gas accumulation might be broadly classified according to its GOR:

GOR (MCF/BBL)	Probable Hydrocarbon
0 - 2,000	Oil, no free gas
1,000 - 20,000	Oil / Gas / Condensate
> 20,000	Dry gas

350

In a typical solution-gas-drive well, the GOR will tend to decrease as the production progresses.

GATHERING SYSTEM - A local pipeline system that connects to several or many natural gas wells in the same area, and transfers the natural gas to a centralized gas processing facility. (From the tailgate of the processing facility, the gas is sold into an interstate pipeline transmission system.) In most cases, gathering systems are intrastate, and hence not subject to FERC rulings such as Rule 636 provisions for 'open access'. This can leave a producer connected to a gathering systems, to some extent, at the mercy of the owner of the gathering system. As of this writing, it is a hotly contested issue in a number of regions of the country.

GENERAL PARTNER - In a *limited partnership,* the general partner is responsible for managing the partnership's activities (and is commonly the party that put the deal together). His liability to the partnership's creditors is unlimited.

GEOPHONES - Microphones placed on the ground to detect sound waves generated during *seismic* surveying.

GEOPHYSICIST - A geophysicist applies the principles of **physics** to the understanding of **geo**logy. Emphasis is generally on the earth's gravitational and magnetic fields, and the travel of sound waves through the earth. Many U.S. universities offer BS, MS, and PhD degrees in geophysics; the Society of Exploration Geophysicists has over 19,000 members.

GROSS ACRES - The number of *acres* in which one owns a *working interest.* A net *acre,* is a gross acre multiplied by one's *working interest* in it.

GROSS INCOME - Total income from an activity, before *deduction* of (1) items that may be treated as *expenses* (such as *intangible drilling costs*), and (2) allowed tax items (such as *depletion* allowance, *depreciation* allowance, etc). See *taxes due*.

GROSS WELLS - The number of wells in which one owns a *working interest*. A net well, is a gross well multiplied by one's *working interest* in it.

GUARANTEED PAYMENTS - Payments by a partnership to one or more of its partners for services rendered. They are paid without regard to the partnership's income (as if to a third party).

HEAVY OIL - Oil that will not flow, (or in any case will hardly flow), having an API gravity of less than 20°API. (To be very technical, some may distinguish between 'crude bitumen' (gravity of 6-14°API) which absolutely will not flow, and 'heavy oil' (gravity of 14-20°API).

HELD BY PRODUCTION (HBP) - Refers to acreage that is leased (and is in the secondary term of the lease), and hence not available to be leased, because of production from the property. See also *secondary term*.

HORIZONTAL DRILLING - The new and developing technology that makes it possible to drill a well from the surface, vertically down to a certain level, and then to turn a right angle, and continue drilling horizontally within a specified *reservoir*, or an interval of a *reservoir*.

HOT OILING - Some *crude oils* contain significant paraffin (waxy) *hydrocarbons* which: 1) reduce the ability of the oil to flow, and 2) remain liquid, only at relatively high temperatures. Production of this type of oil usually tends to decline rather rapidly (as the paraffins in the oil clog the porosity surrounding the well bore).

Hot oiling is a method of (temporarily) alleviating this situation by using heating equipment and special procedures to increase the temperature in the *reservoir* close to the *borehole*, thereby liquefying the paraffin, and unclogging the pore spaces.

Alternatives to hot-oiling include experimental production techniques, injecting chemical additives into the reservoir, etc.

HUCKLEDY-BUCK - Perhaps a corruption of 'hustle for the buck'. Refers to a situation where it is every man for himself. "You and I may be partners in other wells or other projects, but in this project, we're gonna go huckledy-buck." (I'm going to look after my interests.)

HYDROCARBONS - A large class of organic compounds composed of hydrogen and carbon. *Crude oil, natural gas,* and natural gas *condensate* are all mixtures of various hydrocarbons, among which *methane* (CH_4) is the simplest. There are 2 categories: 1) paraffins have the chemical formula C_nH_{2n+2} and a molecular structure that is linear; and 2) aromatics (so named because many of them have a sweet or aromatic odor), which have ring like structure (starting from benzene).

IDC - See *intangible drilling costs.*

INCREASED DENSITY - See *spacing unit.*

INDEPENDENT (OIL COMPANY) - Traditionally, any domestic oil company that is not one of the seven *major* international oil companies. More generally, any U.S. oil company that is not one of the largest 20 or so integrated oil companies. See *major.*

INITIAL POTENTIAL - Flow rate measured during the initial *completion* of a well in a specific *reservoir* ('initial daily rate of production'). It may or may not reflect the ultimate producing capability of the well.

INTANGIBLE DRILLING COSTS - An important tax accounting concept. Please refer to discussion in the text. They include expenses incurred in: agreements and negotiations in obtaining operator for well, agreements and negotiations in obtaining contractors for the drilling of the well, site location and survey work, road construction and earth-moving work on the drill site location, transporting rig to location and rigging-up consumables such as water, fuel, electricity, drilling mud, bits, drilling costs (as calculated per foot or per day), contract services such as logging, drill-stem testing, swabbing, fracturing, acidizing, rental equipment needed for testing, installation and cementing (of casing), transportation of tubing and casing to drill site, perforation of casing, wireline logging, and the cost of injection wells used solely in the course of secondary recovery.[147]

INVESTMENT TAX CREDIT (ITC) - A credit against income taxes, usually computed as a percent of the cost of investment in certain types of *assets* (specified in tax regulations). It directly offsets *tax liability.* See *taxes due.*

JIB (JOINT INTEREST BILLING) - The accounting procedures of billing each *working interest* owner his proportionate share of drilling and *lease operating expenses.*

JOINT - A single section of *drill pipe, casing,* or *tubing,* usually about 30 feet long.

JOINT OPERATING AGREEMENT (JOA) - A detailed written agreement (a contract) between the *working interest* owners (co-owners) of a property which specifies the terms according to which they will jointly develop the property.

JUG-HUSTLER - In the field operations of a seismic survey, the *geophones* (jugs) must be placed on the ground in a particular pattern and connected via electrical cables, to a recording computer. After the sound waves are recorded at one location, the jugs have to be picked up, moved to the next location, and again laid out in the specified pattern. The field-hand who does this is a jug-hustler.

KELLY BUSHING (KB) - Part of the *drilling rig,* the Kelly is a long hollow steel bar that connects to the upper end of the *drill string.* It is square or hexagonal in cross-section. The Kelly bushing is a special 'sleeve' in the rotary table through which the Kelly can freely move up and down during drilling.

The depth to a particular *zone* in a well is generally measured from the KB (Kelly bushing), which may be anywhere from about 5 to 50 feet above ground level (depending on the type and size of *drilling rig* being used).

LACT UNIT - Lease Automatic Custody Transfer unit. A mechanical system for the automatic (unmanned) measurement, testing, and recording of oil automatically transferred from the (producer's) oil storage tank at the wellsite, and pumped into the purchaser's oil pipeline.

LAG TIME - The time it takes for *cuttings* to be carried (*'circulated'*) from the bottom of the *bore-*

hole up to the surface by the *mud* system. It increases with the depth of the *borehole*, ranging up to several hours. See *circulation, bottoms up.*

LAGNIAPPE - Louisiana oil terminology, for 'a little something extra or additional' that is added to a trade to make it acceptable to the other party.

LANDMAN - An oil company employee or agent who negotiates the purchase of *leases*, cures defects in the *title* to property *leased*, and assists the oil company in complying with government regulations and reporting procedures. (Some U.S. universities offer a BA degree in Petroleum Land Management, PLM; there are over 12,000 members of the American Association of Petroleum Landmen.)

LAW OF CAPTURE - A legal concept on which oil and gas law in some states is based: since *petroleum* is liquid, and hence mobile, it is not owned until it is produced ('captured').

Oil and gas law in other states is based on the concept that *petroleum* is a mineral and is treated the same as solid minerals (such as coal).

Consider this analogy: During duck-hunting season, FARMER FRED shoots a duck as it flies over his wheat field. His shot hits the duck, wounding it, but the duck manages to continue to flap along, on its course. It eventually falls from the sky, dead, in LANDOWNER LARRY's front yard, several miles away. Who owns the duck?

(Oil and Gas) **LEASE** - A contract by which the owner of the *mineral rights* to a property conveys to another party, the exclusive right to explore for and develop minerals on the property, during a specified period of time. The conveying party is the 'lessor'; the recipient is the 'lessee'.

The terms of a *lease* are typically negotiated

between a *landman* representing an oil exploration company, and the owner of the *mineral rights* of a property: the *bonus, royalty,* and *delay rentals* to be paid to the lessor, and the *primary term,* and the *secondary term* of the *lease,* among various other terms.

The primary term of a *lease* is established thru negotiation between the *minerals owner* (lessor) and the oil company (lessor), and varies by region. In Oklahoma, three-year *leases* are the norm. In Texas, *leases* executed earlier in this century, with terms or 75 years or more, are not unheard of. These typically date back to an era when the U.S. oil industry was still a new and unknown phenomenon; in certain parts of the country; unsuspecting landowners may have been tricked or duped, or otherwise enticed into signing such extraordinarily long-term *leases.*

LEASE or **SUBLEASE** (classification as) - Any transaction in which the owner of operating rights in a property (for example, a *working interest*) assigns all or a portion of these rights to any other party, either for (1) no immediate consideration or (2) for cash (or equivalent), and retains a continuing nonoperating interest in production (such as an *override*). If AL owns a 100% *working interest* in a property, and assigns all of it to BOB, retaining a 5% *override,* the transaction would be a sub*lease.* See *sale.*

LEASE ACQUISITION COSTS (Leasehold Costs) - Include the following types of expenses: preliminary research of the lease area, geological and geophysical (G&G) expenses to evaluate the property prior to leasing, core-holes drilled to obtain geological samples, payment of lease bonus to landowner, broker commissions to acquire the lease, legal fees: to secure title to lease and or underlying mineral rights or fee simple ownership, as well as legal fees incurred in determining as to ownership of lease.[148]

LEASE HOUND - Someone who goes out and aggressively acquires oil and gas *leases* from the landowner, and then turns around and sells or trades them to an oil company planning to drill a well in the area.

LIFTING COSTS - The expenditures involved in lifting (pumping) oil from a producing *reservoir* in a well, up to the surface. Included in *lease* operating (production) expenses.

LIMESTONE - *Sedimentary* rock largely consisting of *calcite* (calcium carbonate). On a worldwide scale, limestone *reservoirs* probably contain more oil and gas reserves than all other types of *reservoir* rocks combined.

LIMITED PARTNER - In a *limited partnership*, a partner whose liability is limited to the amount of his investment in the partnership (plus any *assessments* and his share of undistributed partnership earnings). A limited partner would lose the limitations on his liability if he were to participate in the control or management of the partnership.

LIMITED PARTNERSHIP - A partnership in which the *general partner* manages the partnerships activities and is solely liable for them. The *limited partners* are liable only to the extent of their *contributions* (and *assessments*), and have only limited control over policy decisions. It is the most common vehicle for investing in oil and gas ventures (by investors who are not oil industry professionals).

LINER - From a layman's perspective, the same thing as casing, except that casing typically extends all the way to the surface. Liner is used to case-off the open-hole portion of the borehole, below the deepest casing point. The liner is suspended down into open-hole portion of the borehole from a hangar that is set in the cased portion of the hole.

LLC (LIMITED LIABILITY COMPANY) - See discussion in text and appendices.

LNG - Liquefied Natural Gas (Methane - CH_4 - that has been liquefied for transportation). 1 MCF is equivalent to 44 pounds of LNG. A ton of LNG is equivalent to 46 MCF natural gas.

LOE - *Lease Operating Expenses.*

LOG, LOGGING - (1) A record of information about the performance of some thing or some process. In the oil field a variety of logs are used in the drilling and *completion* of oil and gas wells. The driller keeps a 'driller's log', which records all mechanical operations undertaken during the drilling of the well. The *mud logger* keeps a daily 'mud log' recording all available information about the type of rock being penetrated and any possible hydrocarbon *shows.*
(2) Wireline logging is the process of lowering a sensing device down into the *borehole* on the end of an electric cable (a **line** made of **wire**). Wireline logs record measurements of various parameters providing information about the type of rock penetrated, the fluids contained in the rock, or the condition of the borehole. Parameters that can be measured include: diameter of the borehole (*caliper log*), electrical resistivity of the rock penetrated (resistivity or electric log,

E-log), density of the rock penetrated (density log and neutron log), acoustic properties of the rock penetrated (sonic or acoustic log), natural gamma-ray radiation of the rocks penetrated (gamma ray log, GR), inclination or dip of the rocks penetrated (*dipmeter log*), borehole temperature (temperature log).

Until fluids have been recovered, wireline logs may be the primary source of information on the quantity and quality of hydrocarbons in the rocks penetrated by the borehole. After drilling the well, the decision to spend additional money to attempt to *complete* the well to produce oil or gas is often based exclusively on the analysis of wireline log data.

LOST CIRCULATION - See *circulation*.

LPG - Liquefied petroleum gas is liquefied natural gas (that has been processed), and consists of propane (C_3H_8) and butane (C_4H_{10}) both of which are in the gas phase at standard temperature and pressure, but can be liquefied at manageable pressures, and hence can be conveniently transported in pressurized tanks and cylinders. Handy source of energy (especially in rural areas) where there are no natural gas pipeline distribution systems in place.

MAJOR (OIL COMPANY) - Traditionally used to refer to the integrated international companies ('the seven sisters'): British Petroleum, Exxon, Gulf, Mobil, Shell, Standard of California (Chevron), and Texaco. (Gulf has since been acquired by Chevron.) Today 'major' may be used more loosely to include any of the twenty or so largest integrated oil companies. See *Independent*.

MANAGEMENT FEE - In oil and gas *limited partnerships:* a fee paid by the *limited partners* to the *general partner* for services he provides in the management of the partnership (according to the partnership agreement). The amount of such fee is spelled out in the partnership agreement. It may be specified as a *guaranteed payment* equal to a percentage of *capital contributions,* or specified as a fee per well, a fee per *leased* property, etc.

MARGINAL WELL - An oil well producing 15 bopd or less. There are about 450,000 marginal wells in the U.S. (1994); they account for about 20% of crude oil produced in the lower 48 states (NPC data). See *stripper* well.

MAXIMUM EFFICIENT RATE (MER) - The experimentally determined flow-rate that permits optimum recovery of oil or gas from a well. Before a well is put on commercial production, different flow rates are tested for their effect on the composition of the oil-gas-water mixture produced, and on the *depletion* of natural *reservoir* pressure.

MCF - Thousands of cubic feet measured at standard temperature ($60°$ F) and pressure (14.65 psi). In the U.S., MCF is the most common unit of measure for volumes of *natural gas.* ('M' is the Roman numeral for 1,000; MMCF indicates millions of cubic feet). See *BCF.*

MEASUREMENT WHILE DRILLING (MWD) - The still-developing technology of measuring various *downhole* parameters during the drilling of a well (without having to pull the *drill string* out of the hole in order to run *wireline logs* or a directional survey, as in conventional drilling procedures). Data recorded by downhole sensors is transmitted up to the surface during the drilling process, by various electric or physical systems.

These MWD systems play a vital role in the new and developing technology of *horizontal drilling*.

METHANE - The simplest of the *hydrocarbon*s, CH_4. It is a colorless, odorless gas which generates about 1012 *Btu* of heat energy per 1,000 cubic feet of gas (*MCF*), when burned.

MIGRATION - The movement of oil and gas through layers of rock deep in the earth.

MINERAL ACRE - A full *mineral interest* in one *acre* of land.

MINERAL INTEREST ('MINERALS', 'MINERAL RIGHTS') - The ownership of all rights to gas, oil, or other minerals as they naturally occur in place, at or below the surface of a tract of land. Ownership of the minerals carries with it the right to make such reasonable use of the surface as may be necessary to explore for and produce the minerals. Only the mineral owner (or *fee owner*) may execute an oil or gas *lease* conveying his interest in a tract of land. See *severance*.

"MINING PARTNERSHIP" - Any co-ownership of minerals creates a partnership. So, in a general sense 'mining partnership' refers to any partnership which comes about as a result of co-ownership of minerals. The specific implications of the term relate to a particular type of partnership allowed under the Internal Revenue Code; such a partnership may elect not to be treated as a partnership under subchapter K of the Internal Revenue Code. To qualify, it must be formed for 1) the purpose of investment (as contrasted with the carrying on of a business) and 2) the joint production extraction and exploitation of a property (but not the selling of products extracted) and meet some other qualifications. This type of partnership is sometimes referred to as a 'mining partnership'.

MOL - "more or less".

MUD (DRILLING MUD) - A fluid mixture of clays, chemicals, and weighting materials suspended in freshwater, saltwater, or diesel oil. See *circulation*.
It (1) cools and lubricates the *drill bit*, (2) carries *cuttings* to the surface, (3) maintains the required pressure at the bottom of the hole, and (4) coats the inside of the *borehole* with a sort of plaster called 'mud cake' which helps prevent the walls from caving into the *open hole*.
'Mud weight' is the density of the mud measured in pounds per gallon (ppg). It can be controlled at the surface by the addition of various substances, such as barite (barium sulfate - $BaSO_4$), a heavy mineral 4.5 times as dense as water:

8.3 ppg	=	the density of water
15 ppg	=	2 x the density of water
20 ppg	=	2.4 x the density of water

The pressure exerted by the column of mud in the borehole must be greater than natural pressures in rocks likely to be encountered during drilling. Drilling with a mud weight that is too low could result in a *blowout*.

MUD ENGINEER - A technician responsible for proper maintenance of the *mud* system.

MUD LOGGER - A technician who uses chemical analysis, microscopic examination of the *cuttings*, and an assortment of electronic instruments to monitor the *mud* system for possible indications of *hydrocarbons* ('*shows*'). See *log*.

MULLET - Don't you be one! (An unflattering reference to someone willing to entertain putting money in an oil and gas venture without actually understanding the specifics of the deal; a sucker.) The term derives from Louisiana bayou country. Mullet is the common name for a species of red fish which is the primary diet of alligators, hence the obvious analogy: "mullet is to alligators as naive investors are to unscrupulous con-men" (who can always be found promoting fraudulent deals in all manner of investment schemes ... including oil and gas ventures).

MULTIPLE COMPLETION - See *dual completion.*

MWD - Original meaning was 'measured well depth' - referring to the actual depth in a well measured from the Kelly bushing. Nowadays: See *measurement while drilling.*

NATURAL GAS - A mixture of gaseous *hydrocarbons* formed naturally, in the earth. Most natural gases contain *methane* as the primary component, mixed with ethane C_2H_6, propane C_3H_8, butane C_4H_{10}, pentane C_5H_{12}, and/or hexane C_6H_{14}. Non-hydrocarbon gases such as carbon dioxide, helium, nitrogen, and hydrogen sulfide may also be present.

NET ACRES - See *gross acres.*

NET PAY (NET FEET OF PAY) - The aggregate thickness (in feet) of the *pay zone* likely to contribute to production from a well. The footage count excludes portions of the *reservoir* having *porosity* lower than a specified cutoff value (5%, for example) and having water *saturation* greater than a specified cutoff value (45%, for example). Cutoff values are established on the basis of historical production data in the same or a similar *reservoir,* in the same or a similar geologic setting.

NET PROFITS INTEREST - A share of gross production from a property that is *carved out* of a *working interest,* and is figured as a function of net profits from operation of the property.
Depending on the specifics of the arrangement, a net profits interest might be required to bear certain expenses of development and operations, but would neither be obligated to advance expenses nor liable for losses (as in the case of the *working interest*).

NRI - See *net revenue interest.*

NET REVENUE INTEREST (NRI) - The percentage of revenues due an interest holder in a property, net of royalties or other burdens on the property. Assume LANDOWNER *leases* his *mineral rights* to OILMAN. LANDOWNER retains a *royalty* of 1/8 (= 12.5%); his net revenue interest is 12.5%. OILMAN'S net revenue interest would be 87.5% (= 100% - 12.5%).

NET WELLS - See *gross wells.*

NGL (Natural Gas Liquids) - Liquid hydrocarbons separated from produced natural gas, generally consisting of propane (C_3H_5) and heavier hydrocarbons. When hydrocarbons lighter than propane are recovered in liquid phase, they may also be considered as 'natual gas liquids'.

NO. 2 FUEL OIL - Competes with natural gas as a heating fuel. A bit heavier and thicker than diesel fuel, widely used in the northeast for residential heating. Many commercial and industrial consumers are organized to switch back and forth between natural gas and no. 2 fuel oil, depending on availability and price.

NO. 6 FUEL OIL - A heavy fuel oil, generally cheaper

than No. 2 Fuel Oil and natural gas, but requires special handling due to low viscosity, etc.

OFFERING MEMORANDUM - A legal document provided to potential investors in a venture (such as an oil and gas *limited partnership*), describing the terms under which the investment is being offered.

OFFSET WELL - A well drilled on the next drilling and spacing unit adjacent to a producing well, as in 'the north offset to the Unruh #1 well'.

OIL COLUMN - The vertical height (thickness) of an oil accumulation above the oil-water contact. In commercial oil fields, oil columns can range from 5 feet to (rarely!) several hundred feet. See *gas column.*

OIL GRAVITY - The density of liquid *hydrocarbons,* generally measured in degrees API (American Petroleum Institute). Degrees API are inversely related to specific gravity: Degrees API = 141.5/Sp Gr @ 60° F minus 131.5
The lighter the oil the higher the API gravity: A tar with an API gravity of 8° API would be heavier than water; motor lubricating oil is typically about 26° API; gasoline is about 55° API.

OIL SHALE - a sedimentary rock, a shale, with a high organic content. It is generally thought that oil shales may represent immature oil source rock (from which the oil gas not been completely expelled); the shale may not contain the specific types of clay minerals that are thought to effect expulsion, or it may not have been subjected to adequate temperatures and pressures for sufficient periods of geologic time.

OPEN HOLE - Refers to a *borehole*, or the portion of a *borehole*, in which *casing* has not been set. See *cased* hole.

OPERATOR - The *working-interest* owner responsible for the drilling, *completion* and production operations of a well, and the physical maintenance of the *leased* property. Responsibilities of the operator and other *working-interest* owners are enumerated in the *joint operating agreement*.

ORGANIZATION COSTS - Direct costs incurred in the creation of a new business organization such as an oil and gas limited partnership: legal and accounting fees, organizational meetings, printing costs. In the calculation of partnership income, these are *amortizable capital* expenditures, generally *amortized* by the partnership over a period of 60 months from the start-up of the business.

OVERRIDING ROYALTY ('OVERRIDE', 'ORRI') - A revenue interest in oil and gas, created out of a *working interest*. Like the lessor's royalty, it entitles the owner to a share of the proceeds from gross production, free of any operating or production costs (but net of state production and *severance* taxes). It terminates when the *lease* expires. See *royalty*.

PACKER - A flexible rubber sleeve that is part of a special joint of pipe (tool). During certain (non-drilling) activities, the tool may be added to (inserted in) the *drill string*. When the *drill string* is lowered into the *borehole*, the packer can be expanded (from operations at the surface), to temporarily block off a portion of the *annulus* of the borehole (as may be done during *drill stem tests* or *squeezing* operations.

PAD* Districts

* Petroleum Admisitration for Defense

PAD - Refers to the "Petroleum Administration for Defense", which groups the 50 states into five regional districts for administrative and reporting purposes.

PAY ZONE or **PAY** - An interval of rock, from which oil or gas is expected to be produced in commercial quantities.

PAYOUT - In the case of an oil and gas investment, the point at which costs of exploration and development (or amount of the investment) are recouped out of net revenues received from production.

In many oil and gas *limited partnerships* (and standard deals within the oil industry) there may be a reallocation of revenues or cash flow among the participants in the investment, after payout has been reached.

PERFORATING GUN - An instrument lowered at the end of a *wireline* into a *cased well*. It contains explosive charges that can be electronically detonated from the surface. When it is at the level of the *pay zone*, the bullets (or 'shaped charges') are shot into the *reservoir* rock, piercing the *casing* (and surrounding cement sheath). The resulting holes allow rock fluids to flow from the *pay zone* into the *borehole*.

PERMEABILITY - The measurable capacity of a rock to allow a fluid to flow through it. Along with *porosity*, it is one of the two most critical properties of the reservoir rock. To be commercially producible, oil or gas must be able to flow from the *reservoir* rock into the well. *See reservoir.*

PETROLEUM - Crude oil. Naturally occurring liquid *hydrocarbons* from which gasoline, kerosene, and countless other 'petrochemicals' are produced. Non-hydrocarbon compounds (often containing sulfur and nitrogen) may also be present as impurities. In the broadest sense, petroleum refers to all naturally occurring *hydrocarbons*, including *oil, natural gas, condensate*, and their derived products.

PETROLEUM ENGINEER - A term including three areas of specialization: DRILLING engineers specialize in the drilling, workover, and *completion* operations; PRODUCTION engineers specialize in studying a well's characteristics and using various chemical and mechanical procedures to maximize the recovery from the well; RESERVOIR engineers design and execute the planned development of a *reservoir*. Many U.S. universities offer BS, MS, and PhD degrees in petroleum engineering; the Society of Petroleum Engineers has over 50,000 members.

PETROLEUM GEOLOGIST - A geologist who specializes in the exploration for, and production of, petroleum. Many U.S. universities have departments which offer BS, MS, and PhD degrees in petroleum geology; the American Association of Petroleum Geologists has about 33,000 members.

PLAY - A geographical trend of one or more geo-logically-related prospects.

PLUG - An object (usually of cast iron or cement) set in a *borehole* to block the passage of fluids. During various operations in the *completion* or the *abandonment* of a well, it may be necessary to isolate certain sections of the well. Some plugs can be drilled through ('drilled out') after the operation is completed.

PLUG BACK - To block off the lower section of the *borehole* by setting a *plug*, in order to perform operations in the upper part of the hole.

PLUGGED & ABANDONED (P&A) - This expression refers to setting cement plugs in an unsuccessful well (a 'dry hole') or a depleted well, before *abandoning* the well.

Ownership of a well includes a potential plugging liability. In 1995, the Oklahoma Corporation Commission spent and average of about $4500. per well to plug 69 wells for which no responsible party could be found to pay the plugging costs. (During the same period, there were more than 122,000 producing wells in the state.)

POOLING - When individual tracts of land are smaller than the *spacing unit*, the separately owned *working interests* (of these tracts) may be brought together ('pooled') in order to obtain a drilling permit.

In states where pooling of separately held *working interests* is required ('compulsory pooling' or 'forced pooling' – notably Oklahoma and Arkansas):

in order to obtain a drilling permit, any *working-interest* owner can initiate a forced pooling order.
A force-pooled *working-interest* owner typically has 3 options: (1) to participate in the well by paying his proportionate share of the costs, (2) to *farmout* his interest to the pooling party, or (3) to sell or *sublease* his interest in the proposed well to a third party.

POOR-BOY - To 'poor-boy' a well means to try to make do without adequate financing: to borrow money, sell interests, make trades, borrow equipment, or otherwise somehow get hold of enough money or credit, to get the well drilled.

POROSITY - The percentage (by volume) of holes or voids in a rock. Commercially productive *reservoir* rocks typically have porosities ranging from about 5% - 35%. The higher the porosity, the more oil or gas that can be contained in the pore spaces, the better the quality of the *reservoir* rock.

PRESENT NET VALUE - The present value of the dollars (income, or stream of income) to be received at some specified time in the future, discounted back to the present at a specified discount rate.

PRIMARY RECOVERY - Production in which oil moves from the *reservoir*, into the *wellbore*, under naturally occurring *reservoir* pressure.

· In a flowing well, the *reservoir* pressure is great enough to force the oil up to the surface.

· In a pumping well, oil is *artificially lifted* to the surface by pumping equipment.

(In reality, these are the same well but at different stages in its productive lifetime.)

PRIMARY TERM - The basic period of time during which a *lease* is in effect. It commonly ranges from 6 months to more than 10 years, but is perhaps most commonly 3 - 5 years. One of the negotiable provisions of a *lease.* See *secondary term.*

PRIVATE PLACEMENT OFFERING - A *securities* (investment) offering not intended for the general public. By meeting certain criteria, such an offering may qualify for exemptions from registration with (1) the Securities and Exchange Commission of the Federal government and/or (2) the *securities*-regulating agencies of the various State governments involved. See *public offering.*

PRODUCTION (OIL) PAYMENT - A specified share of gross production from a property that may be *carved out* of a *working interest,* or *retained* by the transferor of a *working interest.* It is limited: (1) to a specified period of time, (2) until a specified amount of money is received, or (3) until a specified quantity of minerals has been received (in which case it may be referred to as a 'volumetric production payment' or VPP).

PROPPANT, PROPPING AGENT - See *fracturing.*

PROSPECT - The hypothesis that a naturally occurring, commercially exploitable accumulation of oil or gas exists, at a clearly defined underground location. It is described by one or more geologic maps. A single well should be sufficient to test the hypothesis. Surface area of a prospect could range from a 10-acre tract large enough for only a single well, to a tract covering many tens of square miles and requiring dozens of wells to fully develop its reserves.

Prospects are typically named for some nearby geographic or geologic feature, but the name may simply reflect the whim of the moment. A well is commonly named for the *owner of the lease* on which it is drilled. ("The Batholomew Smedley No. 1 was drilled on the Bear Creek prospect, last year.")

PUBLIC OFFERING - A *securities* (investment) offering intended for sale to the general public. It must be registered with (1) the Securities and Exchange Commission of the Federal government and (2) the *securities*-regulating agencies of the various States in which it will be offered. See *private placement.*

QUITCLAIM DEED - A document by which one party (grantor) conveys *title* to a property, by giving up any claim which he may have to *title* (although he does not profess that his claim is necessarily valid). See *deed.*

RECAPTURE - Repayment to the Federal government of tax benefits (such as income tax *deductions* or *tax credits*) that may become necessary upon a development that is contrary to the assumptions on which the tax benefits were originally based.

Assume that an investor in an oil and gas property enjoyed the benefit of *intangible drilling cost deductions* against his *gross income.* If he later sells the property at a gain, some of those *deductions* may be subject to recapture.

RE-ENTRY - Assume that a well was *abandoned,* but subsequent drilling and production in the area suggests that a potential pay zone in the well was missed or 'passed over'. Instead of drilling a second well to evaluate the *zone of interest,* a company might drill out the cement abandonment *plugs* in the original *borehole* to test the potential zone. Such a 're-entry' can be a rather risky operation, but

373

if successful, the cost may be much less than drilling a new offsetting well.

RESERVES - The amount of oil or gas in a *reservoir* currently available for production, usually described as *barrels* of oil, or *MCF* (thousands of cubic feet) of gas, attributable to a well, to a property, or to an entire field. The term should always be qualified by an adjective, since there are many ways of estimating the reserves.
'Reserves in place' describes the amount of oil or gas physically contained in the *reservoir*. The amount of reserves that can actually be gotten out of the ground (can be recovered) using traditional technology may only be 25% to 30% of the reserves in place.
'Recoverable reserves' is an estimate of the amount of oil or gas that can be produced from the *reservoir* in the future. (No one can know what the actual recoverable reserves are until after they have been produced.)
PROVED RESERVES: reserves that are considered to be recoverable under existing technology and economic conditions (based on available geologic and engineering data).
Proved developed producing reserves (PDP; PD): proved reserves recoverable from currently completed intervals in existing wells using existing facilities. These are the numbers a banker might want to see in considering an application for a loan.
Proved developed non-producing (PDNP) include Proved developed shut-in (PDSI) and Proved developed behind pipe reserves: (PDBP). 'Behind pipe reserves' are in zones behind the casing (pipe) in an existing well (which could be produced if the well were re-completed in those zones).

374

Proved undeveloped reserves (PUD): reserves which could be produced, but drilling new wells, deepening existing wells, or secondary recovery methods would be required.

UNPROVED RESERVES: Estimates of recoverable reserves classified as 'probable future reserves' (PROB) and 'possible future reserves' (POSS) may include a wide variety of geologic and engineering assumptions. Estimates of 'undiscovered recoverable reserves' refer to reserves outside of known accumulations and are, at best, a guess developed from geologic and statistical game theory. See *EUR.*

RESERVOIR - Any rock having enough *porosity* and *permeability* to contain appreciable *hydrocarbons.* Most commercial reservoirs are in *sandstone* and *limestone* (limestone/dolomite), rarely in shale or igneous rock.

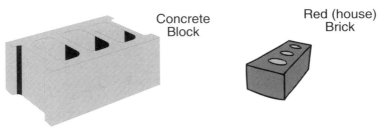
Concrete Block

Red (house) Brick

For relative characteristics of reservoir rocks, consider that concrete block used in building construction might typically have a porosity of 20% and a permeability of 2-5 darcies (making it potentially a very good reservoir rock under the kinds of temperature and pressure common at depths of 10,000 feet). Red brick however, might have a porosity nearer to 5% and a permeability of 25 millidarcies (making it a very poor to noncommercial potential reservoir rock at most temperature and pressure regimes). Of course if either the concrete block or the red brick happened to be extensively fractured, this could vastly improve permeability (and to some extent, porosity), and hence it's quality as a potential reservoir rock.

RESIDUE GAS - Natural gas that comes out of a gas processing plant after natural gas liquids and impurities have been removed.

(Electrical) **RESISTIVITY** - The ability of a substance to impede the flow of electricity through it. Variations in the resistivity of different rocks depends largely on the fluids contained in the pores of the rocks: pure oil, pure gas, and fresh water each have very high resistivity, while salt water can have very low resistivity. Most dry rocks do not conduct electricity (and thus have infinitely high resistivity).

RETAINED INTEREST - A fractional portion of a revenue interest, that is kept by the owner of the whole revenue interest, when he transfers (conveys) the balance of the revenue interest to another party. (Retained interest represents a subset of *carved out* interest.) See *carved out* interest.

REVERSIONARY INTEREST - An interest in a well or property that becomes effective at a specified time in the future or on the occurrence of a specified future event. See *back-in*.

RISK - Literally: 'the possibility of loss or injury'. In oil exploration, a level of uncertainty is associated with the various possible outcomes of the undertaking. Risk usually refers to a numerical estimate of the likelihood of the occurrence of these various possible outcomes.

Drilling a well in an area where: (1) many wells have already been drilled, and (2) the results of previous drilling have been thoroughly analyzed and evaluated, can be a relatively low-risk proposition:

- The technology for drilling wells in this area has already been established.
- There are numerical data from which it is possible to estimate the statistical probability of finding oil or gas.
- Production statistics allow estimates of reserves per successful well.
- Most importantly, there are abundant geologic data from which to synthesize a scientific geologic understanding of the subsurface (which is the key to beating the purely numerical odds of finding oil and gas by random selection of drilling locations).

By contrast, drilling a well at the South Pole would be a very high-risk proposition, indeed.

ROUGHNECK - One of the two or three field-hands on the derrick floor during drilling operations, whose job revolves around breaking out the *drill pipe*, making-up connections, and stacking *drill pipe*. It is a tough, physically demanding, and often dangerous job (not for lightweights or sissies). See *weevil*.

ROUSTABOUT - A semiskilled hand who looks after producing wells and production facilities. The name reflects the great diversity of general maintenance jobs that must be done. The position is frequently offered to former *roughnecks*, who due to age or injury, may no longer be fit for the strenuous work on a *drilling rig* during drilling operations.

ROYALTY - A right to oil and gas (or other minerals) as they naturally occur in place. It entitles the owner to a specified share of oil and gas produced from a property, but bears no costs or responsibility (or rights) for the development of the property. Although he does not pay operating and production expenses the royalty owner does pay state *severance tax* (is subject to Federal income tax); depending on the provisions of the *lease*, he may also pay handling costs or costs required to get the product from the wellhead to a pipeline connection or refinery.

If the *minerals owner leases* his land and retains a 1/8 royalty, he is entitled to receive 1/8 of the gross production from that property, at no cost to himself (either in kind or in value, as agreed upon in negotiation of the *lease*).

In some foreign countries a royalty interest may consist, not of the right to a specified fractional share of oil and gas produced from a property (as in the U.S.), but merely of a claim against the *working interest* owner for oil and gas produced. In such foreign jurisdictions, the royalty owner's claim may represent only one claim among numerous contractual claims against the working interest owner.

ROYALTY ACRE - The (*mineral owner's*) *royalty* on one *acre* of *leased* land.

SALE (classification as) - When cash (or equivalent) is received as consideration, three types of transactions might be classified as a sale:
- the owner of any kind of oil and gas interest assigns all of his interest to another party (or assigns a fractional part and retains a fractional part of that same identical interest),
- the owner of a *working interest* assigns a

378

OIL & GAS INTERESTS, TRANSACTIONS:
Lease/Sublease or Sale/Exchange? (For Federal Income Tax Purposes)

	LEASE / SUBLEASE	SALE / EXCHANGE EXAMPLES		
	1	2	3	4
Original interest held:	operating working interest, **A**	working interest interest, **C**	any type of oil & gas interest, **D**	any type of oil & gas
Interest that is transferred ('assigned'):	all or part of **A**	any type of continuing, non-operation interest	all or a fractional part of **C**, (identical to **C**,	entire interest **D** or a continuing interest in **D** except as to quantity)
Interest that is retained:	non-operating interest in production, **B**	working interest	zero, or the remaining fractional part of **C**, (identical to **C** except as to quantity)	nothing, or a non-continuing interest in **D**
Consideration:	no immediate consideration, cash, cash equivalent or property of unlike kind	cash, cash equivalent, or property of unlike kind	cash, cash equivalent, or property of unlike kind	cash, cash equivalent, or property of unlike kind

EXAMPLES OF POSSIBLE INTERESTS

A: mineral rights or operating working interest.

B: royalty, non-operating working interest, overriding royalty.

C, D: mineral rights, royalty, working interest, overriding royalty, net profits interest, production payment, etc.

(By definition, a production payment is limited by time, amount of cash received, or amount of mineral produced, and is thus a non-continuing interest.)

Source: **1984 Income Taxation of Natural Resources.** See current edition, and also current edition of: **Arthur Young's Oil & Gas Federal Income Taxation.**

Sale - Lease - Sub-lease

continuing nonoperating interest (such as an *override*), but retains the *working interest,*
- the owner of any type of continuing oil and gas interest, assigns that interest, and retains a non-continuing interest in production (a *production payment*).

Classification of the transfer of oil and gas interests as a sale, or as a *lease* or sub*lease,* can have significant economic consequences both to the transferor (affecting the rate at which his income is taxed — ordinary rates or capital gains rates), and to the transferee (affecting his entitlement to *depletion allowance* and the methods by which it may be calculated — percentage *depletion* or cost *depletion*).

SAND LINE - A wire cable used on a swabbing unit to pull swabs from a well.

SANDSTONE - Rock composed mainly of sand-sized particles or fragments of the mineral quartz. Individual grains often occur naturally "glued" together by the mineral *calcite.* Because quartz grains are rigid, the fabric of the rock will withstand tremendous pressures, without being compacted. In this sense, sandstone is very different from *shale.*

SATURATION - (1) Water-Saturation: the fluid contained in the pores of an oil and gas reservoir rock usually consists of a mixture of water plus oil and/or gas. Water-saturation is the percent of water contained in this mixture. A low water-saturation (20% for example) implies a high concentration of hydrocarbons (approximately 100 - 20 = 80%) and suggests that the rock will produce oil or gas. A high water-saturation (greater than 85%) implies that the rock is likely to produce only water.

(2) In a *reservoir* containing oil, the crude oil is said to be saturated when it contains as much dissolved *natural gas* as is physically possible. Any excess gas would accumulate above the oil as a *gas cap*.

SECONDARY RECOVERY - Production in which oil will no longer move from the *reservoir,* into the *wellbore,* under naturally occurring *reservoir* pressure. After *primary recovery* operations have taken their course, various operations may be undertaken to increase the amount of oil that can be produced.

This second stage consists of efforts to increase production by addressing the condition of the *reservoir.* Typical operations involve forcing gas ('*gas injection*'), or water ('water flooding') into the *reservoir.* This serves to repressurize the *reservoir,* which allows recovery of more oil than would be possible from *primary recovery.*

Tertiary (third stage) recovery includes further efforts to recover additional oil from the *reservoir,* by altering the physical characteristics of the oil itself - reducing viscosity, or reducing surface tension. These may be largely experimental procedures, like the injection of CO_2, detergent-like fluids, steam, or chemically treated water into the reservoir; or injecting air (oxygen) into the reservoir and burning some of the oil in place, to raise the temperature of the oil and improve its ability to flow.

SECONDARY TERM - The period of time that a *lease* is automatically extended beyond the *primary term,* as long as there is active drilling or production. See *primary term, lease.*

SECTION - A square tract of land having an area of one square mile (= 640 *acres*). There are 36 sections in a *township*.

SECURITIES - Commonly thought of as stocks and bonds., but as defined by the Securities Act of 1933, securities include any certificate of interest or participation in any profit sharing agreement, investment contract, or fractional undivided interest in oil, gas, or other mineral rights.

SECURITIES ACT OF 1933 - Establishes requirements for the disclosure of information for any interstate offering and sale of *securities*.

SECURITIES EXCHANGE ACT OF 1934 Established the Securities and Exchange Commission which regulates the activities of *securities* markets.

SEDIMENTARY ROCK - Rock that is naturally formed from fragments of other rocks. These fragments result from mechanical abrasion ('weathering') of preexisting rock, and are transported by water, ice, and air. Sedimentary rocks that are important in terms of petroleum include *sandstones* and *limestones*, which are often *reservoir* rocks, and *shale* which may be a *source rock*.

SEISMIC SURVEYING - The procedure of sending pulses of sound from the surface, down into the earth, and recording the echoes reflected back to he surface. By making assumptions about the speed at which sound travels through the various layers of rock, it is possible to estimate the depth to the reflecting surface. It then becomes possible to infer the structure of rocks deep below the earth's surface.

SELLING EXPENSES - Expenses incurred in marketing interests in *securities* (and commonly paid out of the investor's *capital* investment).

SEVERANCE - The owner of all rights to a tract of land (the *fee simple* owner) can sever the rights to his land (vertically or horizontally). In horizontal severance, for example, if he chooses to sell the *mineral rights*, two distinct estates are created: the *surface rights* to the tract of land and the *mineral rights* to the same tract. The two estates may change hands independently of each other. Severed *mineral rights* may be restricted as to mineral type, or limited by depth, (in which case the landowner retains the rights to minerals other than those severed, and to depth intervals other than those severed).

SEVERANCE TAX - A tax paid to the state government by producers of oil or gas in the state. It may be specified either as a percent of the oil or gas taken ('severed') from the earth, or as a dollar amount per *barrel* of oil or per thousand feet of gas (*MCF*) produced (also called 'production tax'). Please see Appendix A.

SHALE - A type of rock composed of common clay or mud. When clay is compacted under great pressure and temperature deep in the earth, water contained in the clay is expelled, and clay turns into shale.

SHALE SHAKER - A vibrating screen or sieve (slightly inclined from the horizontal) that strains *cuttings* out of the *mud* before the *mud* is pumped back down into the *borehole* (in the manner that seeds can be strained out of freshly-squeezed orange juice). See *circulation*.

SHARING ARRANGEMENT - (1) Among oilmen: an arrangement whereby a party contributes to the acquisition, or exploration and development, of an oil and gas property, and receives as compensation, a fractional interest in that property. (2) In a *limited partnership* the basis or formula for the allocation of costs and revenues between the *limited partners* and the *general partner*.

SHOW - An indication of oil or gas observed and recorded during the drilling of a well. Based on experience, a geologist would rate a show as 'good', 'fair', or 'poor', etc.

"SHRINKAGE" - In the case of natural gas: the loss in volume of a quantity of natural gas as it moves from the wellhead along the path of processing at the wellhead, gathering, more processing, and transportation to the purchaser. Because it is more cost efficient to negotiate and agree on shrinkage rates in advance, than it is to make physical measurements along the way and price adjustments after the fact, a shrinkage factor is commonly included in gas sales contracts.
In the case of oil: the decrease in the volume of the produced liquid due to 1) the release of solution gas, 2) removal of bottom sediment and water (BS&W) and 3) contraction resulting from a change in temperature of the oil. It can account for as much as 5-10% of the volume of the oil produced.

SHUT-IN - To stop a producing oil and gas well from producing.

SHUT-IN ROYALTY - A special type of *royalty* negotiated in the *leasing* of a property. It normally pertains to gas production. If a commercially producible gas well is shut-in due to the lack of a gas market, the *lease* will remain in effect so long as the *working-interest* owner (lessee) pays the specified shut-in *royalty* to the *mineral-rights* owner (lessor).

SIDE TRACK - The purpose of a side track is to achieve a different *buttonhole* location. For example: when *fishing* operations have been unable to recover an object in the hole that prevents drilling ahead, the borehole can often be drilled around the obstacle in the original hole. This 'deviated' hole is called the side track hole. Although it is somewhat risky, drilling a side track hole may be much less costly than starting a new *borehole* from the surface. See *whipstock*.

SLANT HOLE - See *directional drilling*.

SLIPS - A heavy wedged-shaped tool handled by two roustabouts that is placed around the drillstring at the derrick floor, to prevent the entire drill string from dropping (slipping) down into the borehole.

SOLUTION GAS - *Natural gas* that is dissolved in the *crude oil* in a *reservoir*. It comes out of solution as pressure is reduced when the oil is produced and flows up to the surface (the way CO_2 bubbles out of a freshly opened can of soda pop).

SOUR CRUDE, SOUR GAS - Oil or natural gas containing sulfur compounds, notably hydrogen sulfide (H_2S) a poisonous gas. When dissolved in water, H_2S forms a weak solution of sulfuric acid. Over time, this can corrode and destroy metal pipes and equipment. Sweet crude and sweet gas do not contain these sulfur compounds, are less damaging to equipment, and hence bring a better price than sour crude and sour gas.

SOURCE ROCK - *Sedimentary* rock, usually *shale* (or *limestone*) containing organic carbon (plant and animal remains) in concentrations as high as 5-10% (TOC - total organic carbon) by weight. After being subjected to high temperatures and pressures during millions of years deep in the earth, the organic material is transformed to liquid or gaseous *hydrocarbons* (which make up *petroleum*). Usually these *hydrocarbons* are (naturally) expelled from the source rock, flowing into nearby *porous* rocks. Because of their natural buoyancy with respect to water, they tend to *migrate* upward, to emerge at the surface as an oil or gas seep unless they become trapped along the way. Oil and gas fields are accumulations of such trapped hydrocarbons.

Some oil shales are believed to represent source rocks in which oil was formed, but from which it was never expelled.

SPACING UNIT - The size (surface area) of a parcel of land on which only one producing well is permitted to be drilled to a specific *reservoir*. It is intended that the single well should drain all (or nearly all) of the recoverable oil or gas from that part of the *reservoir* that lies within the spacing unit. State agencies regulate the size of the spacing unit for different *reservoirs*, to facilitate efficient exploitation of oil and gas from them.

Oil's ability to flow, increases with temperature (which increases with depth). Gas flows more readily than oil. The size of the spacing unit for a particular *reservoir* is set according to its depth and production characteristics, and whether the production is oil or gas.

'Increased density' means the spacing unit is reduced: 2 wells (instead of one) per 640 *acres*, amounts to 1 well per 320 *acres*.

SPOTTING - The mechanical procedure of controlling the circulation in a well in such a way that material (such as cement) put in the mud system at the surface, is placed ('spotted') at a desired depth interval in the borehole - such as opposite a zone of lost circulation, etc.

SPOT MARKET - A short-term contract (typically 30 days) for the sale or purchase of a specified quantity of oil or gas at a specified price.

SPUD - To spud a well means to start the initial drilling operations.

SQUEEZE - The procedure of pumping a slurry of *cement* into a particular space in the *borehole* (often the *annulus* between the *borehole* and the *casing*), so that the *cement* will solidify to form a seal.

STOCK TANK BARREL (STB) - A barrel of oil at the earth's surface. Recoverable oil is measured in stock tank barrels. Due to the complex interplay between pressure and temperature, the volume of a mixture of oil and gas at reservoir conditions is usually different from the volume of the same amount of the mixture at the surface. (In the early days oil from a new discovery was sometimes collected in the **tank**s or ponds on a farm that hold water for live**stock**.)

STRIPPER OIL WELL - An oil well capable of producing no more than 10 *barrels* of oil per day. (At $20/*barrel*, such a well could produce gross revenues of as much as $200 per day).

In 1995, aggregate production from stripper wells accounted for 14% of total U.S. oil production. The average stripper oil well produced 2.1 BOPD with gross revenues averaging about $33.00 per well per day.

A STRIPPER GAS WELL is a well that produces an average of less than 60,000 cubic feet of gas per day, measured over a 90-day period. (At $2.00/*MCF* such a well could produce gross revenues of as much as $120 per day).

In 1995, aggregate production from stripper gas wells accounted for about 5% of total U.S. gas production. The average stripper gas well produced about 16 MCFPD, with gross revenues averaging about $24.00 per well per day.

There were about 434,000 stripper oil wells and 162,000 stripper gas wells producing in the U.S. during 1995. A large portion of these stripper oil wells represent secondary recovery oil production.

SUBSCRIPTION - The manner by which an investor participates in a *limited partnership* through investment.

SUBLEASE - See *lease* and *sale*.

SUPERVISORY FEE - Analogous to a *management fee* in an oil and gas *limited partnership*, it is paid by the partnership to the *general partner* for direct supervision of mechanical operations at the well site.

SURFACE RIGHTS - Surface ownership of a tract of land from which the *mineral rights* have been severed. Surface rights include the same full use and enjoyment rights that belong to *fee simple* ownership, except that surface possession is subject to the *mineral* owners right of access to the land for the purpose of extracting his minerals.

SWAB - A hollow rubber cylinder with a flap (check valve) on the bottom surface. It is lowered into a well, below the fluid level in the well. This opens the check valve allowing fluid into the cylinder. The check valve flap closes as the swab is pulled back up, lifting oil to the surface.

SWEET CRUDE/GAS - See *sour crude*.

SYNDICATION EXPENSES - Expenditures incurred by a partnership in connection with issuing and marketing its interests to investors: legal fees of the issuer for *securities* and tax advice, accounting fees for audits and other representations included in the offering memorandum, registration (with the Securities and Exchange Commission of the Federal government and with pertinent state government agencies), brokerage fees, and printing costs of the offering memorandum and various promotional materials. They are non-*amortizable capital expenditures*.

TAILGATE - The outlet of a natural gas processing plant where the residue gas is discharged (into a transmission pipeline) after processing is complete.

TAKEOFF - A listing and description of documents required to establish title to a given piece of property. Typically prepared by an abstract company, it costs much less than a full-blown abstract of title. When prepared by a landman, basically the same listing may be called a 'run sheet'.

TAKE-OR-PAY CONTRACT - A (long-term) contract between a gas producer and a gas purchaser. The purchaser agrees to purchase (to 'take') a minimum annual amount of gas from the producer, or to 'pay' the producer for the minimum amount, even if the gas is not 'taken'.
In contrast, a market–out clause releases the purchaser from his obligation to 'take' gas, if there is no market for it.

TAR SAND - A sandstone in which the spaces between grains are filled with a highly *viscous* tar. [It is generally assumed that a less *viscous,* flowable oil or oil/gas mixture originally *migrated* into the sand; the gas and the lighter, more volatile hydrocarbons subsequently escaped (into the atmosphere?); the residual tar is what was left behind.]

TAX PREFERENCE ITEMS - Certain items of income, or special *deductions* from *gross income* which are given favored treatment under Federal tax law. If the use of tax preference items reduces a taxpayer's taxable income below specified levels, this may give rise to *alternative minimum tax.*

TAX LIABILITY - See *taxes due.*

TAXABLE INCOME - See *taxes due.*

TAXES DUE (TAXES PAYABLE):

GROSS INCOME
<u>– Adjustments</u> (IRA contribution, alimony paid, moving expenses, etc.)

ADJUSTED GROSS INCOME
<u>– Deductions and Exemptions</u>

Taxable Income x Tax Rate   = Tax Liability
                                 <u>– Tax Credits</u>
                                 Taxes Due (Payable)

Note:
GROSS INCOME is virtually all of your income.
ADJUSTED GROSS INCOME is Gross Income minus certain adjustments such as IRA contribution, alimony, moving expenses.
TAXABLE INCOME is Adjusted Gross Income minus deductions and exemptions.
DEDUCTIONS - see elsewhere in this glossary.
EXEMPTIONS - A set dollar amount (currently $2,450.) subtracted for you and each dependent.

TERTIARY RECOVERY - See *secondary recovery.*

TCF - Trillion cubic feet. See *MCF, BCF.*

"THIRD FOR A QUARTER" - Sometimes also
known as a 'quarter for a third'. A widely used
arrangement for promoting an oil deal to another party. Involves *carried interests, working
interests*. Please refer to discussion in text.

TIGHT HOLE - A drilling well about which the
operator (for competitive reasons) refuses to
divulge any information, except the type of information that is absolutely required by government
regulating agencies (such as the drilling location).

TIGHT ROCK ('TITE') - Potential *reservoir* rock
whose *porosity* and *permeability* turn out to be
insufficient for commercial production of oil or gas.

TIME VALUE OF MONEY - The concept that a
dollar in hand today is worth more than a dollar
that will be received in some future year.

TITLE - The combination of factors that, together,
constitute legal ownership of a property.

TITLE OPINION - An evaluation of the quality of
title to a specific tract of land, written by a title
expert (often an attorney) based on his examination of the abstract of title and other related
documents. The drilling of a well calls for a
drilling (or drill site) title opinion for the specific
tract (spacing unit) to be drilled; it gives the
operator (and working interest owners) reasonable certainty that mineral rights they acquired
are, indeed, valid for the spacing unit in which
the well they are about to drill is located, etc.
Once the well is completed as a producer, a **division order title opinion** is called for. It provides
legal opinion as to the status of the land, royalty,
and working interest ownership of the completed well, and forms the basis on which the
distribution of all production revenues is based.

TOOL PUSHER - The supervisor of drilling rig operations. Also called 'drilling foreman' or 'rig superintendent'.

TOP LEASE - The (conditional) right to automatically lease mineral rights that are already leased to someone else under a preexisting recorded lease, if the preexisting lease expires. The top *lease* would become an effective lease only if and when the existing *lease* expires (or is terminated). In the typical case, the term on the preexisting lease is approaching expiration, and the lessee (is holding on to the lease) but is reluctant or unable to spud a well before it expires.

TOTAL DEPTH (TD) - The maximum depth of a *borehole.* Before the well has been drilled to its planned total depth, the 'current TD' changes from day to day as the well is drilled deeper. If the deeper section of a well is *plugged* off to facilitate mechanical operations on the shallower section, the top of the cement *plug* would be the '*plugged* back *TD* (as distinguished from the drilled *TD*).

TOWNSHIP - A square tract of land six miles on a side, it consists of 36 *sections* of one square mile each.

TRAP - A natural configuration of layers of rock where nonporous or impermeable rocks act as a barrier, blocking the natural upward flow of buoyant *hydrocarbons* from underlying *reservoir* rocks. Most oil and gas fields are believed to be trapped accumulations of oil and gas.

For an exhaustive recent analysis of the many types of trapping mechanisms identified throughout the world, see N.J. Milton and G.T. Bertram's article "Trap Styles - A New Classification Based on Sealing Surfaces" in AAPG Bulletin, July 1992, pp 983-999.

TRIP - Making a 'trip' is the procedure of pulling the entire string of drill *pipe* out of the *borehole* and then running the entire length of *drill pipe* back in the hole. This is done to change *drill bits*, to prepare for *coring* operations, etc. As the *drill pipe* is pulled from the hole, the *drill bit* acts like a piston, sucking fluids out of the *formations* and the *borehole.* Gas which is swabbed into the borehole in this manner is called 'trip gas'. When drilling is resumed, and the *mud* is *circulated* up out of the borehole, an inexperienced *mud logger* might inadvertently mistake 'trip gas' for a true show of gas.

TUBING - Small diameter pipe, threaded at both ends, that is lowered into a completed well. Oil and gas are produced through a string of tubing (which can be periodically removed for maintenance).

TURNKEY - A drilling contract that calls for a drilling contractor to drill a well, for a fixed price, to a specified depth and to adequately equip it so that the *operator* need only turn a valve and oil will flow into the tanks (like when a building contractor builds a house and **turn**s over the **key** to the purchaser when it is completed).
The purpose of drilling a well by turnkey contract may be related to the timing of Federal income tax *deductions.* For income tax purposes, *expenses* are *deductible* from *gross income* as they are incurred. When a turnkey contract is entered into toward the end of the current tax year, the drilling costs may be prepaid at that time. The idea is to give a *working-interest* owner (or investor) in the well, the opportunity to *deduct* the intangible drilling costs (of the well to be physically drilled during the next tax year) from his *gross income* in the current tax year.

UNASSOCIATED GAS - *Natural gas* from a gas *reservoir.* See *associated gas.*

UNDERBALANCED DRILLING - Drilling with a drilling fluid whose hydrostatic head is less than the naturally-occurring pressure in the rock layers being penetrated. The extreme example is drilling with air (using air as the circulating fluid in place of liquid drilling mud). For the purpose of drilling underbalanced, the 'weight' (actually the density measure in pounds per gallon) of liquid drilling mud, can be lowered by the addition of gases including air, nitrogen, natural gas, etc.

UNDERWRITER - One who guarantees the sale of *securities* to investors. He is at risk to the extent he assumes the responsibility of paying the net purchase price to the seller at a predetermined price. He charges a fee or this service.

UNDIVIDED INTEREST - Assume AL owns a 100% working interest in a *section* (640 *acres*) and is willing to sell a 25% (= 1/4) interest to BOB.

DIVIDED interest: AL sells a 100% interest in the northwest quarter of the *section* (a 160-*acre* tract) to BOB but keeps for himself, 100% of the interest in the remaining three quarters of the section (480 *acres*). BOB owns a 25% divided working interest in the section, and AL owns a 75% divided interest in the section. (A *section* is 640 *acres.*)

UNDIVIDED interest: AL sells to BOB a 25% interest in (every *acre* in) the *section.* In this case BOB has a 25% undivided interest, and AL has a 75% undivided interest in (every *acre* in) the section.

UNITIZATION - Consolidation of separate tracts over a common producing reservoir so that exploitation of the reservoir can be managed as a single

entity (in order to promote exploitation efficiency). Every producing state has regulations
addressing compulsory unitization, based on the
consent of a majority of the affected working
interest owners; the percentage ranges from about
60% to 80%.[149] The unitization formula (addressing costs and revenues and the work program, etc.)
is based on extensive engineering and geological
evaluation of the condition of the reservoir, and
the potential the best methods of exploitation.

VISCOSITY - A fluid's resistance to flowing. Honey is
more viscous than water. Oil is more viscous than a
mixture of oil-and-gas. Depending on *oil gravity,* oil
may or may not be more viscous than water.

WAC... - "Weighted average cost of", as in WACOG
(weighted average cost of gas) and WACC
(weighted average cost of capital), etc.

WASTING ASSETS - *Assets* that will eventually
lose their value: though exhaustion as they are
produced (natural resources such as oil, gas,
minerals, and timber), or through the passage of
time (*leased* mineral rights, patents).

WATER DRIVE - The most efficient driving
mechanism to force oil and gas out of the *reservoir.* Due to natural pressures in the *reservoir,*
water moves into the base of the *pay zone,* dis-
placing the oil-water contact upward and flush-
ing the oil ahead of it, as oil is produced. Toward
the end of the life of a water drive well, the fluid
that is produced, contains increasing percentages
of water, until the well becomes watered out and
is abandoned. See also *gas drive.*

WEEVIL - An unglamorous adjective (or noun) used
to describe a "green" hand — anyone new and unini-
tiated, especially to the mechanical operations of an

oil rig. As in: "That weevil geologist over there wouldn't know a Stillson wrench from a 7-iron".

Originally the term 'boll weevil' referred to farm workers who were out of a job picking cotton when insects (boll weevils) destroyed the crop. During boom times in the oil-fields, these workers came to the rigs seeking better-paying work. Although physically capable, they were inexperienced, and had no knowledge of oil-field equipment or the tools, or what they were used for.

If a newly-hired worker were to lose a finger in a piece of machinery, it might be derisively said that he'd gone and done "one of them boll weevil stunts". An uncomplicated piece of equipment is still often referred to as a 'boll weevil device' or simply a 'boll weevil' (meaning that it is so simple, anyone could operate it).

WELLBORE - Physically, wellbore refers to a *borehole* (equipped for, or intended to be equipped for, production); in other words a *completed* well. In some states (notably Oklahoma) a *working interest* owner's rights and obligations might be described as (1) encompassing all oil and gas exploration and development activities within a *spacing unit*, or (2) being limited to exploration and production only from a particular wellbore (*borehole*).

WEST TEXAS INTERMEDIATE - Refers to a grade of crude oil produced in the Permian and Midland basin areas of west Texas (average parameters are 40° API, and 0.4% sulfur by weight; ranges are 34° API - 45° API and up to 0.5% sulfur).

The price paid for crude oil varies according to quality. In the U.S., prices quoted generally specify grade: Alaska's North Slope crude (27° API), California's Kern River crude (13° API),

Wyoming sweet, Oklahoma sweet, Gulf Coas
sweet, Michigan sour, Kansas sweet, Illinois basin
sweet, West Texas sour, etc.

Overseas crudes include: Saudi Arabian light (34°
API), Kuwait blend (3° API), North Sea Brent (38°
API), Indonesia's Minas (34° API), Nigeria's Bonny
light (36° API), Mexico's Isthmus (33° API), along
with many others. See *API, sour crude.*

WET - A *reservoir* rock is said to be 'wet' when it
contains water but no *hydrocarbons.* (Ironically,
a well that encounters only wet *reservoirs,* is
called a dry hole.)

WET GAS - *Natural gas* containing liquid *hydrocarbons* - commonly *condensate.*

WHIPSTOCK - A steel blocking device placed (in
the bottom of) a *borehole.* As drilling is resumed,
the whipstock forces the *drill bit* (as it drills
ahead) to veer off at a slight angle from the
more-or-less vertical *borehole* that has been
drilled down to that point. The new deviated
portion of the *borehole* is called a *side track.* See
directional drilling.

WILDCAT - An exploration well drilled to a reservoir, from which no oil or gas has previously
been produced in the nearby surrounding area.
When the well is located far away from all previous drilling attempts, it might be called a 'rank
wildcat'. These wells naturally involve a high
degree of *risk,* but a small percentage of them
are successful. When a rank wildcat well comes
in a discovery the return on investment can be
very attractive, indeed.

WINDFALL PROFITS TAX - A U.S. Federal revenue-
generating tax on the production of most domestic
(U.S.) *crude oil* (but not on gas). The intent of the

tax was to prevent domestic oil producers from realizing windfall profits when domestic oil prices were deregulated in 1980, and allowed to fluctuate according to the international oil price. Before 1980, domestic U.S. oil prices were regulated by the Federal government.
The tax was repealed as part of the Trade Bill signed by President Reagan, August 22, 1988.

WIRELINE - See *logging.*

WORKING INTEREST - An interest created by the execution of an oil and gas *lease.* The owner of a 100% working interest has the exclusive right to explore for oil and gas on a tract of land, along with the obligation to pay 100% of the costs of *drilling, completion,* and producing any oil or gas found. The working-interest owner is entitled to all revenues from production attributable to a *lease,* after deducting *royalty interests* (and any other burdens on the *lease*). He may reduce his share of revenues by *carving out* revenue interests and transferring them to others: an *override* to an employee, for example.

WRITE-OFF - In common usage: a reduction in *taxable income* that results when allowable *deductions* are subtracted from *gross income.*

WTI - See *West Texas Intermediate.*

ZONE - A layer of rock penetrated by a borehole that has characteristics which distinguish it from other nearby rock; '*pay one*', '*lost-circulation* zone', 'high-pressure zone', etc.

Index

Index

I

Illite 233
Improved oil recovery 342
Income 133
Income funds 184–186
Independent oil company 353
Independent Petroleum Association of America (IPAA 243
India 246
Individual Retirement Account 123
Indonesia 102
Initial potential 353
Intangible drilling costs 72, 90, 128, 206, 266, 354
Interest costs 190
Internal Rate of Return 223
Internal Revenue Code 119–126, 281
Internal Revenue Service 45, 119–121
Internet bulletin boards 231
Interstate commerce 104
Investment contract 178, 180
Iodine geochemistry 237
Iran 244, 248
Iraq 244, 248

J

JIB 354
JOA 354
Joint 354
Joint interest billing (JIB) 65, 268, 354
Joint operating agreement (JOA) 63–67, 77, 162, 180, 270, 354
Joint ventures 268–269
Jug-hustler 355

K

Kelly bushing (KB) 355
Kuwait 248

L

LACT unit 355
Lag time 355
Lagniappe 356
Lagoon 31
Land ownership 52–55
  Louisiana 51
  mineral rights 52–53
  severance 52
  surface rights 52, 52–53
  Texas 51
Land surveys 48
  Mason Dixon line 49
  metes and bounds 48, 49
  National Land Act of 1785 51
  township and range 51
Landman 47–48, 356
Landowner 47
Lateral borehole extensions 234
Law of capture 356
Lease - oil and gas 55, 356, 357
  bonus 55
  delay rentals 55
  lease agreement 56
  leasehold costs 131
  market value of 188
  primary term 55
  secondary term 56
Lease acquisition costs 44, 62, 357
Lease acquisition funds 188
Lease hound 358
Lease operating expenses (LOE) 98, 113, 141
Lifting costs 358
Limestone 358
'limitada' 277
Limited Liability Company (LLC) 173–175, 276
Limited partner 164, 358
Limited partnership 163–169, 274, 284, 358
  agreement 165–169, 192, 194
  costs 189–192
  costs, interest 190
  costs, management fees 190
  costs, offering 189
  costs, organizational 189

403

Page	Personal Notes - People to Contact	Phone

Page	Personal Notes - People to Contact	Phone

A message from the publisher:

Always patronize your local bookstore for any title.Should any **MERIDIAN PRESS** title be temporarily out of stock, however, please order directly, using this form.

Order Form

MERIDIAN PRESS
Marketing Department
PO Box 21567
Oklahoma City, OK 73156

<www.meridianpress.com>

Quantity Discounts

10	Copies	10%
25	Copies	15%
50	Copies	20%
100	Copies	30%
200	Copies	40%

Qty	Title	Price/ea.	Total
	MONEY IN THE GROUND 4th Edition (4.5)	**$79.50**	
	Let's Talk an Oil Deal *1	**$13.50**	
	¡Hablemos de un NEGOCIO PETROLERO!2	**$13.50**	
	Sekiyu Tooshi No Kagi *3	**$39.50**	
	Top 10 Strategies for E&P Investment *4	**$9.95**	

In the U.S.: On orders of 1-4 books, price includes shipment via First Class Priority Mail. For 5 or more books, add 4.5% of the subtotal for freight. **Overseas:** Add $10.00 U.S. per book for overseas airmail.

Sub Total	
Okla. Residents: Sales Tax	
Shipping & Handling #	
TOTAL	

* *1 Let's Talk is a re-print of the glossary in **MONEY IN THE GROUND**. In case English is not your native language, the glossary is also published in *2 Spanish *3 Japanese. *4 This is a practical chart (in English).

☐ VISA   ☐ Mastercard   ☐ Payment Enclosed

Name _____   Email _____

Company _____   Tel _____

Street _____

City _____   State _____ Zip _____

CARD # _____   Exp. Date _____

Authorized Signature _____

Date: _____

1. I found MONEY IN THE GROUND to be: _____
   _____
   _____
   _____

2. Features I would like to see changed: _____
   _____
   _____
   _____

3. Other comments I would like to make: _____
   _____
   _____
   _____

4. In terms of value for money, I would rate this book as:
   Excellent _____ Good ___ Fair ___ Poor ___

In the preparation of future publications, our editorial staff
might like to discuss some of your comments with you.
Would you be willing to accept a phone call at:
   Your office __ or Your home__?
   Area code and phone number _____.

Others might be interested your opinions. May we quote you
in future promotions for MONEY IN THE GROUND?
   Yes ___ no ___.

Signature _____

Title _____

Company _____

A message from the publisher:

Always patronize your local bookstore for any title. Should any **MERIDIAN PRESS** title be temporarily out of stock, however, please order directly, using this form.

_ _

Order Form

MERIDIAN PRESS	Quantity Discounts		
Marketing Department	10	Copies	10%
PO Box 21567	25	Copies	15%
Oklahoma City, OK 73156	50	Copies	20%
	100	Copies	30%
<www.meridianpress.com>	200	Copies	40%

Qty	Title	Price/ea.	Total
	MONEY IN THE GROUND 4th Edition (4.5)	**$79.50**	
	Let's Talk an Oil Deal *1	**$13.50**	
	¡Hablemos de un NEGOCIO PETROLERO!*2	**$13.50**	
	Sekiyu Tooshi No Kagi *3	**$39.50**	
	Top 10 Strategies for E&P Investment *4	**$9.95**	

# **In the U.S.**: On orders of 1-4 books, price includes shipment via First Class Priority Mail. For 5 or more books, add 4.5% of the subtotal for freight. **Overseas:** Add $10.00 U.S. per book for overseas airmail.	**Sub Total**
	Okla. Residents: Sales Tax
	Shipping & Handling #
	TOTAL

✻ ***1 Let's Talk** is a <u>re-print</u> of the glossary in **MONEY IN THE GROUND**. In case English is not your native language, the glossary is also published in ***2** Spanish ***3** Japanese. ***4** This is a practical chart (in English).

❏ VISA   ❏ Mastercard   ❏ Payment Enclosed

Name _____ Email _____

Company _____ Tel _____

Street _____

City _____ State _____ Zip _____

CARD # _____ Exp. Date _____

Authorized Signature _____

413

Listen to what the experts are saying about

MONEY IN THE GROUND!

"... designed for the potential investor. Helpful and simplified ... adequate treatment of every relevant aspect from geology to taxation."
PETROLEUM ECONOMIST – London

"... contains some of the clearest and best- written explanations of oil and gas investments we have ever seen ..."
LIMITED PARTNERSHIP INVESTMENT REVIEW
Springfield, New Jersey

"Anyone with an interest in the subject matter will find this to be good background reading."
JOURNAL OF ACCOUNTANCY – New York, NY

"... explains oil and gas investment in simple terms ..."
JOURNAL OF PETROLEUM TECHNOLOGY –
Richardson, TX

"... new and comprehensive. Provides specific deals with examples."
OIL & GAS JOURNAL – Tulsa, Oklahoma

Comes highly recommended!

"...don't lay a nickel down on the table until you've read this book."
DOUG BENTIN – Columnist, Oklahoma Gazette

"MONEY IN THE GROUND ... is now the book I would heartily recommend to anyone interested in learning about oil and gas investment."
ROBERT A. STANGER – Chairman of the Board
Robert A. Stanger & Co., Shrewsbury, NJ

"Well written and informative ... does not assume a level of knowledge that the reader may not have."
RICHARD D. CLEMENTS – Director Energy Division
Oklahoma City Chamber of Commerce

"... we rate your book as excellent ... and would recommend it to others."
WILLIAM R. McHUGH – President
Royalty Information Systems, Inc.,
Covington Louisiana

"I was looking for just this sort of book ... both up to date and written in a style which a 'non-oily' can understand ..."
GENE A. CASTLEBERRY – Partner
Castleberry & Kivel
Attorneys at Law, Oklahoma City, Oklahoma

"Excellent value for money. An excellent informative book."   **JOHN L. PIESEK** –Vice President
Stockmen's Bank and Trust Co.
Gillette, Wyoming

John Orban III is an experienced oil & gas consultant.

Following graduation from Princeton University (BSE in Geological Engineering), he spent three years in the Naval Civil Engineer Corps as division officer with the Seabees in Vietnam (for which he was awarded the Navy Achievement Medal), and as Officer In Charge of Construction in Yokohama, Japan.

He has worked as roustabout for Sun Oil, mud-logger for Baroid, and explorationist for: Mobil, Aramco, a four-man start-up oil company in Oklahoma City, and Callon Petroleum.

Founded in 1983, J. Orban & Company has been providing strategic assistance to the international petroleum industry for 23 years. The firm specializes in upstream oil and gas opportunities.Corporate clients include multi-national corporations, from both the U.S. and the Pacific Rim (where Mr. Orban studied Japanese at Keio University in Tokyo, and Mandarin Chinese at Nanyang University in Singapore and Taiwan Normal University in Taipei). Individual clients include private investors from the U.S. and from overseas.

Mr. Orban lives with his wife in Oklahoma City.

If you're participating in upstream oil and gas ventures, you need to have an expert on *your* side of the table.

Contact:
john@JOrbanCo.com

J. ORBAN & COMPANY, LLC
PO BOX 21785
OKLAHOMA CITY, OK 73156

www.JOrbanCo.com